SECRET NAMES of The Strongmen & Their Agendas

Strongmen Information & Study Guide
Prayer Guide

H. A. Lewis

This book is about strongmen of the spirit world, which bring negative influence in the lives of people and countries. Generations upon generations of people's lineages are effected by strongmen which they have no knowledge about. Cities have been challenged by the adversary to keep it from operating in God's plan which again influence the people and churches.

When we know the names of these spirits, we can by God's mercy and grace call them out and interupt their plans and establish God's will for the cities, churches and people that were once held in bondage by these spirits.

Secret Names of the Strongmen
ISBN: 978-0-9904360-0-3   Soft cover

All rights reserved. No part of this book may be reproduced or transmitted in any form or by any means, electronic or mechanical, including photocopying, recording, or by any information storage and retrieval system, without permission in writing from the copyright owner.

Copyright © 2014 by Dr. Henry Lewis, Joshua International dba H.A.Lewis Ministries

This book was printed in the United States of America.

Dedication

This work is dedicated to all my Christian brothers and sisters in Christ who have stood faithfully in spiritual warfare on the behalf of those who could not. This teaching is to help those to give a **direct attack using their names** against the enemy of their souls so victory will be theirs.
May the Lord bless you and keep you safe.

A Special Thanks

To my wife, Patricia, Co-President of Joshua International.
A special thanks for organizing and editing of all my books for printing and publishing
as well as coordinating my ministry and material.

To my secretary, Grace Miller,
who typed and formatted this challenging book.

To my graphic artist and production manager, Debbie Wheat,
for the work of the cover(s) and charts.

Harry Baxter,
for proofreading and advice.

I am blessed to work with them.

And He (Jesus) asked him, **"What is thy name?"** And he answered, saying, "My **name** is Legion: for we are many."
Mark 5:9

Contents

Introduction 9
Chapter 1:   Strongmen of War 13
Chapter 2:   Strongmen of Sex 23
Chapter 3:   Strongmen of Idolatry 31
Chapter 4:   Strongmen of the Storm 37
Chapter 5:   Strongmen of Infirmity and Disease 43
Chapter 6:   Strongmen of Death 49
Chapter 7:   Strongmen in Serpent Form 57
Chapter 8:   Strongmen of Mystical Legends 63
                      Part 2: Cannibals 75
                      Part 3: Shape-Shifters 81
Chapter 9:   Strongmen of Destruction 95
Chapter 10:   Strongmen of Slavery 99
Chapter 11:   Strongmen of the Occult 103
Chapter 12:   Worldwide Leaders of the Strongmen ... 108
Chapter 13:   Hebrew Strongmen 115
Chapter 14:   The Watchers of Enoch 119
Chapter 15:   Strongmen of Emotions 128
Chapter 16:   Strongmen of False Religions
                      Part 1: Vodou (Voodoo) 133
                      Part 2: Santeria 154
Summary on the Strongmen 167
Prayer(s) Deliverance and Healing 185-194

If you call out a spirit by <u>his name</u>, then you will get his attention. Actually in many cultures of the world, people will **not** reveal their real birth names to strangers. They believe if you know their real name, then you have power over them.

I will give you the keys of the kingdom of heaven; whatever you bind on earth will be bound in heaven, and whatever you loose on earth will be loosed in heaven **Matthew 16:19**

Introduction

A few years ago, my wife and I were ministering at a prophetic meeting. My wife who is a prophetess, had a vision of a baby that concerned a dear couple that was there. She had prophesied earlier that this joyous event would happen. The good news was confirmed that they were going to have a child. We were immensely delighted at their news and the fulfillment of the prophecy in their lives.

After returning home, we received a phone call from this couple. They were extremely distressed because the wife was developing complications and was losing the baby.

My wife and I began to intercede for the life of the unborn child. We prayed in every way we knew how. We bound the spirit of death and infirmity. However, the couple sadly lost their child.

My heart was broken over their loss. I cried out to the Lord, asking Him what went wrong. I told the Lord I bound the spirits of death and of infirmity. I didn't understand what went wrong?

The Lord answered me and told me I did pray, and I was earnest in my prayer; however, the spirits I was praying against was not the spirit causing the problem. He directed me back to my studies and showed me the name of the strongman responsible for the death of the child.

The Lord informed me the name was given to me so the next time I received a call concerning a similar situation, I would know the name of the spirit who was behind the assault.

A short time later we received a telephone call from the same couple. The wife was once again carrying a child and the same problem was happening during this pregnancy as it did with the previous one. The doctor's prognosis was that she would lose this child as well, and she would never be able to conceive again.

My wife and I began to intercede once again for this young couple and their unborn child. The Lord reminded me of my studies. I now knew the name of the strongman behind the attack. The Lord instructed me to bind this spirit **using his name.** My wife and I joined together, calling this spirit by his name and binding him in Jesus' name.

The name of the spirit was **Kasdeja**. It was he who taught mankind how to destroy the embryo in the womb. This time **Kasdeja** was dealt with. The child, who was a girl, was born healthy. In fact, this couple had two more children besides her.

Now, I am **not** saying if you don't know the name of the spirit operating in the life of a person or persons, God will not honor your prayer. What I am saying is if God reveals a specific demon or strongman by his name, **take advantage of knowing this information, and use it. You will be amazed at the result.**

A poor allegory of what I am trying to say is: if you are in a crowded area and wish to gain a specific person's attention, you don't yell, "Hey you!" No one will know whom you want.

You get the person's attention by calling out his name.

When he hears his name, there will be a reaction by the person as a result of you calling him by name.

It is the same in the spirit world. If you call out a spirit by the name, then you will get his attention

Actually in many cultures of the world, people will not reveal their real birth names to strangers. They believe if you know their real name, then you have power over them.

Isn't it interesting that, in the Mormon temple rites, only the priest knows the secret name given to the husband? The man's wife doesn't even know the secret name. Yet the husband knows the secret name of his wife.

That at the **name** of Jesus every knee shall bow, of things in
heaven, and things in earth, and things under the earth; And that
every tongue should confess that Jesus Christ
is Lord, to the glory of God the Father.
Philippians 2:10-11

Neither is there salvation in any other:
for there is none other **name** under heaven
given among men,
whereby we must be saved.
Acts 4:12

For whosoever shall call upon the **name** of the Lord
shall be saved.
Romans 10:13

Chart 1: Strongmen of War

1. **Abigor** – warrior demon	6. **Jestan** – Hindukusch demon of disease, famine, and war	11. **Siva (Shiva)** – the destroyer
2. **Agaliarept** – Hebrew commander of armies	7. **Mars** – Rome's strongman of war	12. **Thamuz** – god of war, said to have started the inquisition and to have invented artillery
3. **Aries** – Greek god of war	8. **Mont** – Egypt's strongman of war	13. **Udl** – Austrian god of war.
4. **Azazel** – Hebrew god of war	9. **Pruflas** – facilitates quarrels, wars, discord, and poverty	14. **Zaebos** – god of war that appears as a soldier
5. **Busas** – another name of Pruflas	10. **Rama** – Hindu god of war	15. **Zepar** – god of war that appears in the form of a soldier

Chapter 1
Strongmen of War

I remember as a child reading about the gods and goddesses of the Roman and Greek mythology as well as the gods of Norway. I encountered names like **Zeus**, the father god of the Greeks and his Roman counterpart **Jupiter** and **Odin** the father god of Norway. I read about **Thor** the Norse god of thunder and **Loki**, his evil half brother.

Like so many people, I read the stories, legends and fables of these mystical beings which were created in the minds of ancient civilizations. In actuality, they were trying to explain things they simply did not understand.

As a youngster, I did not understand every story is based on a fable, which is based on a legend, which in turn is based on a foundation of truth. Take for example the legend of **Hercules**.

In **Rome**, he was the son of **Jupiter** and an earthly mother. He was famous for his great strength. Everyone knew who he was by the lion skin he wore. One of his nicknames meant 'the spotted one'. In Greece he was called **Heracles**, the son of **Zeus**, the father of the gods and an earthly mother, **Alcmene**. **Heracles** was known for his great strength and by the skin of a lion he wore. Coincidence? I don't think so.

In **Egypt, Osiris** was the same as **Heracles** or **Hercules**. Just like his **Roman** and **Greek** counterparts, he was identified by the lion skin he wore, and one of his nicknames meant 'the spotted one'. We have three gods of three different cultures. All have the same power, nicknames, and the sign of their identity – the lion skin they wore.

My question is this: how did these three cultures come up with the same mythological being, especially if there was no truth behind the character? If we look closely at **Heracles, Hercules** and **Osiris**, we find they all died a violent death. They all went from being above-average humans to becoming gods.

As **Heracles** and **Hercules'** bodies were being consumed by fire, their godhood was being released. **Heracles'** godhood was to **Olympia** while **Hercules** was to Asgartoh. When **Osiris** was brutally killed, his spirit ascended and became the constellation **Orion.**

Amazingly, these three mythological characters can be traced back to an actual human being found in **Genesis 10.** His name is **Nimrod**, the mighty hunter before God. He was known for his great strength and was a fierce warrior. He had a nickname, which meant 'the spotted one'. He received this unusual name because of the skin of a leopard he wore, which was as a sign of his being a leader and having great strength.

Many of these gods and goddesses, or what we refer to as strongmen, can be traced back to a human being or to what the Bible calls the offspring of the sons of God and the daughters of men. Skeletons of these creatures, which so many people try to deny or explain away, have been found in almost every country in the world.

These strongmen are behind almost every terrible thing that has happened in the world from the beginning of creation until now and until the coming of the Lord Jesus and the millennium kingdom. The strongest of these beings was responsible for the rebellion of one-third of the sons of God in heaven.

He was also the one who *deceived Adam and Eve*, causing them to disobey the command of God in the Garden of Eden. Yes, his name in Greek is **Lucifer**, son of the morning. The Hebrew calls him the Adversary and the rest of mankind calls him **Satan** or the devil. Yes, *He is very real, and he heads up a very organized evil kingdom.*

His kingdom consists of strongmen and their legions, which are many.

I will cover as many of these beings that I can. I will endeavor to provide you with as much information on their background as I can and what their assignment is on the earth.

Knowing their names and how they work secretly in our lives and in the lives of our loved ones helps us to know how to pray against them.

We begin with the strongmen of war, which not only affects countries, but history itself. We will follow with many other strongmen and end with the strongmen of false religion, which will lead us into the days of the Great Tribulation.

The Strongman of War – Rome, Greece, Egypt

Ares, the *Greek god of war and of battle*, cared for nothing else. The Greeks loved and cared for the other gods because they felt they were loved and protected by them. The gods came to their help in times of trouble, but this was not so with **Ares**.

The only help they would receive from **Ares** would be in battle. **Ares** was quite untrustworthy because he was very double-minded and would quite often change sides in the midst of battle. **Ares** only cared for the fight. In fact, the more the numbers in the armies increased, and the more violent the battle as well as the more warriors that died, the happier he was. Although a *god of war*, he was, according to legend, a poor warrior.

The goddess, **Athena**, defeated him in battle by using her intelligence against his brute strength. **Heracles** battled **Ares** using strength for strength and finally knocking him out. The good news is when this spirit of war comes into your life or the life of a loved one, there is One who can easily defeat him at all times. His name is Jesus!

Rome's *strongman of war* was **Mars,** the counterpart to the Greek god of war, **Ares**. Both were gods of war, but this is where their familiarity ended. Where the people of Greece despised **Ares**, **Mars** was highly esteemed by Rome. He was so honored by the Romans, he was second to **Jupiter**, the father of the gods.

Mars made up the head of the Roman gods, including **Jupiter** and **Quinnus** (the latter had no Greek counterpart). **Numas,** the legendary *second king of Rome* elevated the importance of **Mars** as a god when he built an altar for him in Campus Martius. That's right, this area was named after the god,

Mars. Unlike his Greek counterpart, **Mars** was really a father to the Romans. According to the legends of Rome, **Mars,** along with **Rhea Silvia,** gave birth to **Romulus** and **Remus**.

The number of temples built to him shows the importance of **Mars** as a *god to the Romans.* With all the positive portrayal of **Mars** by Rome, you must remember he is just the Roman's version of **Ares**, a *violent strongman of war.* Like the old saying, a rose by any other name is still a rose; therefore, a demon of war by any other name is still a demon.

Egypt's strongman of war, Mont, is also known as Month, Menthu, or Mentu.

He was a falcon-headed god of war whose cult was at **Hermonthis** (present day **Armant**).

The kings of the *eleventh dynasty*, who used his names as part of their own, favored **Mont**. Sometimes pictured as a bull-headed man, he was reputed to incarnate himself in the bull called **Buchis**, which was kept in the shrine at **Hermonthis**. **Mont** also had solar characteristics; the *symbol of the bull* often *represented the heat and power of the sun.* He was shown with the *curved saber* called a **khepesh**. For a time, **Mont** was considered the supreme god of the south until he was placed in the triad of the Theban. He was replaced and demoted by the god **Amun** of Thebes, who went on to become the king of the gods.

During the war against the **Hittites, Rameses II** saw he was losing, so he called on the name of **Amun** and rallied his troop to counterattack. He was victorious over the Hittites, so he declared himself to be like **Mont**, the god of war. Other cultures may have had a god to help them on the battlefield, but the Egyptians had a god on the battlefield which fought with them, and it was their king who was the earthly symbol of their celestial god.

Although **Mont** had many qualities the Egyptians looked for in a god, he was finally dropped from the triad of Theban in favor of **Khons**, the moon god. Yes, **Mont**, like **Mars** and **Ares**, was a *violent god of war and destruction*; however, the great commander of the armies of the Lord, our Lord and mighty Savior, Jesus Christ, can also overcome him.

In many nations, there are different gods of war with different names, like **Thamuz**, **Zepar** and **Zaebos**, but they are exactly the same in attitude and attributes. They are known as the gods of wrath, anger, violence and destruction. As destroyers of peace and unity, they pit country against country, families against families, and man against man.

These so called gods of war hate unity with a passion and strive with all their might to spread chaos and destruction.

No country or community is beyond these gods' touch or their vile poison. No one is safe from their anger and hate. There is no defense against their destructive power on this earth. Every generation has been plagued with their violence.

Yet there is coming a day very soon where it doesn't matter what name these spirits go by because they will all be destroyed forever. Their strength and power will be no more because of the champion of champions, our Lord and Savior, Jesus Christ.

Strongman of War – India

Rama, Hindu god of war is a hero war god, an avatar, and an incarnation of **Vishnu**. **Rama** was born into a royal family, but he had to leave because of his stepmother's plotting. His wife, **Sita**, went with him despite the dangers of the jungle and wilderness. **Ravana**, the demon king of the Rakshasas tricked **Rama** by having him pursue a phantom deer. While **Rama** was busy, **Ravana** stole his wife, **Sita**.

She was held captive in **Sri Lanka** until a helpful eagle discovered her prison. **Rama's** ally **Hanuman**, king of the monkeys, made sure she was still alive. When he discovered she was, **Rama** gathered an army and set out to rescue his wife. He tried to convince the ocean to divide and allow him to cross over, but the ocean refused. **Nala**, son of the smith god, **Visvakarma**, instructed **Hanuman's** monkeys on how to build a bridge.

They worked so well and so hard the bridge was completed in five days. **Rama's** forces crossed over to **Sri Lanka** and battled with the demon **Ravana's** army. **Rama** and **Ravana** came together like two ferocious lions. Taking accurate aim with his bow, **Rama's** arrows shot off the ten heads of **Ravana**. However, through the use of magic, the ten heads grew back. Therefore, **Rama** selected a mythical arrow made by **Agastya** and shot it at this king of demons. The arrow pierced **Ravana's** chest, passed through his body, and returned to **Rama** as loyal as any well-trained dog.

Even though **Rama** defeated **Ravana**, he would not take his wife, **Sita**, back until she was proven to be pure publicly. He did not want there to be any rumors she had been molested or abused by the demon king, **Ravana**. **Sita,** who was completely in despair, built a funeral pyre and climbed alive into the flames.

The flames refused to hurt her, and, taking the form of a divine being, they bore **Sita** up. After such a dramatic display of his wife's purity, **Rama** took her back as his wife.

It is true these are stories and legends, but what do they have to do with the strongmen over our lives? *By sharing these legends or myths of the strongmen in different countries, you will discover the spirit and purpose are the same.* The **names are different**, but they <u>all seek to make your life miserable</u> and will <u>eventually destroy you and your loved ones.</u>

By reading these legends, we can see the deception these spirits use to ensnare man in their lies.

Many of these stories will portray these demons as beneficial and helpful to the societies which worship them.

They are represented as heroes and protectors of mankind. They show their enemies, or their opponents, as demon spirits when in reality they are in league with each other. Basically, they are working together to destroy man and lead him into damnation.

According to **Hindu** folklore we find that **Ravana**, who was the *demon king* of the **Rakshasas**, was a fallen angel. He had disgraced himself in heaven and was given the choice of returning to the earth three times as the enemy of **Vishnu** or seven times as his friend. After meditating on his choices, he realized **Vishnu** could dispatch with all of his enemies quickly.

Not wanting to spend any more time on earth than he had to, he chose to be **Vishnu's** enemy. Seeing his stay and confinement on earth as punishment, he decided to take the shortened stay so he could get it over with as soon as possible.

Therefore, he was *incarnated as the demon*, **Hiranyakashipu**. **Vishnu** incarnated himself as the *lion-headed man* and quickly destroyed **Hiranyakashipu**. The fallen angel quickly reincarnated himself as **Ravana** and abducted **Sita**, the wife of **Rama**, who was another incarnation of **Vishnu**.

According to this version of the story when **Rama** caught up with **Ravana**, he admitted he kidnapped **Sita** in order to be killed quickly. He wanted his punishment of banishment to the earth to end straightaway. Of course this wasn't very flattering to **Sita**.

Ravana's *third incarnation* was as a prince called **Sisupala**. In this incarnation he was born with three eyes and four arms. When his parents planned to abandon the child they were stopped by a mysterious voice, which said the child was highly favored and that his destined slayer was already alive.

The destined *slayer* would be revealed when **Sisupala** sat on his knee. When he did, his extra limbs and eye would vanish. This sign would assure them of who his murderer would be.

Soon **Vishnu** as **Krishna** came visiting the family. When the child, **Sisupala**, sat on **Krishna's** knee, *his third eye closed* forever, and his extra arms fell off. Seeing this, **Sisupala's** mother made **Krishna** promise he would forgive her son if her son ever did something to offend him.

Several years later at a public ceremony, **Sisupala** brought the meeting to a screeching halt over a disputed point of precedence. There was a vicious argument, and **Sisupala** insulted and threatened the worthy old men and honored guests.

Sisupala was told of the prediction concerning him and **Krishna**. This only added to his anger; therefore, he increased his insults and threats until they could no longer be forgiven. At last given no choice, **Krishna** raised his divine weapon, the magic disc, and threw it toward **Sisupala**, splitting him from his helmet to his sandals. This was the third and final incarnation of **Ravana**, the king of demons, and his ultimate end here on earth.

Unfortunately we find in these legends that the heroes and demons are actually working together to blind man to the truth.

In the lie of reincarnation, we are told we have many lives to live so we can reach Nirvana and become one with the cosmos.

There is no need to fear hell because, if we fail in this lifetime, we get another chance in another life.

We keep living until we get it right. This is deception! There is no **Wheel of Karma**! We do not keep coming back if we don't get it right the first time.

> **If we miss it, sorry; there is no second chance once you're gone.**

The Bible says, *"Today, if you hear His voice, is the day of salvation. When you heard Him, do not harden your heart as they did in the desert."*

> **As you study about these gods and heroes of these different religions, you will find it interesting that they are often worshipped to keep them away from you and not to bring them near.**

Another **Hindu** god of the *triad* is **Brahma**, the creator and father of gods and men. He is the *supreme* Hindu god next to **Vishnu (Krishna)**, the **Hindu** god of love. Finally the *most feared* of all the **Hindu** gods and one even greater than **Brahma**, god of creation is **Siva (Shiva)**, *the god of the dance*, which is the *great destroyer*.

This Hindu god, *known as the destroyer*, and I have had a history together.

Thank God that through the power of Jesus' name, he was bound and overcome.

> **Shiva has a *double side, like all the Hindu gods have*.**
> **Shiva is considered both destroyer and savior.**

He is mainly worshipped to keep him away from someone than he is to bring him near. **Siva** or **Shiva** is a complex god with many conflicting attributes and names. He is known as **Lingodbhava**, the phallic deity; **Rudra**, lord of beast; **Pashupa**, protector of cattle;

Bhutapati, father of demons; **Tryambaka**, accompanied by three mother goddesses; **Digambara**, clothed in space or sky clad; **Nataraja**, king of the dance.

Siva indicates benevolence, but the name was propitiatory for he is dangerous, destructive, and lethal. Around him collects all the negative deities of the Dravidians, the original inhabitants of southern India.

Siva is not a **bhagavat (blessed one)**; instead, he is an **isvara (a master)**. He is the *leader of all the outcasts of society* like *vampires, demons and ascetics*. Although destructive, he is supposedly merciful. (*Let me assure you there is no truth to this statement. Although I was known as the son of Shiva, I never received mercy from him at all.*) Even though he is considered a *phallic god*, he is also *ascetic*. He combines contrasting characteristics and points the way to an *underlying principle of unification*.

Siva wears a tiger skin and a snake collar. His hair is tied in the knot of the ascetic and adorned with the crescent moon and trident. He is shown with his third eye open and has a variable number of arms, usually four. **Siva** rides on a bull and is considered so holy by the Hindus; even his mount is considered a god.

Compare **Shiva** with the strongmen or gods of other countries. **Shiva** wears the robe of a tiger skin to show his power. This is also a sign of power of the **Greek** god, **Heracles** and its Roman counterpart, **Hercules**, and also of the **Egyptian god**, **Osiris**. The fact he is a phallic god is another tie to **Osiris**.

> **Let me reiterate a statement I made previously.**
> **There may be different countries and different names for the gods or strongmen, but the same demonic strongman**
> **is working to enslave and destroy mankind.**

The last image of **Siva** is of **Nataraja**, the dance king. **Siva** fills the whole cosmos with his so-called joyous dance called **tandava**. He will continue to dance and dance until all of creation is brought to the point of annihilation. According to **Siva** philosophy, in order to be reintegrated into the absolute, the universe must first be destroyed.

His intoxicating and revelatory dance was often the cause of the conversion of the heretics. Isn't it amazing that **Siva** wears the crescent moon as the sign of his deity! It is exactly like that of the moon gods: **Allah** of the Moslems; **Khons**, an Egyptian moon god: **Adural**; and **Adriel**. They use force to convert the heretics like the Moslems use the sword and threats to convert people to Islam.

> **Important Point**: The God of Christianity is the complete <u>opposite</u> of these moon gods. He loved man so much He gave His Son so we could be united with Him by choice and not by force. You can study any religion and their so-called gods, but you will not find a God of love and compassion for mankind outside of the Bible.

Prayer Against the Strongman of War

Dear Lord Jesus, You are Lord and the strongest of the strong. You are our cover and our banner. **(Exodus 17:15)** *You are our hiding place, our strong tower, and we take refuge in You, Lord.* **(Psalm 32:7)** *We do this knowing we are securely protected from these strongmen of war.*

Lord, as we bind these spirits, **(Matthew 12:29)** *we loose the spirit of peace, which You gave unto us just before Your return to Your Father. Peace, not as the world gives, but peace that passes all understanding. We pray this in the name of Jesus, the Prince of Peace. Amen.*

Footnote

Why do we bind? Jesus commented on the need for binding evil in **(Matthew 12:29)**. Jesus explained that we must first bind the strongman before we can plunder his house. When we are facing an evil stronghold in life, we must first use our inherited authority as children of God to bind the evil forces involved. After that, we can loose, or call forth God's plans for restoration.

Study Notes

Chart 2: Strongmen of Sex

1. **Agrat-bat-mahlaht** – spirit of prostitution and sex slavery	7. **Druj** – Iranian demon of lies and uncleanness, rape, and incest	13. **Ornias** – spirit of homosexuality
2. **Ashtaroth** – Phoenician goddess of lust and seduction	8. **Erzulie** – spirit of fornication and adultery	14. **Philatanus** – Jewish strongman of sodomy
3. **Ardhanarisvara** - bisexual personality of Siva	9. **Hermaphroditos** or **Hermaphroditus** – spirit that is both male and female	15. **Proserpine** – spirit who helps in establishing the act of sodomy
4. **Chil Gazi** – seducer of women	10. **Incubus** – male demon of sexual lusting	16. **Succubus** – female demon of sexual lusting
5. **Daevas** – demon of addiction, drunkenness, sexuality, death by starvation and contagious diseases	11. **Jaldabaoth** – spirit that rapes women and seduces men into sexual immorality	
6. **Dantalion** – three-face spirit of sexual perversion, bisexualism, gender confusion, mind reading and the worship of the occult	12. **Lilith** – spirit of sexual seduction	

Chapter 2
Strongmen of Sex

These strongmen of sexual perversion are alive and well on Planet Earth. The spirit of **pornography** is growing by leaps and bounds because of the internet. It is a sad truth that even pastors and church elders are ensnared in this trap.

What's worse is these pastors, elders, teachers, scout leaders and police officers have been found guilty of the terrible crime of **pedophilia**. These child molesters are everywhere and in various occupations.

Society has definitely returned to the conditions which were dominant in the days of *Noah and in the days of Sodom and Gomorrah*. Jesus said it would be so in the time of His return. Homosexuals, lesbians and the occult grow so strong in their lobbying in Washington, D.C., they have even been able to change the laws of America.

> **If you dare to speak against the perverted sins of homosexuality or witchcraft, you will be considered narrow-minded and can be arrested for hate crimes. We are truly living in a time of spiritual darkness.**

There are several different spirits of perversion, which I will address. According to legend, **Dantolien** is a *three-faced spirit* and is considered a *grand duke* of **Satan's** kingdom. He is in charge of *thirty-six legions of sexual perversion and is the strongman behind bisexualism and gender confusion.*

He works well with **Daevas**, who is a *perversion demon of addiction, drunkenness, sexuality and envy.*

Therefore he is **behind** many of the *plagues* like the *HIV virus, AIDS, syphilis and herpes*. **He is also behind the** hate religions **and tries to** mislead the righteous.

According to legend, **Agra-bat-Maklaht** is one of the wives of **Satan** and is the spirit which *leads women into prostitution and sex slavery.* **This spirit hates women** and *seeks to destroy and belittle them.*

She works well with a spirit named **Ashtaroth** who is a **Phoenician** goddess of lust and seduction and is the same type of spirit as **Ishtar**. In Christian legend, **Ashtaroth** is a *male spirit* who is the lord high treasurer of **Satan's** kingdom. He is the **leader** of the *accusers of the believers*. He is a *demon of vanity and sloth or laziness* and, according to Jewish myth, he is one of the *seventy-two spirits of Solomon.*

Druj is an **Iranian** demon of *lies and uncleanness*. A lot of evil and terrible things are cause by him like *rape and incest*. He uses evil men to do these vile acts.

He calls evil good and good evil.

Druj works well with a spirit of Hunza society known as **Chil Gazi**, the seducer of women. Her husband is supposedly of **Yachemi**, an anthropophagous female demon spirit which attacks and devours men.

Erzule is a spirit which is *very active in today's permissive society*. Moreover, it is a very powerful spirit – *operating behind the sins of fornication and adultery*. It is also the *spirit behind the philosophy*: **if it feels good, then do it**. Therefore, it's not surprising it is the **same spirit behind the witch's rite**: *if it harms no one, then do what you will*. (Does this sound familiar?) It was the same spirit at work behind the people in Noah's time and led every man to do what was right in his own sight.

Philatanus works with Belial.

Philatanus works with **Belial**, the Jewish strongman of sodomy. According to legend, he was one of the sexual perverted spirits working in Sodom and Gomorrah, the twin cities of perversion. I personally believe it is the same spiritual strongman over Provincetown (known as P-town) in Massachusetts, as it is completely inhabited by homosexuals and lesbians. **Philatanus** works with another spirit called **Proserpine** who also helps **Belial** in establishing the act of sodomy.

Jaldabaoth is a *Gnostic spirit-being* who, according to myth, is *the powerful lord of the underworld*. He is the spirit who supposedly *raped the first women and seduced man into sexual immorality*.

Ardhanarisvara is another personality of the *Hindu spirit*, **Siva**, the destroyer. This personality is a strange combination of both male and female. It is made up of **Siva** and **Siva's shakti**, the *female power*. Interestingly, this figure is divided right down the middle. Its torso displays one female breast and its high-domed head represents the lingam, or male power, of **Siva**. **Ardhanarisvara** works hand-in-hand with another spirit called **Hermaphroditos**.

Hermaphroditos was the son of **Hermes** and **Aphrodite**. According to legend, **Hermaphroditos** was pretty much the outdoorsy type who roamed wild on Mount Ida.

One day, he was bathing in the lake and was being observed by the nymph, **Salmacis**, who was dazed with love for him. She literally threw herself on him in a very passionate embrace. **Hermaphroditos**, however, did not feel the same way about **Salmacis** and struggled in vain to get free from her passionate embrace. **Salmacis** called upon the gods to make them one, so the gods caused their bodies to become one.

They created a creature never seen before. It was *neither male nor female*, yet **both** a *hermaphrodite*. Before he was dragged down to the watery depth of the lake, he called out a request: In the future whoever bathed in those waters should lose their virility.

There are many legends concerning spirits of lusts and sexual perversion, but they are more than legend.

> **There are very real spirits out to destroy the purity of the gift of sexual relations between a man and his wife.**
> **They work hard to replace true love and the proper sexual relationship which exists between a husband and his wife.**

With the lust of perversion, natural sexual relations between man and woman become unnatural.

> **Now relations exist between men and men, women and women, adults and children, and humans and animals.**

> **In Romans 1:21-32, God gives us a warning.**

If we refuse to obey Him and do not walk in alignment with His Word, then He will have to turn us over to a reprobate mind, becoming filled with all kinds of wickedness, evil, greed and depravity. These unclean strongmen are very real and are out to destroy our relationship with the Lord, as well as destroy our relationship with family and friends.

> **Scripture shows us over and over again the power the spirits of sexual sin have.**

We see it with **Samson**, the strongest man whoever lived. He succumbed to the temptations **Delilah** offered and lost his strength. We also see it with David and Bathsheba. His heathen wives influenced Solomon, the wisest man whoever lived. Sexual temptation was the only temptation that Paul, the great Apostle, told Timothy, his young disciple, to run from.

> **Yes, this is great advice: flee from this to the shelter of God.**

Prayer Against the Strongman of Sexual Sin

Lord, we admit we are not strong enough in our own strength to defeat this unclean spirit. Father, we are asking You in the precious name of Your Son, Jesus to cover us with His blood and hide us from the eyes of these unclean spirits.

Lord, we willingly submit our bodies to our minds, and our minds to our spirits, and our spirits to the Holy Spirit.

We ask, dear Lord, that You make us vessels of honor for Your namesake in Jesus name. Amen.

Footnote

Satan offers us instant gratification with demonic "enhancement": You can be "spiritual"... You can be "wise"... You can be "attractive"... You can have "fun"... You can "cope"... As soon as we've been lured in, satisfaction becomes ever more elusive, and death is the sure result.

Satan gives temporary power to those who believe his lies. He becomes their "father", and they become his possession. Let us not take the bait of temptation

God gives everlasting power to those who wait upon Him to perform what He has promised. What we receive through faith will last forever. Seek the presence of God.

PRAYER FOR FORGIVENESS FROM SEXUAL SINS

Father, I confess that at various times in my life I have been powerless against the continuing attacks of the enemy on my sexuality. I have chosen to sin in various ways and ask You to forgive me for the following: **(specifically confess each and every sin)**. *I now agree with Your verdict on my sin. I renounce all pleasure associated with these sins. I ask You to cleanse my memories, heal the hurts and forgive me. In Jesus' name. Amen*

ANOTHER PRAYER FOR SEXUAL SIN

Loving Heavenly Father, I thank you for the gift of human sexuality and the high and holy purpose for which you created it. In the name of the Lord Jesus Christ and by the power of His blood, I resist all strongholds of sexual pervertedness assigned to manipulate and rule over _____. I specifically resist demons and strongholds of **(name the areas of sexuality where they are being defeated)**, *I command all of Satan's forces to cease all activity and leave _____ and go to where the Lord Jesus Christ sends them. In Jesus' name I pray. Amen*

PRAYER TO BREAK UNGODLY SOUL TIES

In the name of the Father, the Son and the Holy Spirit, I ask God to break all ungodly spirit, soul and body ties that have been established between me and **(name person)**. *I sever that linking supernaturally and ask God to remove from you all influence of the other person* **(name him/her)** *and drawback to myself every part that has been wrongfully tied in bondage to another person. I now speak directly to every evil spirit that has taken advantage of this ungodly soul tie. You no longer have any rights here and I order you to leave now without hurting or harming me or any other person and without going into any other member of the family. In Jesus' name. Amen*

One of the most important passages in scripture is **II Corinthians 10:3-5**

One of the most important passages in scripture is **II Corinthians 10:3-5**: For though we walk in the flesh, we do not war after the flesh: (For the weapons of our warfare are not carnal, but mighty through God to the pulling down of strong holds Casting down imaginations, and every high thing that exalteth itself against the knowledge of God, and bringing into captivity every thought to the obedience of Christ." Cross reference this with **James 1:12-14**: "Blessed is the man that endureth temptation: for when he is tried, he shall receive the crown of life, which the Lord hath promised to them that love him. Let no man say when he is tempted, I am tempted of God: for God cannot be tempted with evil, neither tempteth he any man: But every man is tempted, when he is drawn away of his own lust, and enticed".

Study Notes

Chart 3: Strongmen of Idolatry

1. **Aamon** – Egyptian sun god	7. **Amon** – Egyptian king of the gods	13. **Khons** – Egyptian moon god
2. **Abduxuel** – moon god	8. **Anamelech** – moon goddess	14. **Men** – Anatolian moon god
3. **Adriel** – moon god	9. **Apollo** – son of Zeus, god of the sun	15. **Osiris** – Egyptian strongman of sun worship
4. **Allah** – moon god in Arabic mythology	10. **Diana of the Ephesians** – spirit behind the worship of the moon. Queen goddess of all divisions of witchcraft	16. **Ra** – Egyptian god of the sun and creator god
5. **Amaimon** – Egyptian sun god	11. **Horus** – Egyptian god of the sky and sun	17. **Tammuz** – Egyptian vegetation god
6. **Ammon** – another name for **Amon**, the Egyptian king of the gods	12. **Isis** – Egyptian strongman of moon worship	

Chart 3
Strongmen of Idolatry

In today's society, men are worshipping many gods and goddesses. They really have no idea who they are submitting themselves to. Therefore, these spirits must be exposed. The following deals with the many names of the spirits, which are being worshipped and what they represent. Unfortunately, the list is long. It shows that if man will not worship the one true God who made them in His image, then they will worship the gods, which are made in man's image.

Many of the strongmen of idolatry are associated with the worship of the sun and moon.

Aamon is the Egyptian sun god also known as **Amun**, **Anmon** and **Amen**. He was originally the local god of the city of Thebes (**Nut Amun**). As the city grew in size, so did the importance of **Aamon**.

He replaced the war god, **Mont,** and went on to be regarded as the chief god of Egypt. Originally, he was just a wind god or an air god. Somehow, he rose to a position to where he became the patron of the Pharaohs. He even came to the attention of Alexander the Great, who after consulting the oracles of **Amun** took the title of **Son of Amun**.

Amun is the *Egyptian's Lucifer,* except that **Amun** *controls reproduction and life.* **Amun**, along with his wife **Mut** and son **Khons** make up a **triad**. Another name of this spiritual triad is **Amaion**.

Horus is another Egyptian sun god and was the son of **Osiris** and **Isis**. According to legend, when **Set** killed **Osiris**, **Isis,** who was both sister and wife to him, found his body. Upon finding his body, **Isis** took on the *form of a hawk*. She then settled on **Osiris'** body where her warmth revived **Osiris'** sexual power long enough to impregnate her.

The child born was **Horus**, the hawk-headed *solar god of Memphis*. **Horus**, often indistinguishable from the great **Ra**, is *god of the sky* as well as *the sun* and was widely worshipped and faithfully served. His images are universal, and he has many names and aspects.

Legend says **Horus** was *secretly raised* in the Nile Delta swamps around *Buto* until he was old enough to challenge his father's murderer, his uncle **Set**.

The battles with **Set** were long, fierce and inconclusive. They were just as much verbal as they were physical. Finally, **Horus** received vindication at a formal trial where judgment was ruled in his favor.

Horus *was more than just the son* of Osiris.

He was the *incarnated form* of **Osiris** on the earth and was the intermediate between his father and the men or women who died. The *dead* would stand before **Horus** and tell of their good deeds they performed.

Horus would then take the *person's heart* and place it on the scale opposite of a feather. *If the person were good, the heart would be less in weight than the feather.* If the heart were light, they would be resurrected. If not, a jackal sitting by the scale would eat the heart, and the person would not be resurrected. This portrayal of **Horus** as the *incarnation of his father* and the *only mediator between men and god* is a **perversion of the office of Jesus who is the only way to God the Father and the only true mediator between God and man.**

Horus came to eventually inherit his father's kingdom – restoring order, justice and prosperity. **Osiris** was a counterfeit to God the Father; **Horus,** a counterfeit to Jesus the Son; and **Isis** to the Holy Spirit, producing a perversion of the Trinity which started with **Nimrod, Semiramis** and **Tammuz.**

Osiris' brother, **Set,** is the **Egyptian's** evil god. He compares to **Hades,** the **Greek** *god of the underworld* and evil god brother to **Zeus.** He is also comparable to the Roman evil god, **Pluto** and his brother **Jupiter** as well as the *evil Norse god* **Loki,** son of **Odin,** and half brother to **Thor,** *the storm god.* Finally, he is likened to **Lucifer,** *the fallen angel and enemy of all mankind.*

> ### As we study the circumstances surrounding Horus' birth, we not only see *incest, but sex with the dead.*

Do Not Be Shocked; this is the norm for many of the gods and goddesses worshipped by man. For instance, **Zeus** slept with many goddesses and human females; **Diana** slept with her brother and then with her own son. **Poseidon** slept with **Aethra, Medusa,** and **Theophane. Aphrodite** slept with her brother. These so-called holy gods and goddesses lived very permissive lives.

Once **Horus** took his father's place after avenging his death from **Set's** hand, he assumed *many different names and positions.* He was known as **Haroeris (Har-Wer)** meaning '**Horus** the *elder*' or '*Horus the great*'. Another name was **Horkhenti Irti** meaning '*Horus who rules the two eyes*' which was what he was known as in **Letopolis.** Interestingly, his *two eyes were considered the sun and the moon.*

In **Pharboethos,** he was called **Hor Merti** meaning '**two eyed Horus**'. It is in this name, which describes the constant battle with his uncle, **Set.** In fact, in one particular battle, **Set** tears out **Horus'** two eyes, and **Horus** castrates **Set.** Therefore because of this action, **Horus** is known as **Hor Nubti** meaning '**Horus the conqueror of Set**'.

> ### According to Egyptian legend, Set is the oldest evil god in existence, even older than Satan.

In **Edfu (Behtet)** he is shown as a winged solar disc. This sign is found over the porches of the temple. Here **Horus** appears as a great bird of prey, a hawk, and his victim is always Set.

In **Heliopolis,** the *center of sun worship*, he was linked with **Ra** in the form of **Ra Harakhty** whose symbol was the rising and setting sun.

Horus was also known by the following names: **Hor-Sa-Iset** meaning 'the son of Isis' and **Heru-Pa-Khut** meaning 'Horus the child'. This is the image the Greeks adopted as the *god of secrecy and discretion*. Another name was **Har-End-Yotef (Harendotes)** meaning '**Horus protector of his father**'. This name put him in this position as a *god of war* also known as **Hartomes**, 'Horus the spear man'.

Finally he was **Har-Pa-Neb-Taui**, '*Horus of two lands*' and **Heru-San-Taui (Harsomtus)** 'Horus united of two lands'. With this name, the symbol appears as a youthful god with two crowns.

The Pharaohs use the title '**living Horus**' to strengthen their claims to kingship and divinity. In every portrayal of **Horus,** you see a god of anger and war who is constantly seeking revenge on his father's behalf.

Take a moment and give God glory!

You must understand – every one of these **gods of Egypt**, including the *Pharaoh's* boast of godhood, was totally defeated by the God of Israel.

The one true God of Israel is greater and more powerful than any other god – no matter the culture.

Continuing on, there is **Tammuz** who was originally a *tree god*, son of **Nengishzeda** meaning '*lord of the tree of life*'. Later, **Tammuz** became a *rising and dying vegetation god*. His lover, **Ishtar**, caused his death. Afterwards, she sought for him in the underworld and brought him from there to stand at the gate of **Anu**, *the heaven god of Mesopotamia*. With his horned headdress, **Anu** signifies the example of leadership and royalty. Subsequently, **Enlil** replaced him.

Tammuz's only strong point was that he would be faithfully *resurrected every spring*; although he was cut down every year. The name of **Tammuz** can be traced back in history.

Tammuz was the son of Nimrod and Semiramis and was the sun god.

The Egyptian god **Tammuz** and his lover **Ishtar** were worshipped in many countries. In Assyro-Babylonia, they were known by the same names. In Sumerian, it was **Dumuzi** and his lover **Inanna**. To the Phoenicians, he was **Adoni,** and she was **Astarate** or **Ashtoreth**. For the Greeks, they were **Adonis** and **Aphrodite,** and for the Romans, they were **Adonis** and **Venus**.
In fact, this was the **Tammuz** which *the women of Jerusalem* were guilty of weeping over and worshipping (**Ezekiel 8:13-14**). To reiterate, many of these other gods and goddesses who were sun and moon deities can trace their origin back to **Nimrod** and **Semiramis** and **Tammuz**.

These individual gods and goddesses, as well as the triads, are Satan's attempts to take away the truth about the miracle of the birth of Jesus. It is his attempt to deny the divinity of our Lord and Savior.

Prayer Against the Strongmen of Idolatry

Dear Lord, we are reminded of Your command in **(Exodus 20:1)**. *You alone are our Lord and God, which brought Your people out of bondage in Egypt. Lord, we will have no other gods but You. Neither will we make any image of anything in heaven above or in the earth below, or in waters.*

We will not bow down to them or worship them. Lord, **(Exodus 20:5),** *we know that You are a jealous God who truly loves us. You alone sent Your son to take our place to prove Your love for us.* **(2 Corinthians 5:2)**

Lord, we acknowledge that there is salvation in no other name **(Acts 4:12)** *but the name of Jesus. We thank You, Lord, that You protect us from these fallen angels who try to portray themselves as gods.*

There is no God but You, Lord, and no name greater than the name of Jesus. **(1 Chronicles 17:20)** *Our God does not need to die at the end of every summer and to be reborn every spring. Our God has no beginning and no end. He is forever eternal. Amen.*

However, what the disciples didn't understand then, and what most people don't understand today, is there was a strong spirit behind the storm. This strongman was trying to stop the Lord from getting to the other side. The reason was the Lord had an appointment to meet a demon-possessed man and set him free.

The word used for '*storm*' in this passage of scripture was speaking not only of a *physical storm, but a spiritual one as well*. The spirit or strongman of the *whirlwind behind the storm* could have been the spirit called **Ugallu,** meaning '*big weather beast*', or another spirit called **Umudabrutu,** the 'strong man of the *violent storm*' such as the **whirlwind, hurricanes, and tornadoes, as well as tsunamis**.

Chart 4: Strongmen of the Storm

1. **Adad** – Babylonian storm and thunder god	6. **Chango** – in Santeria, he is the god of thunder and lightning	11. **Thor** – Norse god of thunder
2. **Addu** – another name for Adad, Babylonian storm and thunder god	7. **Focalor** – spirit that has power over the winds and the sea and is the cause of death by drowning	12. **Ugallu** – big weather beast
3. **Agau** – in Vodou, he is the violent god of storms	8. **Jeretik** – in Russian mythology demon that spreads bad weather, storms, and sickness	13. **Umudabrutu** – strongman of the violent storm
4. **Babuala** – strongman of the storm	9. **Nicor** – water demon that causes hurricanes and tempests, causes death by drowning	14. **Vaya** – Iranian demon of wind and causes death by numbing the body
5. **Bade** – in Vodou, he is the god of wind	10. **Shango** – another name for **Chango**	

Chapter 4
Strongmen of the Storm

Luke 8:22-24 depicts the power and authority Jesus has over nature. This portion of scripture begins with Jesus and his disciples getting into a boat to go to the other side of the lake. Jesus falls asleep in the back of the boat as the disciples launch out to cross the lake.

From out of nowhere a severe storm arises, and the boat is suddenly in danger of sinking. Extremely terrified, the disciples wake Jesus from his sleep. He immediately rebukes the storm, the water becomes calm, and the wind and rain ceases. The disciples are totally amazed at the Lord because even the weather has to obey Him.

However, what the disciples didn't understand then, and what most people don't understand today, is there was a strong spirit behind the storm. This strongman was trying to stop the Lord from getting to the other side. The reason was the Lord had an appointment to meet a demon-possessed man and set him free.

The word used for '*storm*' in this passage of scripture was speaking not only of a *physical storm, but a spiritual one as well*. The spirit or strongman of the *whirlwind behind the storm* could have been the spirit called **Ugallu**, meaning '*big weather beast*', or another spirit called **Umudabrutu,** the 'strong man of the *violent storm*' such as the **whirlwind, hurricanes, and tornadoes, as well as tsunamis.**

> **There are just two names of the strongmen behind the storms that bring destruction, sickness, poverty and death.**

However, in every nation or culture there is a legend concerning a god of storms and lightning, and the destruction wrought by them.

The **Babylonians, Phoenicians, Syrians** and the **Hittites** worshipped **Adad**, who was also known as **Hadad** and **Addu**. He was *the storm and thunder god* who later became equated with **Rammon** or **Rimmon**. Not only was he the *storm and thunder god*, but he was also supposed to bring forth fertilizing rains.

In his **Phoenician** form, he was a *storm and cloud god* known as **Amurru** or **Martu** the Ammorite, and **Kurgal** the 'great mountain' and perhaps the Baal of Lebanon. He crossed over different cultures but was always a violent storm god. It was **Adad** the storm god who supposedly gave the gift of great courage to the legendary Gilgamesh the king of Uruk.

In **Norse** *mythology,* **Thor** was formerly known as **Donar**, which meant *thunder.* He was the god of thunder, *the sky, weather and crops.* **Thor** was a huge, red-bearded irascible and *loud-voiced god* (thunder voice). He wore a girdle of strength, iron gloves, and of
course his magical hammer, **Mjollnir**, which he held in his hand and could be thrown to execute judgment in battle.

Actually, **Thor** was a *very popular god*, and the worship of him continued even up to the time of Christianity. Archeologists have discovered miniature hammers in the same silversmith shops along with crosses and crucifixes.

Thor was the absolute *man of action*, yet was uncomplicated. He had a great love for food and drink. The common people adored him because he controlled everything they needed for life - namely the weather, the crops and even the seas, which affected trade and fishing.

Men would swear sacred oaths on holy rings kept in **Thor's** shrines. The images of **Thor** were framed in such a way that they could be used to produce holy fire. It is quite possible the pebble in the head of the image of **Thor** was for the followers of this *god of thunder* to remember his battle against the giant **Hrungnir**.

Mjollnir, **Thor's** *hammer*, shattered the giant's whetstone in pieces. Some of the pieces of the whetstone embedded into the head of **Thor** and was never removed. This story of a stone imbedded in the head of the giant **Thor** reminds me of another giant who had a stone embedded in his head. His name was Goliath.

The acceptance of Christianity in **Iceland** in A.D. 1000 brought pagan belief to an end in that country. Moreover, in the next few centuries following this conversion, **Odin** and **Thor** *became demons in the minds of the people. These former gods now existed as evil spirits who tempted men to do evil deeds or to have evil thoughts.*

Coincidentally, the occult sign for Satan is the lightning bolt.
(Harry Potter scar)

One thing which stands out about these *storm gods*, whether it is **Adad** of the *Babylonians and Phoenicians,* or **Thor** of the *Norsemen,* or **Ugallu** the big weather beast, or **Umudabrutu** the *spirit of violent storms, hurricanes and tornadoes*: they all have one symbol declaring their power and authority. *It is the lightning bolt*. Coincidentally, the occult sign for **Satan** is the lightning bolt. **(Harry Potter scar)**

This shouldn't be too surprising to us because all these so-called *gods of the storm*, like **Loki** the *god of mischievousness*, are all actually built on the foundational image of **Lucifer** himself, the son of the morning (**Isaiah 14:12**). If you take the time to look behind the images of these false gods and goddesses, you will always see the demonic strongman.

The devil and his fallen angels do not care what shapes
they have to take to ensnare and deceive man.

They will even take the shape of an angel of light.
Satan wants to be worshipped.

Satan wants to replace the God of creation
and keep mankind in darkness and despair.

He walks about seeking whom he can deceive and destroy.

Yes, just like **Thor**, *master of the storm*, he will bring *chaos in your life and use the lightning bolts of accusation and lying to keep you down and enslaved all the days of your life*. Then *he rejoices greatly* as **you are forever separated from God**. If he can never return to heaven, then he will do what he can to stop you from getting there yourself.

Be on guard, for the enemy of your soul is still looking for a victim to devour.

Prayer Against the Strongmen of the Storm

Lord, we see the storm clouds gathering all around us. We see the lightning and hear the rumble of the thunder. The darkness of this spiritual storm seems to hide the light of the Son from our spiritual eyes.

We can feel the forces of the windstorm of accusation and slander. We feel the power of the lie and the result of unity-shattering. Lightning is being felt everywhere.

*Father, in the name of Jesus we ask that You will do here in this situation what Your beloved Son, our great **Adoni Elohim**, did in the boat. When the storm tried to stop him from crossing the lake to do the miracle of deliverance for the demoniac, He spoke to the storm, and it ceased.*

***Speak** to the **strongman Ugallu**, the big weather beast, and to **Umudabrutu**, the power of the violent storm, both physically or spiritually in our life. Speak to **Thor**, the thunder god, or **Addu**, the Babylonian god of destruction and chaos, which is just another name of **Baal**. **Baal** is the adversary, **Satan**.*

***Peace be still!** For we know that, according to (**John 14:27**), You gave to us peace. You gave us Your very own peace, not the peace as the world gives. This peace soothes the troubled heart, removes all fears and calms the raging storms in our life.*

We thank You, Father, that You never leave us or forsake us, **(Deuteronomy 31:6)** *but when the storms of Satan assault us on the sea of life, You are there in the boat with us to bring peace and joy to us.*

Father, we thank You that at the end of the storm, there will be a rainbow promising You will always be there with us. Yes, the storms of life may last for the night, but in the morning the Son of promise will arise with healing in His wings. We pray this in Jesus' name. Amen.

Study Notes

Chart 5: Strongmen of Infirmity and Disease

1. **Aclahayr** – spirit of mental illness	7. **Jeretik** – spirit of storms and sickness
2. **Ahazu** – spirit of night seizures	8. **Jestan** – spirit of disease, war, and famine
3. **Asakku** – spirit of disease and death; plagues	9. **Shabriri** – spirit of blindness
4. **Daevas** – demon of addiction, drunkenness, sexuality, death by starvation and contagious diseases	10. **Xtabal** – spirit of infirmity
5. **Impundulu** – vampire spirit of disease and death	11. **Zarich** – spirit of weakness and illness
6. **Iya** – cannibal spirit of sickness and death	

Chapter 5
Strongmen of Infirmity and Disease

One of the most heartbreaking facts in life is when we see loved ones suffering from incurable diseases. We helplessly watch as their lives slip away bit by bit and stand by feeling so useless because it is out of our hands.

When an elderly person passes away from a disease like cancer, it is hard to deal with – even though they may have lived a long life. But, when a child dies from a terrible disease, or is confined to a wheelchair, or is institutionalized and can never run and play like other children, it tears your heart out.

In times like these, the reality of the adversary becomes very real in a personal way. Of course, **Satan** uses many names to hide behind – even in infirmity and disease. There are names such as **Ahazu**, spirit of the night seizures, and **Aclahayr**, *spirit of mental illness*. Then, there is **Asakku**, spirit of disease and death, **Iya**, *cannibal spirit of sickness and death*, **Shabriri**, the *spirit of blindness*, **Xtabal**, spirit of infirmity, and **Zarich**, spirit of *weakness and illness*.

> **It doesn't matter what the names are in each culture;
> it all goes back to the spirit known as Satan.**

He is the **leader behind all illnesses.** When looking at the attributes associated with the names of these spirits of infirmity, you see the very nature of **Satan** behind everyone.

For example, the **Semenic spirit** called **Ahazu** *attacks at night*, causing its victim to go into a *seizure. Many people have died in their sleep because of these attacks.*

Numerous times people have gone to the doctor's because of these *night seizures*, but **no** *physical evidence* could be found to ascertain the cause of them. Instead, they were told they had a *form of epilepsy* which happens only at night in their sleep.

We **cannot** blame all seizures on demons, however;

> **We must also understand that many times
> there is a spirit behind the illness.**

> **Therefore, we need the *gift of discerning of spirits*
> so we can truly understand the cause of these seizures.**

My own father suffered from epilepsy, and I worked for a few years with children who suffered from this terrible disease. **None** of them were demon-possessed, but, in over thirty-five years of ministry, I have seen many who were.

When dealing with illness, we must be careful *not to give the enemy too much credit*. Whether it is a spirit of infirmity or a natural disease, **Jesus is still our answer.**

If you go to a doctor, and he prescribes medication, follow his instructions, and ask the Lord to increase the effect of the medicine which will help speed up the healing process. If you go to a doctor, and he or she cannot find a cause or a reason for the illness, then call on the name of the Lord to bind up the spirit of infirmity and loose the healing power of the Holy Spirit in your life or the life of the person you are praying for.

Another strongman, who can make it hard to know whether it is a *natural disease* or a *spiritual assault*, is the spirit **Aclahayr** or **Dibbux**, the *spirit of mental illness*. This spirit is on an increase today. All you need to do is look around at the many homeless outcasts of society. Some are people who have been turned out of institutions which no longer have the funds to stay operating, so they have to close down and turn their patients out on the streets.

Thankfully, many of these poor souls can be helped through therapy and medication. Sadly, *unclean spirits of insanity or mental illness drives others*.

> **Years ago, my wife and I were used to set a young girl free from more than a legion of demons.**

The deliverance took place in a *state-run institution* with the permission of the girl's parents. It happened in front of doctors, psychologists, social workers and nurses. Needless to say, God did a wonderful job, and the medical geniuses didn't know what to say.

I have seen God set many people free from the bondage of *mental illness*. One of the best testimonies I ever read on deliverance was the story of **Karen Kingston**. As a young girl, she was institutionalized because of a mental problem. Given up by medical experts, God rose up a young preacher who prayed for her, and using the name of Jesus gave this girl back her life. Karen went on to become a math teacher.

> **Yes, these *spirits are strong and can do great harm*, but our God is stronger and does much greater work than any fallen angel can ever do.**

These spirits of infirmity, in the form of **Asakku** and **Daevas**, are the spirits behind *plagues like the* **Black Death** that took thousands of lives, to *AIDS, HIV and other sexually transmitted diseases*.

> **The devil does not care how he destroys a life, he just cares that life is destroyed.**

It doesn't matter if it is hepatitis, mononucleosis, chronic fatigue, cancer, heart disease, meningitis or even the common cold – as long as it kills you.

> **Thank God the Lord bore our infirmities,
> and by His stripes we have been made whole.**

These words are **not** meaningless to me; neither are they just someone else's testimony. I have had God miraculously heal me of spinal meningitis when I was young. Later when I was much older, He delivered me again. This time it was from multiple sclerosis.

> **The word of God is a standard against any disease
> and any spirit behind the illness.**

I have seen the power of God work in **Nigeria, Egypt, Switzerland** and here in America. Absolutely nothing is too hard for our God.

I have seen the *spirit of blindness*, **Shabriri**, *defeated in the name of Jesus* in Salem, Massachusetts, in Egypt, and in Nigeria. I have seen the power of the *deaf and dumb spirit* defeated in all these places as well to the glory of God. I have seen **Zarich**, the *strongman of weakness and illness*, overcome by the strongman of life, the Holy Spirit of the living God.

> **The Orientals have an interesting outlook
> on the familiar spirits and the spirits of illness.**

They feel God has promised twenty years of life on earth to man, and if man should die in his sin before fulfilling his quota of years, then he is doomed to wander the earth as an earth-bound spirit of the disease he died from. If he had any infirmities, like blindness, deafness, mute, lame or crippled, then he will become a familiar spirit of that disease with which to trouble his family until his time of twenty years on earth is fulfilled. Afterwards, he will be brought down to hell to wait until the final judgment.

No matter what we may think a **spirit of infirmity** is, we must bear in mind it **is an enemy of God and of man.** Some day very soon all unclean spirits are all going to be judged along with their master and leader **Lucifer**, *the son of the morning*. Also known as **Satan**, he along with the place called *hell*, the *false prophet*, the *antichrist*, and all his *evil minions* shall be cast into the lake of fire.

Prayer Over the Strongmen of Infirmity and Disease

(**1 John 1:7**) *Father, we thank You for the Blood of Your Son which washes us clean.*

Although it grieves us to imagine what Your Son endured, we thank You for the stripes on His back that brings to us healing. (**Isaiah 53:4-5**)

We, oh Lord, are most fortunate, for we have a God we can call on for healing. Lord, You are forever faithful. Just as You promised that wherever two or more people agree on anything according to Your divine Will, it shall be done according to their faith. (**Matthew 18:19**)

Lord, sometimes when we are sick, it seems as if we are traveling through the valley of the shadow of death, in that I will fear no evil. We do not travel alone, for You are there with us. Your rod and staff comfort me, (**Psalm 23:4**)

You anoint me with the balm of Gilead. You restore my soul and heal my broken body.

You have redeemed us from every sickness and every plague

You cause me to rise up with the wings of an eagle. (**Deut. 28:61 and Gal. 3:13**)

You renew my youth and return my strength to me. (**Isaiah 40:31**)

Oh that man should praise You, oh Lord! (**Psalms 107:8**)

For You have sent Your Word (Your Son Jesus) to heal us. (**Psalm 107:20**)

We thank You Lord, that your Word has not changed.

You are the same yesterday today and forever. (**Hebrews 13:8**)

Those who will call on His glorious name and receive it will be saved. (**Joel 2:32**) (**Romans 10:13**)

Praise You Lord forever and ever, for You are worthy. Let all who have breath praise Your holy name. Kodesh, Kodesh, Kodesh Elohim Adoni. Holy, Holy, Holy are You, Lord God. (**Psalm 150:6**) ***Amen***

Study Notes

Chart 6: Strongmen of Death

1. **Abaddon or Apollyon** – angel of bottomless pit and death	21. **Imdugud** – Sumerian spirit of death of domestic animals
2. **Amducious** – in Hebrew, the destroyer	22. **Impundulu** – vampire spirit of disease and death
3. **Ankou** – death spirit of the elderly and the sick	23. **Iya** – cannibal spirit of disease and death
4. **Aosoth** – spirit that specializes in passion and death	24. **Jahi** – death by poison
5. **Astovidatu** – spirit of death	25. **Jigarkhvar** – cannibal spirit of death; witch-like vampire
6. **Bajang** – death spirit of newborns	26. **Kasdeja** – spirit of death by abortion and by miscarriage, a former Watcher
7. **Banshee** – Irish death spirit	27. **Maahes** – Egyptian spirit of massacre
8. **Baron Samedi** – Vodou spirit of the dead	28. **Meshabber** – spirit of death over wild and free animals
9. **Basilisk** – spirit of violent death	29. **Milcom/Moloch** – Ammorite demon who causes the death of children
10. **Befana** – Italian spirit which destroys children	30. **Nicor** – water demon that causes hurricanes and tempests, causes death by drowning
11. **Buda** – spirit of the death of children	31. **Siva or Shiva** – in Hindu, the destroyer
12. **Daevas** – demon of addiction, drunkenness, sexuality, death by starvation and contagious diseases	32. **Vanth** – Etruscan spirit of death
13. **Dengelmaennie** – Alpine spirit of death	33. **Vaya** – Iranian demon of wind and causes death by numbing the body
14. **Dimme** – Sumerian spirit of sickness and death	34. **Vepar** – fallen angel who brings storms and causes death by gangrene
15. **Dre** – spirit of death and destruction	35. **Virikas** – West Indian spirit of death
16. **Drude** – spirit of nightmares and death by strangulation	36. **Wasco** – demon who brings death to children by eating them
17. **Duppy** – spirit of terrible death	37. **Wraith** – death spirit
18. **Focalor** – spirit that has power over the winds and the sea and is the cause of death by drowning	38. **Yama** – West Indian god of death
19. **Flauros/Haures** – spirit of death by fire	39. **Yukki-Onna** – Oriental spirit of death by freezing
20. **Hemah** – Hebrew spirit of death over domestic animals	***Kabala** – Hebrew spirit of crib death called **Lilith** (supposed first wife of Adam and mother of all demons)

Chapter 6
Strongmen of Death

These particular spirits dealing with **death** are the **most feared in all cultures** of the world. On every continent, sacrifices are made to appease the wrath which seems to be associated with these strongmen of death.

Every person on earth knows he or she will eventually die, and there is nothing he or she can do to stop it from happening. Even though man knows he cannot stop death, he does everything in his power to stop the aging process and to delay it as long as possible.

> **In every culture of all people groups on earth,
> there is a *spirit or angel of death* and a *legend surrounding it.***

In the **Hebrew legend**, there is **Amducious**, *the destroyer*. The destroyer in **India** is **Siva**. In **Bretagne, France**, there is **Ankou**, a *graveyard watcher* who appears to the elderly and sick. Then there is **Aosoth**, who in the *pantheon* order of the nine angels, specializes in passion and death.

The Bible speaks of **Abaddon** or **Apollyon,** the *angel of the bottomless pit and of death*. In Iran, **Asto Vidatu**, the spirit who *hunts for the souls of the dead* with **Aeshma**. In Malaysia, **Bajang** is known as the *death spirit of newborns*. You also have **Basilisk**. **Befna** is the Italian spirit which destroys children. There is the Irish banshee – the one who brings death. **Baron Samedi** is the *voodoo cult spirit of the dead* who wears a top hat and dresses in all black.

In the **legend** of **Baron Samedi**, he is the *lord of all the Gede* and one of the most *powerful and most feared* of the **lwa**. He *controls passage between the world of the living and the dead*. Without his help, no soul may pass between the world of the living and the dead or into the ancestral homeland of **Ginen**, and **no** spirit may return to the physical world to become an ancestor spirit or immortal **lwa**.

> **The Baron knows everything that is going on in the world of the dead.**

Through possession, he often passes on information about what is happening to someone's ancestor family member. Anyone who wants to talk with the dead must first invoke **Baron Samedi**. Without his help, no one can communicate with the dead, and the gates to the underworld stay closed. *The symbols of this spirit of the dead are the cross, symbolizing the crossroad between the living and the dead, and also the coffin.*

In addition to the *previous death spirits*, there is also **Daevas**, the **Persian demon** *of addiction, drunkenness and death*. The Alpine spirit is called **Dengelmaennie**, the cousin to the Irish banshee. *Its call also announces the death of a person.*

The **Sumerians** have a spirit called **Dimme** who brings *sickness and death to children*. In Tibet, there is **Dre** who brings death and everything harmful to people. **Focalor**, whose real name is **Lucifuge Rofocal**, is the *spirit of the seas and the wind and is the cause of death by drowning*.

Flauros Haures is the *spirit of death by fire*. She supposedly *knows all secrets and will destroy all her enemies by fire*. In South Africa, there is **Impundulu**, *the spirit of blood and death*. You even have **Imdugud**, the spirit of *death of domestic animals*. He is a **Sumerian** demon who has a twin Hebrew spirit called **Hemah**, the spirit of *death over domestic animals*. **Hemah** works with **Meshabber**, the spirit of *death over wild and free animals*

The Lakota Indians of North America have a spirit called Iya. He is a *cannibal spirit of death and disease.*

In the West Indies, there is **Duppy,** a spirit of terrible death. The **Hindu** has the spirit **Jahi**, the one who *poisons*. The female of Indian mythology, **Jigarkhvar**, is a *cannibal spirit* which *kills and then eats the victim's liver.*

Spirit of Abortion and Miscarriage

Then there is the **spirit of abortion and miscarriage**, which I spoke about in the introduction of this book. His name is **Kasdeja**, a *watcher, a fallen angel* found in the **book of Enoch**. According to **Hebrew legend**, he was one of the *seven main angels who led the rebellion in heaven.*

Child Sacrifices and Drowning

Then there is the Ammorite demon, **Milcom**, who *demands child sacrifices,* and **Nicor**, the spirit of *death by drowning*. We also have the Etruscan demon of the underworld, **Vanth**, who *brings death*.

Death by Numbing

Vaya is an **Iranian** *demon of wind* and causes *death by numbing the body*. There is also **Vepar**, the *Hebrew fallen angel* who can bring *forth storms and causes death by gangrene*. **Virikas** is the West Indies' cousin to the Alpine spirit **Dengelmaennie** and *Irish banshee spirit*. These spirits *announce and cause death by their screams.*

Death to Children

In **Nutka-Indios** legend, **Wasco** is a *demon spirit* who brings *death to children*. In the Hebrew kabala there is **Lilith**, the **first wife of Adam** who became the **mother of all demons** and is the *cause of crib death and death before the eighth day* – especially boys.

Yama is the **West Indian god of death** who *pulls the soul from the body*, and **Yukki**

Onna is the *Oriental spirit of death by freezing.*
As you can see, there is a legion of these spirits and a legend concerning each one in every society of the world. It does not matter by what name these strongmen go by for they are one and the same. It is the enemy of mankind who seeks to destroy us.

Civilized and uncivilized people try everything they can to avoid death.

> **There is no human power over the spirit of death.**

You cannot buy it off; you cannot out-think it; neither can you hide from it. There comes a day, and we must face it head on.

> **The only power greater than death, hell and the grave is the power in Jesus' name. No matter what spell or incantation or secret name you use, death will not bow to it.**

There is only **one name** that causes death to flee, and that **name is Jesus – the Name above all names**. **(Deuteronomy 32:39) (Philippians 2:9)**

The name of **Buddha** will **not** do it! The name of **Allah** has no power over sickness or death! **Siva's** name cannot conquer it! **Krishna** and **Brahma** lack the power! Only the precious name of Jesus causes death to tremble!

> **ONLY the creator holds the power and no other god.**
> **(Revelation 1:18) (Colossians 1:16,17)**

Three times I have prayed the name of Jesus over people who have passed away, and three times they have come back to life. All three were extremely happy because before they died they did not know Jesus as their Lord. When they came back from death, they happily accepted Him into their lives. Yes, these spirits are real and are looking to destroy as many as they can, but we can trust in the Lord for protection.

I remember the days when I was involved with the occult, I saw the spirit of death and feared it greatly. I saw what it had done in the lives of many who were caught up in witchcraft, and I knew there was no protection against the spirit. Then Jesus entered my life and filled me with His Holy Spirit, and I saw an amazing thing. I saw the death spirit tremble in the presence of the Spirit of the Lord.

If you don't know Jesus as your Lord and Savior, you are absolutely right in fearing death. But if you do know Him, then you can say along with the apostle Paul in **(1Corinthians 15:55)**, "O death where is thy sting? O grave, where is thy victory?" The sting of death is sin, **(1 Corinthians 15:56)** and the strength of sin is the law.

But thanks be to God, which gives us the victory through our Lord Jesus Christ. **(1Corinthians 15:57)**

We can also say with Paul in (**Romans 8:37-39)**, "Nay, in all these things we are more than conquerors through him that loved us. For I am persuaded, that neither death, nor life, nor angels,

nor principalities, nor powers, nor things present, nor things to come, nor height, nor depth, nor any other creature, shall be able to separate us from the love of God, which is in Christ Jesus our Lord."

Praise God! Just like David when he went out to face Goliath, he did **not** go on his own or in his own strength. The Lord God of Israel was with him and is truly with us. We do not ever have to walk alone. (**Hebrews 13:5**)

Prayer Against the Strongmen of Death

Praise you, Father, even though we walk through the valley and shadow of death (**Psalm 23**), *we are not alone for You are with us. We need fear no enemy for You are our strength.*

You, oh Lord, are our hiding place, our strong tower, our city of refuge. (**Psalm 61:3**)

You are Jehovah Nissi, the Lord our Banner. (**Exodus 17:15**)

At the sound of Your name, the enemy trembles and his army flees. (**Hebrews 12:26**)

Yes, arise oh Lord and let Your enemies be scattered. (**Psalm 68:1**)

I call on You Lord in the time of trouble, and You answer me. (**Psalm 91:15**) *No one, Lord, can take me from the palm of Your hand.* (**John 10:29**)

The heathen may rage, and the enemy may threaten, and the storms of life may blow fiercely against my boat, but my anchor stays firm, and the waves do not overflow me. Your voice speaks so far and no farther and the waves stop and the wind ceases its blowing and all the weapons of the enemy fall harmlessly to the ground. (**Psalm 35**)

Yes Lord, the armies of the enemy may come at me in one way, but when I call on You, they will scatter in a hundred different ways. (**Deuteronomy 28:7**)

Yes Lord, the spirit of death is a giant to me, but to You he is nothing. Even if he takes my life, he cannot take my soul and spirit, and I, Lord, like the psalmist said, shall dwell in the house of the Lord forever. (**Psalm 27:4**)

I will be with my loved ones who have been promoted before me, and all my trials and hardships will come to an end forever. Amen and Amen

Death, be not proud. Oh grave, do not boast, for the sting of death has been removed, and the victory of the grave has been destroyed forever by the power of the sacrifice of our Lord and Savior, Jesus Christ, the wonderful Lamb of God and the mighty Lion of the tribe of Judah.
(**1 Corinthians 15:56-28**)

Purpose for attack- Jn.10:10 "...steal, kill, destroy..."
- He has your faith targeted for attack.

He knows that if he attacks your faith and you yield to the attacks, then he can cripple your anointing.

Your anointing is what makes you effective to minister. **Isa.10:27- Lk.4:18,19- 1Jn.3:9- Acts10:8**. *steal*- 2813 klepto. *Kill*- 2380 to slaughter for any purpose.

Destroy - 622 perish, lose, die, to destroy fully.

Our entire belief system in Christ is linked to our faith. **1Jn.5:4**.

No faith - no joy, no peace, no confidence, no anointing.

Why is your faith his main target? **Heb.11:6**.

Study Notes

Chart 7: Strongmen in Serpent Form

1. **Anantaboga** – Hindu giant dragon-like creature	9. **Mehen** – Egyptian divine serpent
2. **Apep** – Egyptian snake spirit	10. **Musilinda** – the great cobra
3. **Apophis** – Greek snake spirit	11. **Mushussu** – furious serpent
4. **Aspis** – Hebrew snake spirit of evil and stubbornness	12. **Musmahhu** – exalted serpent
4. **Banda** – serpent that binds or ties men up	13. **Nagas** – Hindu serpent deities
5. **Basmu** – a poisonous serpent	14. **Nehebkau** – serpent god of the underworld
6. **Basuki** – Hindu giant dragon-like creature	15. **Ra Uraeus** – divine cobra
7. **Botis** – snake spirit	16. **Satan** – that old serpent, the devil
8. **Kundalini** – spirit that is a coiled serpent at the base of the spine and is invoked during yoga	17. **Usumgallu** – great dragon

Chapter 7
Strongmen in Serpent Form

There are strongmen who take on the appearance of giant serpents or snakes. In my travels across America and in other countries, I have come face to face with many of these 'serpent' strongmen. They are all very evil and dangerous to mankind and have the same attribute as a serpent. Ever since the serpent tempted Eve in the Garden of Eden **(Genesis 3:1-6), Satan** has been using the serpent to deceive man.

In many cultures and various cults, the serpent is considered sacred and is worshipped. In **Numbers 21:8-9**, Moses is instructed by God to make a fiery serpent. The children of Israel rebelled against the God who delivered them from slavery, so He sent fiery serpents among them and they were bitten. Although they offended God, He had mercy on them and had Moses to make the image of the serpent. Therefore, any who were bitten and would humble themselves and look upon the image, they would be healed.

God had a reason to use this particular image. It was to remind the people of their sins of rebellion. I believe it was the serpent which tempted Eve to rebel against God's command and was now tempting the people of the **Hebrew nation** to rebel against the God who was their deliverer. He wanted them to see the enemy who was out to destroy them.

The very first time I ever saw one of these spirits was in 1978 while flying over the city of **Boston, Massachusetts**. We had just entered the Boston airways when the Lord showed me a vision of a giant *golden serpent* wrapped around the city of Boston.

I asked the Lord what this vision meant, and He told me this giant boa was the strongman of idolatry and false religion. This strongman did not only have Boston in its terrible grip but also all of the New England states.

A few years ago, a Brazilian pastor friend of ours was ministering in California with my wife and I. One night when he retired to his room, he was awakened around midnight by a giant golden boa. The Brazilian brother told us in the morning how this serpent challenged his reason for being there. When he told the serpent he was there by my request, the serpent told him he knew who I was, but wanted to know who he was. The brother took authority over it in Jesus' name, and the serpent turned and slowly left the cabin.

In **Nigeria, Egypt**, and even in **Switzerland**, people have told me about these encounters with these strongmen in serpent form. During the deliverance of a brother in Switzerland, snakebites appeared all over his face and body. His eyes took on the shape of a snake's eyes, and his tongue kept flickering in and out of his mouth. When he was finally set free, all of these effects vanished.

One of the strengths of a serpent is the ability to blend in with the landscape and remain hidden in plain sight and also to be able to mesmerize their victims with their eyes. The serpent is a *silent enemy and will not expose himself* until he is ready to strike. By then it is almost impossible to defend oneself against the attack.

> **Always be on guard against the enemy so you can avoid his snare. Like the serpent, the enemy works in silence and can remain hidden in plain sight. He patiently bides his time – waiting for the perfect moment to strike. Thank God we have the power to not only stop him, but to bind him so he cannot continue his assault.**

There are several names and titles these strongmen work under. In the **Hindu** religion **Nagas**, which is an evil race of snakes that lives in the underground kingdom called **Patala**. In **southern India**, several of the **Nagas** are regarded as gods and are worshipped. One of their kings is called **Takshaka**, and he rules over a kingdom of precious stones.

Many of the *royal families* see **Nagas** as being their ancestors. When they have statues of these snake gods erected, they make sure the land all around the statues is not cleared of vegetation. It is believed that if you give them enough of their own space, then they will leave your space alone.

Though these *snake gods* are very *destructive and evil*, there are many stories how these *violent creatures* have been very helpful to the **Hindu gods**. **Vishnu**, the **Hindu god** of *love*, laid down on the thousand-head serpent to sleep. He used another to churn the sea of milk. **Buddha** was supposedly sheltered from a storm while meditating by the hood of the great cobra **Musilinda**.

Some of these serpents, like **Musilinda** the cobra, are **Naga Basuki** and **Naga Anantaboga**. According to Hindu myth, **Basuki** and **Anantaboga** are *two giant dragon-like creatures* which help the gods, even though they are *extremely dangerous and evil*. There is also **Naga Banda**, which binds or ties men up. In the southern part of India, there is a **festival** called **Nag Panchami**. During this festival, snakes are honored, fed and basically worshipped.

The **Hindu** also practice a **form of yoga** in which they try to raise the **Kundalini** spirit, which is a *coiled serpent at the base of the spine*. <u>Through meditation</u>, the serpent *travels up the spine into the brain* and supposedly produces an intensely blissful experience. The truth is, many people have died trying to do this. It is only another deception and a form of demon possession.

Egypt has **Mehen**, the so-called *divine snake* whose coils protected **Ra**, the sun god, as he *journeyed on his boat through the waterways* of the night kingdom. **Mehen** is usually seen *draped in protective coils* about the deckhouse in which **Ra** stands.

Mehen is the enemy of another giant serpent called **Nehebkau**, *serpent god* of the *underworld*. **Nehebkau** is a *serpent with human arms and legs*, which lurks in the <u>underworld</u> as a constant menace to gods and men. He was a subject of **Ra** and would often give food to the dead. He is sometimes <u>portrayed as having two heads</u> at one end of <u>his body and another at the other end.</u>

Egypt has another serpent god called **Apep**, who is also called **Apophis** in the **Greek**. He is referred to as the *demon enemy of the sun* and is a huge snake symbolizing *darkness, storm, night, the underworld and death*. Every night he fought against **Ra**, the sun god, and was defeated every night in order that the sun could rise and shine again upon the earth.

Apep lived in the depths of the celestial Nile and had the occasional near victory during the eclipse where he swallowed the boat of the sun god – sometimes partly and sometimes completely. However, he always had to vomit it back up, as **Mehen** protected **Ra**. **Apep** was often paired with the *dark god* **Set**, producing the wickedest pair of gods ever imagined. The children of **Apep** attacked the god **Shu**, who after beating them off, was so weakened and exhausted he abdicated his position to **Geb**, the *earth god*.

Ra also had another serpent besides **Mehen**. This serpent, which he kept in a box was **Ra Uraeus**, the divine cobra. This cobra's extremely poisonous breath killed two of **Geb's** companions and severely burned **Geb**, the earth god.

Now, in the **Akkadian Epic** of Creation, we have the record where the female monster of chaos fashions eleven monsters to battle deities in order to avenge the death of a god called **Apsu**. These monsters were: **Basmu**, a giant venomous snake; **Usumgallu**, the great dragon; **Musmahhu**, the exalted serpent; **Mushussu**, the furious snake; **Lahmu** the hairy one; **Ugallu**, the big weather beast; **Uridimmu**, the mad lion; **Girtablulu**, the scorpion man; **Umu Dabrutu**, violent storms; **Kulullu**, the fish man; and **Kusarikku**, the bull man.

These entities are recorded in the most primitive records, and we can find astonishing parallels in later literature. From the **Sumerian**, to the **Akkadians**, to the **Hebrew**, these legends *remained consistent*. Even the Romans and Greeks had creatures, which were a mixture of man and beast, besides their gods and goddesses. This is also quite evident in the **Egyptian**, **Norse** and **Hindu** myths of mixed creatures. No matter what country or name these serpent strongmen are called by, they are your enemy, and like the snake, they lay hidden and in secret, waiting patiently for the opportunity to strike.

With Basmu, the *giant poisonous serpent*, we see how Satan, the original serpent, spreads his poison through slander, accusation, lies and defamation of character.

With **Musmahhu**, the exalted serpent, we see the arrogance of Lucifer who thought more of himself and wanted to replace God. With **Mushussu**, the furious serpent, we see the anger of the adversary being loosed upon man without mercy.

Aspis, the *Serpent of Evil and Stubbornness*:
Unrepentant, Hardened Heart of Satan – Refusing to Listen to God

With **Aspis**, the *serpent of evil and stubbornness*, we see the unrepentant, hardened heart of **Satan** refusing to listen to God and refusing to be contented with what was given to him. He demands what was not his to be his. He wanted the worship, glory and honor, which belonged to God only.

**With Apophis or Apep, the *dark serpent*, the *enemy of the sun*,
we see the devil's deep hatred of the light,
preferring the darkness of the lie to the brightness of the truth.**

**Just as Apophis hated the sun,
so Satan hates the Son and everything He stands for.**

Prayer Against the Strongmen in Serpent Form

Father, we come to You in the name of the One whose heel crushed the head of the serpent as was foretold in Your Holy Word. It is in the Name above every name, **(Philippians 2:9)** *the name of Jesus. We ask that these serpent strongmen who glide in and out of our lives to be bound, so they cannot continue to spread their poison in our lives.* **(Psalms 91)**

We ask that the false accusations, the slanderous remarks, the defamation of character and the lies, come to an end. **(Isaiah 54:17)** *No weapon that is fashioned against you shall succeed, and you shall confute every tongue that rises against you in judgment. This is the heritage of the servants of the Lord and their vindication from me, declares the Lord."*

Lord, as Israel looked to the image of the brazen serpent in the wilderness, which Moses and Aaron lifted up so the people could be healed, so we look to You, **Adoni Elohim***, to be delivered from the power of these serpents.* **(Numbers 21:9)**

Lord, in **(Luke 10:19),** *You gave to us power over scorpions and snakes. You said that nothing by any means would harm us, and we would have authority over all the works of the enemy.*

Yes, dear Lord, because of You and Your sacrifice, we are more than conquerors. We are forever victorious through Christ who strengthens us. **(Romans 8:37)**

We can do all things through Christ Jesus to the glory of God the Father. (Philippians 4:13) Amen and Amen.

Chart 8: Strongmen of Mystical Legends
Part 1: Vampires

1. **Adze** – ghost-like vampire from Ghana	22. **Hantu- Dor Dong** – Indian vampire
2. **Alu** – vampire spirit of the night	23. **Hiadam/Haidam** – Hungarian vampire
3. **Asanbosam** – in African folklore, vampire-like creatures	24. **Impundulu** – vampire spirit of disease and death
4. **Aswang** – Philippine vampire spirit	25. **Jaracaca** – Brazilian snake vampire
5. **Aulak** – temple vampire	26. **Jigarkhvar** – cannibal spirit of death; witch-like vampire
6. **Baital/Baitala** – race of vampires	27. **Kali** – wife of Sita/Shiva, fierce vampire
7. **Baobhan** – vampire spirit	28. **Kuang-Shi/Chiang-Shi** – Chinese vampire
8. **Bhutas** – vampire shape-shifter	29. **Mah'anah** – vampire spirit
9. **Charmo Vetr** – Hindukusch vampire spirit	30. **Mmbyu** – mischief-making vampire from India
10. **Chordewa** – vampire witch	31. **Nachzeher** – vampire spirit
11. **Churel** – vampire spirit in India	32. **Neuntoter** – German vampire that is a carrier of plagues and pestilence
12. **Civatateo** – Aztec vampire	33. **Pacu-Pati** – vampire race from India
13. **Danag** – Oriental spirit	34. **Penanggalan** – Malaysian vampire
14. **Dearg-Due** – Irish vampire	35. **Pisacha** – Indian vampire
15. **Eretica** – Russian vampire	36. **Rakshasa** – unrighteous Hindu vampire
16. **Estrie** – Jewish vampire	37. **Swawmx** – vampire creature from Burma
17. **Gayal** – vampire ghost from India	38. **Talamar** – vampire creature of the Banks Islands
18. **Gierach** – Prussian vampire	39. **Vetala/Vetal** – similar to Baital/Baitala, race of vampires
19. **Hanh Saburo** – vampire from India	40. **Vrykolakas** – vampire on the island of Chios/Khios
20. **Hannya** – Japanese vampire	41. **Wichan Alwe** – Araukanian vampire
21. **Hant-pare** – Indian vampire which clings to the wounds of a person	

Chapter 8
Strongmen of Mystical Legends
Part 1: Vampires

In 1999 while living in Georgia, I received a call for help. The young lady on the phone was in a panic. Her friend was in serious spiritual turmoil. At the time she was actually possessed by a very violent spirit which was threatening to take her life.

When I entered into the house and began to go up the stairs, a very masculine voice shouted obscenities, telling me to leave. The young lady who called me began yelling, "Come quick, Pastor! We're up here! Help us! Please!"

When I entered the room I couldn't believe what I was seeing. The young lady's friend was hanging in the air in the shape of a cross. There were two large fangs hanging out of her mouth, and blood was pouring out of her mouth, hands and feet.

The spirit which possessed her identified itself as a vampire spirit. It had entered her when she had joined one of the five families of the vampire cult headquartered in Anderson, South Carolina. The spirit claimed that it and its fellow vampire spirits were trapping hundreds of young people through the books, movies and television programs they were being exposed to.

By God's grace this young lady was set free and given her life back. She accepted Jesus as her Lord and is living a wonderful life. However, there are many, many young people ensnared by these spirits which most people believe are not real.

My wife and I have faced these unclean spirits manifesting through their victims in places like *Asheville, NC; Salem, MA; Norcross, GA; and in Anderson*, SC., just to name a few.

These strange cults are growing by leaps and bounds.

The **new** vampire books and the shows are recruiting young people into these cults in large numbers, just like *Harry Potter* is doing for the cults of witchcraft and Wicca.

The names of the following spirits, which are ensnaring the young people into vampire cults, are found in the myths and legends of many different cultures and are very real in these particular lands.

I have spoken to many mature Christian people across the world that have had experiences with these supernatural beings ranging from *shape-shifters* (*werebeasts*), to *vampires*, to *cannibalism*, and even with what the Africans call the *underwater people*. We may consider these testimonies as pure fantasies but to the hundreds of people who have seen them, it is **no fairy tale, but reality.**

Adze drinks the blood of children and can possess humans.

The people from the **Ewe tribe** in Ghana speak of a creature called **Adze**. He is a *ghost-like vampire* who **drinks the blood** of *children and can possess humans*. There is also a **Semitic night demon that brings death by seizures**.

Asanbosam are vampire-like creatures.

Asanbosam are vampire-like creatures in **African** folklore with iron-like teeth and whose feet are shaped like hooks. They appear in three forms, male, female, and little children. They supposedly suck blood from the thumbs of sleeping victims.

In the **Philippines,** there is a creature called **Aswang** which appears as a woman in the daytime and as a flying monster at night. When it's the flying monster at night, it drinks the blood of sleeping people.

In **Arabia**, there is a terrible *vampire spirit* which eats women and children. In **Scotland**, there is a terrible *vampire* spirit which appears as a young girl dressed in green to attack young men and drain their blood.

There is a very strange spirit which is a combination between a shape-shifter and vampire. It drinks blood and eats the meat of their victims, and they roam about in the shape of horses, pigs and giants.

Charmo-Vetr is a **Hindukusch** *demon* of the **Kam tribe** and preys on travelers in the villages. In order to appease her, *animals have to be sacrificed*. In **India**, there is a *vampire ghost spirit*, which **hates all life**. It is a belief that when a pregnant woman dies during <u>Diwali</u>, which is the **Hindu** festival of lights, she becomes a <u>churel.</u>

In the **Philippines**, there are *vampires who had become vampires* by *drinking a drop of blood*.

In **Ireland**, there is what is called the **Dearg-Due**, meaning *red bloodsuckers*. They are *female vampire spirits*. Each night, they rise from their grave and lure men with their beauty. Then they attack and kill the men by sucking all their blood.

South Africa has what is called the **Impundulu**. These are *demons* of the people who live at the Cape of South Africa. These creatures are known to *drink blood* and to *bring disease and death*.

Finally we have **Wichan Alwe,** a *vampire* from the **Araukanians** who are believed to be the *souls of the evil dead. They drill a hole into the heart of the person and drink the blood.*

In the **Banks Islands** near **Australia**, there is a legend concerning a creature called **Talamar** which can be either male or female. The **Talamar** is supposedly able to *communicate with ghosts*; thereby, establishing a close relationship with the deceased person and turning it into a dreadfully dangerous familiar spirit or servant that can be sent forth to affect the living.

Another kind of **Talamar** was an individual who could send out his or her soul to consume the lingering life essence in a new corpse. The approach of a **Talamar** could be detected by a scratching at a door or a rustling sound near the corpse.

In **Burma**, there is a *vampire* creature called a **Swawmx** which was considered a god creature and was worshipped. In **India** you have a *vampire ghost* called a **gayal.** It is believed to be the spirit of a man who died unmarried or without a male heir; therefore, depriving him of someone who can properly perform the funeral rites. When the **gayal** returns, he focuses his attention on the sons of others as well as his relatives. This threat is a guarantee someone will see that the proper funeral rites are done.

Among the **Punjabs**, the **gayal** is given a small platform with a hemispherical depression, which has milk and the water from the Ganges poured into it as a sacrifice. Then lamps are placed around the depression. Mothers in the local area hang a coin around the necks of their sons to keep them safe from attacks by the **gayal**.

Germany is a country with a *large variety of vampire traditions*. These traditions are reflected in its diverse history of the area and have shaped the character of the nation. Aside from the traditional Slavic form of the creature found in the east of Germany, the country has been faced with many other types, such as the **Nachzeher** which *kill their relatives.* There is the **neuntoter**, a vampire considered to be a *carrier of plagues and pestilence.* This is the Alps and Prussian form of the **gierach.**

In **France**, there are **no fables of vampires,** but their **historical** *evidence of living vampires are very interesting.* You have the cases of Gabrielle de Launay, the *Marques de Moueve,* the *Marquis de Sade, Sergeant Bertrand, Antoine Leger, Alexander Simon, Victor Ardisson,* and *Giles de Rais.*

In **Serbia**, **Bulgaria**, and **Romania**, there is an extremely evil clan of vampire creatures referred to as the children of **Judas**. Their **red hair** is the distinguishing characteristic of these creatures. They are known mainly through traditions and are considered the worst of the Balkan undead.

These supposedly *red headed spawn of Judas Iscariot has the incredible ability to drain all the blood from their victims with a single bite or kiss.* They leave behind the symbolic sign 'XXX', which represents the thirty pieces of silver – the price for betraying Christ.

In **China**, there is the legend of the **Kuang-Shi** (or **Chiang-Shi**), which was the name used to describe the most *fearsome type of vampire* in China. It was a creature with red eyes, sharp fangs, talons, and white or greenish hair covering the entire body. This spirit sometimes has *the ability to fly or to appear as a mist or vapor and even to become invisible.*

Chios (also known as **Khios**) is a mountainous island in the **Aegean Sea**, where the inhabitants of the isle believe firmly in a *vampire* known as the **vrykolakas**. To stop a person from becoming a **vrykolakas**, *a cotton or wax cross is placed on the lips of the corpse*, and during the funeral, the priest would place a shard of pottery with the words *'Jesus Christ conquers'*.

The **vrykolakas** was believed to *rise from the grave and knock on doors calling out the name of someone in the house.* If there were any responses given, the next day the person would die. Since the **vrykolakas** never called out twice, the *people of Chios* always waited for the repetition of their name before responding.

In **Bangladesh** among the **Oraon tribe**, is a *vampire* witch called a **chordewa** who is able to turn herself into a black vampire cat, and in this shape enters the dwelling of the sick and dying. She'll eat the food of the person who is dying and lick their lips, causing their doom.

The **chordewa** in its *cat form* can be distinguished by its strange mewing and the *superhuman effort* it takes to capture it. Any injury the cat receives would be found on the human witch. **If the cat was caught, the witch would fall into a coma** in which she remained until the cat was free and able to reenter her own body. Women who were suspected of being a **chordewa** were burned.

Other witch vampire creatures were also found among the **Aztecs of Mexico**. They captured the attention of the Europeans in the sixteenth century as a result of the *Spanish Conquest*. These **Aztec vampires,** or **Civatateo,** were the servants of the moon god, **Tezcatlipoca,** and the *moon goddess*, **Tlazolteol**. The **Civatateo** were given the title **civapipiltin** (princess), as they were noble women who died in childbirth. Their favorite victims were children. Because of the **Civatateo's** power, the children died horribly of a wasting disease.

In **India**, the **Churel** is a *vicious and vengeful ghost-like vampire*. This was normally a woman who died while *unclean in childbirth* or during pregnancy at the *Diwali festival*. If she was treated badly by her family, she would return to harass them and dry up the blood of the male family members.

In **Russia**, there is a *vampire creature* called an **Eretica**. It was believed in this region that *heretics who died became vampires*. The **Eretica** was *always* a woman. These women, according to legend, had *sold their souls to the devil during their lifetime. Returning to life after their death*, they would assume the disguise of an old woman in rags. When night came, they would meet with other **ereticy** in a ravine and have a Sabbath. They were active only in the spring and the late fall – sleeping at night in the coffins of those who in life had been impious. To fall or sink in the grave of an **eretica** would cause a person to waste away. The most **dangerous** was to <u>**look into the evil (eye gate)**</u> of these creatures, because in doing so a person would die a slow painful withering death.

Even Israel <u>does not</u> escape the *vampire legends*.

The *'Jewish vampire'* or strongman of the undead demon creature is called an **Estrie**. It is a *feared Hebrew spirit* connected **both with demons and witches** and is *always female*. The **Estrie** was held to be one of the *incorporated spirits of evil*, which had taken on flesh and blood. It lived among the living in order to fill its need for blood and the favorite prey was a child. If no children were available, it would attack adults.

The **Estrie** could change its appearance at will but would always revert back to its demonic form to fly around at night. If the **Estrie** was wounded or was seen in its natural shape by a human, the creature would have to eat the bread and salt of the person who saw it, and it would lose its powers. When prayers in a service were said for a woman who was suspected of being an **Estrie,** at the conclusion of the prayer no one said 'amen'.

At the burial of a person suspected of being an **Estrie**, the body was examined to see if the *mouth was open.* <u>If it was found to be open,</u> then it was believed it would continue in its activities for another year. Placing dirt in the mouth of the creature rendered it inactive.

> **In Japan, the most hideous *monster* of their culture is a *child-eating, blood-drinking ghoulish vampire* called a Hannya.**

In **1720** in a village near the **Hungarian border**, a strange historical story took place concerning a creature referred to as the **Hiadam (or Haidam)** *vampire*, which was fully investigated by officials of the **Holy Roman Empire**. This resulted in one of the *best documented cases* of *true vampirism* of the time.

In **Brazil, one of the *species of vampires* which *appears in the shape of a snake, feeds from the breasts of a nursing mother*. The jaracaca *will push a baby out of the way and keep the infant quiet by shoving its tail down the child's mouth.***

> **There are so many more legends concerning these creatures or strongmen of the undead referred to as vampires.**

It would take a whole separate volume of books to cover every legend. Many experts feel *the root of the vampire legends* may have begun in **Egypt**. Others believe it started in India with its culture of many gods and goddesses. In India alone you have the **Bhutas** – ghosts of a deceased person, the **Rakshasa** – an unrighteous spirit, and a **Jigarkhwar** – a witch-like vampire found in the Sind region.

Also in **India**, there is the **Hanh Saburo**, the **Hant-pare** the **Hantu-Dor Dong**, the **Mah'anah** and **Pacu-Pati** whose name means *master of the herd* and known also as **Mmbyu**, an earlier personification of death. It is deemed the lord of all mischief including different kinds of *ghosts, ghouls* and, of course, the *vampire*. He is seen at night, surrounded by his entourage of servants, frequenting cemeteries and places of death.

The **Penanggalan** is a *dreadful Malaysian vampire. It is very unique because it appears as a detached female head and neck with its stomach and intestines dangling beneath.* The creature is *always* female and *delights* in *sucking the blood of children and pregnant women in labor.*

There is the **Pisacha** and finally, the **Vetala** which is a type of **Indian** *vampire also considered a chief of demons*. It is known in some regions as a **baital**, the **baitala** or the **vetal**. This creature is described as being white, green or wheat colored and riding a green horse. It can also appear as an old hag sucking the blood of women who are insane or drunk.

> **India's most notorious vampire-like creature is also one of its most popular goddesses. It is the *wife of the notorious Siva, god of destruction*. Her name is Kali, the great dark goddess.**

She is pictured with many arms – all holding a weapon or shield or the head of a demon.

Her mouth is covered with blood and around her neck is a necklace of human skulls. Her cult of thieves worshipped her with bloody human sacrifices. These **Thugees,** who were finally put down by the British in the nineteenth century, made death and blood a lasting aspect of **Kali** *worship*.

Looking at the different stories concerning these creatures called vampires makes it almost impossible to believe in their actual existence.

The logical mind says they cannot be real; **yet**, in every country of the world, civilized or uncivilized, both educated and uneducated people truly believe in their existence, and they have affected many lives.

We have a tendency to ridicule and laugh at these stories. We believe there cannot be any possibilities of there being any truth to them.

> **However, to *repeat a statement made earlier*:**
> **Behind every fable is a myth, behind every myth a legend,**
> **and behind every legend is a foundation of truth.**
> **What we need to do is separate fact from fiction – the truth from the lie.**

No matter what we believe or what we think is fantasy or fable or a lie, just keep in mind that someone somewhere is experiencing a very real problem due to a very real and dangerous strongman posing in one of his many disguises.
He does this to ensnare and destroy the person and his family.

In the incident of the young girl at the beginning of this chapter, you may actually doubt her testimony; however, to her *it is a reality*. She doesn't need anyone's approval for her to know the truth of what she lived through. Am I saying this was a real vampire as in the legend of Dracula? My answer is no! What I am stating is *this was a spiritual strongman using a disguise to hide his real identity.*

I believe the actual spirit is referred to as **Bhuta**. The **Bhuta** in legends around the world is the one **most feared** and is **considered to be the power behind all other vampire spirits**. Yes, **Satan** will even use fairy tales or horror stories to work his destructive evil throughout the world.

> **The emotions of fear and anxiety are to Satan**
> **what faith and trust is to God.**

When we walk in faith and have complete trust in God, He can work fully in our lives to bless us and to help us to live free from bondage. On the other hand, when we allow fear and anxiety to control us, we give an invitation to the devil to work in our lives and to keep us in bondage.

Do I believe there is a *Dracula-like creature* hiding in the darkness of night to spring unaware on its victim, to drink its blood, and turn it into an undead being like itself? The answer is no, but I do believe there are spirits out there, which seek to drain all of the joy, peace and happiness from you and your loved ones.

To drain a person completely of all hope and spiritual strength leaves the victim a dried out hollow husk of what they once were. They are completely drained of all emotions and the essence of life.

These spirits may not drink your blood like the Hollywood version of the vampire, but they will definitely drain you of your spiritual life force. They'll leave you every bit of an undead creature as *Dracula's blood sucking could ever do.*

Prayer Against the Vampire Strongmen

Father, we acknowledge that the life of a man is in the blood, and if we ever wanted to end the life in man or animal, all we need to do is drain the blood from them.

Yes Father, we know our physical blood sustains our physical life, but Lord, it is the Blood of Your son Jesus, which gives us eternal life.

*Just as we would **not** allow a vampire to drain our life force from us physically, neither Lord, will we allow a psychic or spiritual vampire to drain the spiritual Source of our eternal life. We take a determined stand against these strongmen in Jesus' name, binding them from off our lives and the lives of our loved ones.*

Lord, we command these spirits of darkness to not only stop their assault, but to also return the peace, joy and happiness they have stolen from us. Lord, we also command these spirits of darkness to return our rest and to stop the storms which troubles and disturbs our minds.

We thank You Father, that You have given us power and authority over all the works of the enemy and his allies, no matter what dark disguise they may take. No weapon formed can harm us in any way whether it is physical, mental, emotional, financial or spiritual.

Thank You Father, for the Blood of Jesus, which covers us completely so no vampire, real or spiritual, can touch us in any way. Thank You for the precious Blood which protects and gives to us life and much more.

Yes, that awesome Blood which protects us and hides us from all of our enemies and contains the gift of eternal life that we wear as the armor of God – making us victorious and over comers through Jesus Christ, the ultimate vampire slayer. Amen.

Psalms 27

The Lord is my light and my salvation—
whom shall I fear?
The Lord is the stronghold of my life—
of whom shall I be afraid?
² When the wicked advance against me
to devour me,
it is my enemies and my foes
who will stumble and fall.
³ Though an army besiege me,
my heart will not fear;
though war break out against me,
even then I will be confident.
⁴ One thing I ask from the Lord,
this only do I seek:
that I may dwell in the house of the Lord
all the days of my life,
to gaze on the beauty of the Lord
and to seek him in his temple.
⁵ For in the day of trouble
he will keep me safe in his dwelling;
he will hide me in the shelter of his sacred tent
and set me high upon a rock.
⁶ Then my head will be exalted
above the enemies who surround me;
at his sacred tent I will sacrifice with shouts of joy;
I will sing and make music to the Lord.
⁷ Hear my voice when I call, Lord;
be merciful to me and answer me.
⁸ My heart says of you, "Seek his face!"
Your face, Lord, I will seek.
⁹ Do not hide your face from me,
do not turn your servant away in anger;
you have been my helper.
Do not reject me or forsake me,
God my Savior.
¹⁰ Though my father and mother forsake me,
the Lord will receive me.
¹¹ Teach me your way, Lord;
lead me in a straight path
because of my oppressors.
¹² Do not turn me over to the desire of my foes,
for false witnesses rise up against me,
spouting malicious accusations.
¹³ I remain confident of this:
I will see the goodness of the Lord
in the land of the living.
¹⁴ Wait for the Lord;
be strong and take heart
and wait for the Lord.

PRAYER FOR DELIVERANCE FROM OCCULT INVOLVEMENT

I unreservedly forgive all my ancestors for all the things they have done that have affected me and my life. I specifically renounce the consequences of their sins in Jesus' name. As a child of God I now claim that the power of the blood of Jesus is setting me free from the consequences of generational sins. I claim my freedom from the consequences of all occult activity on either my father or my mother's family lines **(name specifically)**, *from curses and pronouncements that have had an effect on my life, from hereditary diseases and from the effects of any of their sins that have influenced me. I put any and all sins of an occult nature that I may have committed under the blood of Jesus and ask for Your forgiveness for each of them (specifically name as many of them as you can). I take back any access I have given to any of Satan's forces through these sins. I pray this in the name of Jesus, who became curse for me on Calvary and died that I might be set free. Amen*

PRAYER FOR FORGIVENESS FROM IDOLATRY BASED SINS

Dear heavenly Father, You have said the pride goes before destruction and an arrogant spirit before stumbling **(Proverbs 16:18)**. *I confess that I have not denied myself, picked up my cross daily, and followed You* **(Matthew 16:24)**. *In so doing I have given ground to the enemy in my life. I have believed that I could be successful and live victoriously by my own strength and resources. I now confess that I have sinned against You by placing my will before Yours and by centering my life around self instead of You. I now renounce the self-life and by so doing cancel all the ground that has been gained in my members by the enemies of the Lord Jesus Christ. I pray that You will guide me so that I will do nothing from selfishness or empty conceit, but that with humility of mind I will regard others as more important than myself* **(Philippians 2:3)**. *Enable me through love to serve others and in honor prefer others* **(Romans 12:10)**. *I ask this in the name of Christ Jesus my Lord. Amen.*

PRAYER OF SUBMISSION TO THE HOLY SPIRIT

Dear heavenly Father, You have said that rebellion is as the sin of witchcraft and insubordination is as iniquity and idolatry **(I Samuel 15:23)**. *I know that in action and attitude I have sinned against You with a rebellious heart. I ask Your forgiveness for my rebellion and pray that by the shed blood of the Lord Jesus Christ all ground gained by evil spirits because of my rebelliousness would be canceled. I pray that You will shed light on all my ways that I may know the full extent of my rebelliousness and choose to adopt a submissive spirit and a servant's heart. In the name of Christ Jesus my Lord. Amen.*

PRAYER OF THE ARMOR OF GOD

Heavenly Father, I desire to be obedient by being strong in the Lord and the power of Your might. I see that this is Your will and purpose for me. I recognize that it is essential to put on the armor that You have provided, and I do so now with gratitude and praise that You have provided all I need to stand in victory against Satan and his kingdom. Grant me wisdom to discern the tactics and sneakiness of Satan's strategy against me. I delight to take the armor You have provided and by faith to put it on as effective spiritual protection against the spiritual forces of darkness present in the world today

I confidently take the belt of truth that You offer me. I take Him who is the truth as my strength and protection. I reject Satan's lies and deceiving ways to gain advantage against me. Grant me discernment and wisdom to recognize the subtle and sneaky ways in which Satan seeks to cause me to accept his lies as truth. I desire to believe only the truth, to live the truth, to speak the truth, and to know the truth. I worship and praise You that You lead me only in the ways of truth. Thank You that Satan cannot stand against the truth.

Thank You for the breastplate of righteousness which you offer me. I eagerly accept it and put it on as my protection. Thank you for reminding me again that all of my righteousness comes from You. I embrace that righteousness which is mine by faith in the Lord Jesus Christ. It is His righteousness that is mine through justification. I reject and repudiate all trust in my own righteousness which is as filthy rags. I ask You to cleanse me of all the times I have counted my own goodness as being acceptable before You. I bring the righteousness of my Lord directly against all of Satan's workings against me. I express my desire to walk in righteousness before God today. By faith I appropriate the righteousness of Christ and invite Him to walk in His holiness in my life today that I might experience His righteousness in total context of ordinary living. I count upon the righteousness of my Lord to be my protection. I know that Satan must retreat from before God's righteousness.

Thank You, Lord, for the sandals of peace You have provided. I desire that my feet should stand on the solid rock of the peace that You have provided. I claim the peace with God which is mine through justification. I desire the peace of God which touches my emotions and feelings through prayer and sanctification **(Philippians 4:6).** *Thank You that as I walk in obedience to You the God of peace promises to walk with me* **(Philippians 4:9),** *I thank you that as the God of peace You are putting Satan under my feet* **(Romans 16:20).** *I will share this good news of peace with all others that Your Spirit will bring into my life today. Thank you that You have not given me a spirit of fear but of love and power and a sound mind.* **(II Timothy 1:7).** *Thank you that Satan cannot stand against Your peace.*

Chart 8: Strongmen of Mystical Legends
Part 2: Cannibals

1. **Bachbakuala-Nuksiwae** – man-eating creature among the Kwakiutl Indians	11. **Wendigo** – shape-shifter, flesh-eating beast in the outback and woods of Canada
2. **Baka** – Haitian cannibal spirit	12. **Wolba** – flesh-eating spirit
3. **Belu** – man-eating spirit in Burma	13. **Wutr** – female cannibal
4. **Blutschink** – man-eating cannibal	14. **Xastur** – kills people in their sleep and devours them
5. **Bolla** – a cannibal spirit in Albania	15. **Yachemi** – female cannibal
6. **Cherufe** – giant cannibal spirit, which eats young girls	16. **Yama-Onna** – cannibal spirit of greed
7. **Curiysira** – shape-shifting cannibal from the Amazon	17. **Yamale** – giant cannibal
8. **Iya** – cannibal spirit of disease and death	18. **Yara-Ma-Yha-Who** – Australian cannibal
9. **Jigarkhvar** – cannibal spirit of death; witch-like vampire	19. **Yush** – red giant cannibal spirit
10. **Wasco** – demon who brings death to children by eating them	

Chapter 8
Strongmen of Mystical Legends
Part 2: Cannibals

The story of the *vampire spirit seems almost unbelievable*, and so does the next spiritual strongman which deals with *cannibalism*. However, the *flesh-eating* creature of our worst nightmare is so much easier to accept because of the accounts given in history of those who have been confronted by the cannibalistic tribes of **Africa** and uncivilized nations.

When we first heard these *tales of horror* of how people were killed and eaten in the **Congo** and other jungle areas, we were completely devastated and could not believe a human being could be so animalistic as to do something like this repulsive act of eating another human. Then our next thought was, "Well, this only happens in the uncivilized jungles of the world. These savages didn't know better. They weren't people of culture after all."

However, we suddenly began to receive reports of *cannibalism* which was not from the Congo or in the other remote jungles of the world. Instead we were hearing of *cannibalism* right here in **America**, and in **England**, and in other so-called civilized nations.

It was now not just an uncivilized tribal custom of vicious savages of the wild. It was now an emotional sick form of a depraved mind. Nevertheless, it is more than just being uncivilized or having a depraved mind. It is because of the strongmen of *cannibalism* who are submitted to the most evil depraved mind of the Adversary of man. We call him **Satan**, who is the strongest of the strongmen.

The word *cannibalism* comes from the **Spanish name** for the **Carib** people. This people group lived mostly in the Lesser Antilles of the **West Indies** and acquired the reputation of being *cannibals*. *Cannibalism* has also been well documented around the world from **Fiji** to the **Amazon Basin** to the **Congo** to Ma' on, **New Zealand**, even to modern day America.

Reports of Cannibalism

In the 872 day siege of **Leningrad** in *1941-1942*, reports of cannibalism among the **German** soldiers began to appear. In *January 1943*, roughly *100,000 soldiers* were taken as *P.O.W.s*, and almost all of them were sent to camps in Siberia or Central Asia. There was such a severe lack of food in these camps; reports began to filter from there that the prisoners were resorting to cannibalism to stay alive. Out of the 100,000 prisoners taken at **Stalingrad**, only 5,000 survived.

In February 1945, a *Japanese* soldier ate *five American airmen*. In 1947, thirty Japanese soldiers were put on trial and five were found guilty on charges of cannibalism and were hung.

October 24, 1986: Self-proclaimed emperor of the Central African Republic Jean-Bedel Bokassa was placed on trial for many mass murders as well as the crime of cannibalism.

During the famine of 1990, reports of *cannibalism* began appearing all over **North Korea**. In 2006, there was a report that three people were executed for the eating and selling of human flesh in **North Korea**; and in 2013, it was reported that a man was executed for killing his two children for food.

In 1993, the **Chijon family** was a **South Korean** gang of *cannibals* founded by Kim Ki-hwan, an ex-convict, and six former prisoners and unemployed workers who hated the rich. A member of the gang admitted that *cannibalism* fired up his courage and helped him to renounce his humanity.

In the 1950's, there was the notorious **Mau Mau tribe**, which were the ultra-violent **Kikuyu** rebels of **Kenya**. They opposed British rule and conducted bloody ritual oaths to ensure the loyalty of its members. This tribe was so violent that in 1952, the British waged war against these rebels with just determination that by 1956, 11,000 militants were slain and another 20,000 were confined to prison camps.

Among the **Kwakiutl Indians**, there is a creature called **Bachbakuala-Nuksiwae** which is a man-eater. In Haiti, there is the **Baka** which is a form of zombie cannibal that thrives on human flesh. In **Tirolian** *mythology*, you have the **Blutschink**, a man-eating *cannibal*. In **Albania**, there is the **Bolla**, a *dragon-like creature* who, according to legend, awakes on the day of Saint George and eats whoever it sees first.

In **Burma**, there is the **Belu** who appears human with sharp teeth that feed on human flesh. **Chile** has the evil creature, **Cherufe**, whose *appetite for destruction* can only be appeased by *eating young girls*. In the **Amazon region**, there is the legend of the **Curiysira**, a *shape-shifting cannibal* which appears human, except for his backward facing feet.

Among the **Lakota tribes** in America there is the creature called the **Iya**. He is the *embodiment of all evil and eats humans*. His breath brings *disease and death*. In **India** mythology, there is a **Jigarkhvar**, a *female demon* who makes *people faint* by the *power of her eyes(gates)*, and then *eats their liver*. In connection with the **Nutka-indios** there is another spirit called a **Wasco**. These demon spirits *hunt little children* and *devour* them.

Even in a civilized country like **Canada** there are tales of *flesh-eating monsters* called the **Wendigo**. Then there are the women of the **Yush** that *feed upon humans*. There is also the **Xastur,** another *female spirit*, which *kills people in their sleep* and then *devours the bodies*. Another *feminine spirit* from **Hindukusch** is called a **Yachemi**, which kills her victims and then eats half of them. The **Hindukusch** male counterpart to the **Yachemi** is the **Yamale**, who *live in caves and hunt humans*.

In **Japan**, you have what is called **Yama-Onna**, a spirit of *intense greed* who is a *cannibal*. **Australia** has the **Yara-Ma-Yha-Who**. This creature has a large head and mouth, and its hands and feet have suckers on them *like an octopus*. Finally from the **Kafir** mythology, there is the **Yush**, which is a *giant red demon* with *six fingers* on his hands. He hunts humans to eat them.

Creatures of Myth and Horror Stories

Once again, we are looking at creatures of *myth and horror stories*. Fairy tales are made up to scare little children into behaving, or short scary stories are told to share around the campfire. Sorry to say these creatures called cannibals do exist. We have seen the horrible results of their unnatural appetites.

Modern Day Cannibals

When modern day *cannibals*, like **Jeffrey Dahmer**, are on trial, we sat stunned to think humans could be so depraved.

In the case of **Hamilton Howard** "Albert" Fish, who was an American serial killer was also known as the *Gray Man*, the *Werewolf of Wysteria*, the *Brooklyn Vampire*, the *Moon Maniac*, and *The Boogey Man*. He was a *child rapist and cannibal*, who bragged that he had over a hundred children. We don't know if he was talking about *rapes or cannibalism*. He was finally found guilty for the kidnapping and murder of Grace Budd, and on January 16, 1936 at the age of 65 was executed in Sing Sing correctional institution in Ossining, New York.

The other famous modern American serial killer and cannibal was **Jeffrey Lionel Dahmer**. He was known as the Milwaukee Cannibal. He was guilty of *the rape, murder, and dismemberment of seventeen men and boys between 1978-1991*. **Dahmer** was also *guilty of the crime of cannibalism and necrophilia* which is having sexual relations with the dead. **Dahmer** was sentenced to seventeen life sentences, and on November 28, 1994, another inmate at the Columbia Correctional Institute beat him to death.

Although both men were thought to suffer from a borderline personality disorder, they were declared completely sane enough to stand trial for their crimes.

Today's Society's Way of Thinking

It is amazing to think that in today's society, every form of lifestyle is accepted. Instead of calling it a sin, society labels it as a result of a birth defect. It is just another alternate lifestyle as in a sexual choice, or it is a sickness as in cases of addiction and alcohol abuse. However in the case of *cannibalism*, it is not a case of an emotional sickness, but a spiritual one. It is a soul sickness, which comes from the most evil and perverted mind in all of eternity. The act of cannibalism can only stem from a mind rooted in the cesspool of hell itself. Only the most criminally depraved mind or a mind lacking any Godly thought; a mind totally in the realm of darkness and evil could act against nature like this.

This reprobate mind is the mind of Satan, which is the power behind the spirit of *cannibalism*.

Prayer Against the Cannibal Strongman

Dear Lord, we stand in absolute amazement at how evil the human mind can sink to. When we look around and see the horror of the darkness which has come into Your perfect creation, we are ashamed. Because of the entrance of sin into this world by the disobedience of man to Your commandments, all that You meant to be so beautiful has become tainted and polluted by the cancer of sin.

Father, we pray for those whose minds have become so darkened by the lies of the father of lies. It is abhorrent how they would turn to perform so terrible of an act against God and nature. We pray they would be exposed to the light and truth of Your Word.

We pray the darkness will forever be destroyed by the power of Your Spirit. We also ask that the victims from the diabolical snare of the Adversary be set free.

Thank You Father, for watching over us and being our Protector against the rabid attacks of the enemy and his allies.

Thank You that You hide us and our children, our grandchildren, and our friends from these terrible things and have given us Your Word and the name of Your Son, Jesus as a strong sword and shield in which to protect our loved ones in Jesus' name. Amen.

PRAYER OF SUBMISSION TO THE HOLY SPIRIT

Dear heavenly Father, You have said that rebellion is as the sin of witchcraft and insubordination is as iniquity and idolatry **(I Samuel 15:23)**. *I know that in action and attitude I have sinned against You with a rebellious heart. I ask Your forgiveness for my rebellion and pray that by the shed blood of the Lord Jesus Christ all ground gained by evil spirits because of my rebelliousness would be canceled. I pray that You will shed light on all my ways that I may know the full extent of my rebelliousness and choose to adopt a submissive spirit and a servant's heart. In the name of Christ Jesus my Lord. Amen.*

Chart 8: Strongmen of Mystical Legends
Part 3: Shape-Shifters

1. **Achelous** – river spirit with head of bull and head of man	12. **Chindi** – Navajo shape-shifter
2. **Adlet** – dog people	13. **Chordeva** – East Indian shape-shifting cat spirit
3. **Almasti** – Russian creature that was part man and part beast	14. **Curiysira** – shape-shifting vampire spirit
4. **Anubis** – Egyptian jackal-headed god of the underworld	15. **Jestan** – Hindukusch dog spirit
5. **Bhutas** – shape-shifting vampire spirit	16. **Kusarikku** – bull man strongman of the half man and half animal mutations
6. **Bisclaveret** – French werewolf	17. **Lahmu** – spirit of the beast man
7. **Bogies & Boggarts** – English shape-shifters	18. **Maahes** – lion-headed man, Egyptian strongman of war and massacre
8. **Boxenwolf** – German werewolf	19. **Mont** – bull-headed Egyptian strongman of war and destruction
9. **Bruxsa** – Portuguese shape-shifter	20. **Wendigo** – shape-shifter, flesh-eating beast in the outback and woods of Canada
10. **Caacrinolaas** – strongman of darkness, appears as a black dog	21. **Were-being** (can take the shape of any animal – record of cases in every nation)
11. **Canaima** – notorious shape-shifting spirit	

Chapter 8
Strongmen of Mythical Legends
Part 3: Shape-Shifters

Here in America we tend to look down on people who believe a man can change his shape to that of an animal. When I was growing up, I remember wanting so badly to see the movie *Frankenstein meets the Werewolf*, starring Lon Chaney, Jr. in his famous character, *The Wolf Man*.

For millions of people around the world, the image of a werewolf brings to mind that of Lon Chaney, Jr. in *The Wolf Man* (1941). We all felt great sympathy for Larry Talbot, the character played by Mr. Chaney.

Mr. Talbot was an innocent victim of the curse of the werewolf. A mild-mannered man turned into a rabid murderous animal. When in the form of the werewolf, Mr. Talbot was invincible to all weapons except a silver bullet. This legend of the silver bullet is found throughout the movies such as: *I Was A Teenage Werewolf* (1957), starring Michael Landon, *An American Werewolf in London* (1981), *An American Werewolf in Paris* (1997), and *The Howling* (1981).

A very interesting fact in these later movies is the difference in the beasts themselves. In the older versions, the creature walked about on two legs and appeared to be more man than wolf. He also wore the shirts and pants of the man even after his transformation into the wolf. In the more recent versions, all clothes are removed and when the transformation is over there is no resemblance of man in the beast. The wolf creature is all animal and is larger than a normal wolf, with a silvery sheen to its fur and has red eyes. These modern versions are actually more characteristically true to ancient records of the beast that ran on all fours.

**If the wolf were killed in its animal form,
it would return to its human shape completely nude.**

This book is about strongmen in the spirit world, which operate in the lives of people. So, how do creatures like the cannibal, vampire, and *shape-shifter*, and all mythological creatures of legend fit in the world of demonic strongmen?

The truth is you may never see a true to life *shape-shifter* or a *werewolf*, which I pray you never do, but it doesn't mean that the spirits behind the legend do not exist. Just as in the actual historical cases of the existence of people who were cannibals and those who were affected by the spirit of *vampirism*, there are those who are oppressed with the spirit of the *shape-shifter*.

Seaside Court Case

We have a known case about a *werewolf* in the seaside resort of **Southend on Sea in England**. The man became known as the Werewolf of **Southend**. The man turning into a werewolf was witnessed by police officers and finally set free from this spirit by an exorcism performed by *Bishop Robert McKenna*. You can read about this case in the book, Werewolf: A True Story of Demonic

Possession, by *Ed and Lorraine Warren* with *William Ramsey* and *Robert David Chase*.

We also have the strange case of a creature called the **Almasti**, which was told to the famous Russian monster hunter, *Dr. Jeanne-Marie-Therese Koffman*, by *Mr. Didanov*, a highly respected person of his **Russian** village. By the time the creature left the village of **Kabardin**, nine people of good character and reason had seen this dark hairy creature. *Professor V.K. Leontiev*, who was tracking a *leopard*, came across some very strange human tracks. *Professor Leontiev* caught sight of this creature and had him in view for about seven to eight minutes. He stated that the beast was *about seven feet tall and had extremely large shoulders and a very large hairy head*.

In 1210, *Abbot Ralph of Coggeshall Abbey*, **Essex, England** wrote in his chronicles of a raging thunderstorm that lashed the countryside on the night of St. John the Baptist in June of 1205. Lightning struck and killed a certain strange monster at **Maidstone in Kent**. According to his record, this creature had the head of a strange beast, the trunk of a human, and its limbs were that of animals unlike each other, and the stench which came from its body was so terrible that few people could stand being near it. Also on July 29, 1205 after another terrible storm, tracks of another *monstrous creature half man and half animal* were found.

Even history speaks of these half-man and half-animal-like creatures.

In the **Epic of Gilgamesh**, which was written around 2000 B.C., a character named **Enkidu** becomes the first literary expression of a *werewolf* being.

1000 B.C. – Stories depicting the power of transformation are immensely popular among the Greeks. Heroes and deities freely change themselves and others into various animals and serpents.

850 B.C. – is the suggested date for *Homer's Odyssey*, a work filled with were-beasts and shape-shifters such as **Circe**, who transformed his lovers and suitors into swine.

540 B.C. – The Biblical King Nebuchadnezzar is turned into a beast for seven seasons.

500 B.C. – The **Scythians**, a nomadic **Eurasian** people, record their beliefs that the Neuri tribe turn themselves into werewolves during an annual religious festival.

175 B.C. – **Pausanias**, a **Greek** traveler, geographer and author visits **Arcadia** and sees the **Lycaonian** *werewolves*.

410 A.D. – **St. Augustine** relates in his writing, The City of God, about certain sorceresses who, after giving a certain cheese to their victims, turn them into beasts of burden.

435 A.D. – **Saint Patrick** arrives in **Ireland** and discovers that among his flock are many families of *werewolves*.

731 A.D. – Venerable Bede's Ecclesiastical History of England describes a host of were-animals which haunt the night.

774 A.D. – The Chronicles of Denys of Tell-Mahre describes the wolf-like monsters that terrorized the region known today as Iraq.

840 A.D. – **Agobard**, the *Archbishop of Lyons*, writes in his *Liber contra insulam vulgi opinionem* of the evil demons of the mountains that appear as man-beasts.

1101 A.D. – *Prince Vseslav of Polotsk*, an alleged **Ukranian** *werewolf*, dies.

1182 A.D. – *Giraldus Camrensis*, a **Welsh** historian and author of *Itineraium cambraie*, learns of an Irish tribe whose members transform into wolves during their Yuletide feast.

1257 A.D. – *The Catholic Church* officially sanctions torture as a means of forcing *witches, shape-*

shifters, and other heretics to confess.

1275 A.D. – A woman in **Toulouse** is found guilty of sexual intercourse with an **incubus**, a demon in male form, and giving birth to a child who is half wolf and half snake.

1407 A.D. – *Werewolves* are tortured and burned during witchcraft trials in Basel, Switzerland.

1440 A.D. – *Gilles de Rais* is tried and burned for child murder and for worshipping **Satan** in human and animal form

1521 A.D. – Three *werewolves* of **Poligny, France** are accused of having *eaten children* and consorting with wild she-wolves. They confess to having received their ability to be able to transform into a wolf by a magic salve. They are burned at the stake.

1541 A.D. – A **Paduan** *werewolf* dies after being tortured. His legs and arms are hacked off in search of wolf hair.

1550 A.D. – Witekind interviews a self-confessed *werewolf* in **Riga, Latvia.**

1555 A.D. – *Olaus Magnus* records his observation that the *werewolves* of **Livonia** put on a girdle of wolf skin, drink a cup of beer, and utter certain magic words to accomplish their transformation from the human to the wolf.

1573 A.D. – *Gilles Garnier* is burned as a *werewolf.*

1589 A.D. – *Peter Stubbes* is executed as a *werewolf* in **Cologne**.

1598 A.D. – *Jacques Roulet* is tried as a *werewolf*, but his sentence is commuted. The *Werewolf of Chalons* is a tailor accused of eating children in his tailor shop. He is executed in **Paris**. The *Gandillon family* are burned as werewolves in the **Jura**. A wolf is killed while in the act of attacking a village girl and is witnessed by the mob to return to human form of *Perrenette Gandillon*.

1603 A.D. – *Jean Grenier* is tried as a *werewolf* and is sentenced to life in prison.

1610 A.D. – Two women are condemned to death as werewolves in Liege, Belgium. Jean Grenier dies.

1612 A.D. – In *L'inconstance, Pierre de Lancre*, a noted judge of **Bordeaux, France** writes of his visit to the cell of *Jean Grenier* and declares that the werewolf had sharp, protruding teeth and appears more comfortable walking on all fours than walking upright.

1692 A.D. – The Livonian werewolf **Theiss** is interrogated.

1697 A.D. – *Charles Perrault's Contes* includes the legend of *Little Red Riding Hood*.

1764 A.D. – The Beast of Gevaudon starts a *werewolf* scare in Auvergne, France.

1812 A.D. – *The Brothers Grimm* publish their version of Little Red Riding Hood.

1824 A.D. – *Antoine Leger* is tried for *werewolf* crimes and sentenced to life in a lunatic asylum

1922 A.D. – *The Fraternity of the Inner Light*, which was founded by *Dion Fortune*, has a dramatic and frightening encounter with a *werewolf*.

1940 A.D. – *Harry Gordon*, the *Werewolf* of **San Francisco**, is arrested.

1957 A.D. – *Ed Gein*, the **Wisconsin Ghoul**, is arrested.

1982 A.D. – The notorious gang, the *"Chicago Rippers"* who were guilty of rape and mutilation, are apprehended. They confess on their own to not only crimes of rape and mutilation but also to *cannibalism*. They ate the left breast of their victims.

1987 A.D. – *Michael Lupo*, the Werewolf of **London** (the real one, not the movie), is arrested.

1989 A.D. – In **Paris**, *Francis LeRoy*, the *Werewolf of Dordgone*, is imprisoned for life.

1997 A.D. – Real life *"Werewolves on Wheels"*, the Cobra and the Butcher, two motorcycle slashers are apprehended for the death of thirty-seven **Shiite Muslims** in **Karachi**. Police in **Paris** engage in nine desperate searches for the *"Bastille Slasher"*, a vicious rapist who slashes the throats of his victim.

<u>1998 A.D.</u> – Hanoi's *"Werewolves on Wheels"*, a crazed pair of motorcycle slashers who prey on children, are sought by police as the number of young victims continue to rise high. The *Ripper of Genoa* is finally caught by Italian police after slashing to death at least eight women.

<u>1999 A.D.</u> – The *U.S. Patent and Trademark* Office rejects an attempt to patent a technique for creating animal-human hybrids.

The Adlet

There are various cultures, which believe in what is referred to as *werebeasts*. For instance, the **Inuit tribal** people have a legend about the **Adlet**, known as the dog people who were, according to their legend, offspring of a great red dog and an **Inuit** woman. This marriage of two species gave birth to five ugly *werebeasts* (*weredogs*) and five regular dogs, and the mother, being full of disgust, set them all adrift on rafts. The five dogs eventually reached the shore of **Europe** and gave birth to the variant white race. The *weredogs* evolved into horrible, *bloodthirsty monsters* which still roam **northern Iceland** in search of human flesh.

Animal Ancestors

In the **Algonquin** legend of **New England**, *C.G. Leland* tells of a common *Native American myth*, which proclaims that as animals are now, man was once, and how man is now, animals once were.

The mythologies of the aboriginal people of **South America** echo the belief that in the beginning, people were a mixture of men and animals. These myths proclaim that the spiritual aspect of beings one day evolved to human. However, they found its first physical expression in the form of animals.

Numerous legends from various tribes across **North America** give reports of *wolf-men, bear-men, cougar-men*, and other *were-beings*. Stories of women who gave birth to animal children are common as well as tribe men who took animal brides.

Many *Native American* tribes have legends, which tell how the first tribes that ever existed were *wolf-people* who walked at first on all fours - then eventually evolved to walking on two legs, and then becoming fully human.

Anubis (Egypt)

Anubis is the *Egyptian jackal-headed god* of the underworld – *the judge of the dead*. He was also known as the <u>great dog</u>. **Anubis** was mated to **Nephthys**, the underworld aspect of the goddess, **Isis**. For Christians in the Middle Ages, images of **Anubis** reinforced folk legends of were-jackals that attacked unwary desert travelers. Some ancient cults saw **Anubis** as a healer; while many felt the priest wearing jackal-headed masks were stealing the souls of hapless victims they only pretended to cure.

Badger People

The **Native American** people see the badger as the smaller brother to the bear, and they greatly respect its strength and courage. They also believe that the evenly marked stripes of black and white makes the badger a creature that can stand between the night and day – the darkness and the light.

Many *shamans* believe that the badger is the *perfect ambassador* to unite the world of the spirit to the world of the human.

Its powerfully secured body makes him the perfect host to hold the *shape-shifting* spirit of the shaman.

The **Japanese** also value the badger because of its strength and courage but unlike the Native Americans, they see the badger as a creature of extreme violence and believe that the badger is the favorite form chosen by the dark magician to *shape-shift* into in order to work great evil.

Elizabeth Bathory (1560-1614)

Elizabeth Bathory was a Hungarian countess responsible for the torture and murder of at least six hundred girls and young women. Many considered her to be a vampire, but many, including her own cousin, the Prime Minister who led the actual raid on her castle, Csejte, on New Year's Eve – 1610, felt that the countess was an actual werewolf.

Bear People

Many tribes of **Native Americans** worship the bear because of its great strength and its endurance. The shaman of various tribes felt it had the power to transform into a *werebear*.

The Beast of Le Gevaudan

Le Gevaudan is a barren, 75-mile stretch of hills and valleys in the rugged mountain range that runs along the edge of the **Auvergne plateau in southern France**. In 1760, rural residents of the area were terrorized by a *werewolf* which allegedly killed hundreds of people during a bloody three-year period. Shouts of *loup-garou, werewolf,* became the cry that terrified the whole region of Le Gevaudan. The crimes of the beasts finally came to the personal attention of *Louis XV at Versailles*. The king ordered a detachment of dragoons to search the mountains for the creature.

After the soldiers left the area, the murderous rampage of the beast increased. The years between 1765 and 1767 are spoken of as the time of death in the mountains. Parish reports revealed daily attacks by the *werewolf* who seemed to specialize in the killing of housewives and children. Finally, the *Marquis d'Apcher* organized a posse of several hundred armed men, who after tracking the creature for many days, finally surrounded it in a grove of trees near the village of *Le Serge d'Auvert*. As dusk turned into darkness the werewolf charged the men and was finally killed.

Jean Chastel was given the credit for the kill. According to *Mr. Chastel's* testimony, he had retired a short distance from the group to read his prayer book. As he glanced up from his reading, he saw the beast coming directly toward him – walking completely erect.

Chastel stated he had prepared himself according to ancient traditions. His double-barreled musket was loaded with silver bullets made from a *sliver chalice* which had been blessed by a priest. The first bullet from the musket struck the *werewolf* directly in his chest. The beast did not go down, but savagely charged at *Chastel*. The second bullet struck the creature in the heart – killing him immediately. He died at *Chastel's* feet.

Many people who weren't even there claimed the creature was a rare form of *leopard or possibly a wild boar*. *Chastel* described the beast as possessing *strange feet, pointed ears* and a body completely covered with dark coarse hair. The opinion of the men of the hunting party was that the creature was indeed a true *werewolf*.

Beaver People

The **Osage tribe** has a legend stating that until **Wabashas**, the first human, was created, the **Great Spirit** had appointed the *beaver* to be chief over the birds, beasts and fish of the forest. *Chief Beaver* considered disputing the Great Spirit's decision that he should turn the covert decision of chief over to **Wabashas.**
Beaver was not willing to submit until he saw the sharp arrow of **Wabasha**s. It was then he decided that *beavers* and men should be brothers. In fact, Chief Beaver offered the hand of his beautiful daughter to Wabashas as his bride in order to seal their friendship.

In the eyes of the **Osage people**, and many other tribes, the *beaver* is referred to as the **Little Wise People**. The beaver is believed to provide great healing power to those who are in need of it.

To the shaman of many tribes, the *beaver* serves as a *familiar spirit* being that journeys with them outside of the body. To be able to transform into a *beaver* while still an apprentice, enables the person to learn well the way of the spirit and healing.

Bisclaveret

A *Bisclaveret* is a **French term** used to describe a *werewolf*. In **Brittany**, **Bisclaveret** is used to describe a person who has been transformed by black magic into a *vicious beast (werewolf)*.

Not only are there actual historical cases from cultures and persons whose lives were affected by these *werebeasts*, but there are also actual cases of people who were tried and even confessed to being a *werebeast*. The orders of kings like Louis IX of France and by prime ministers, governors, mayors, commissioners and chief of police subsequently executed them.

Jean Bodin 1530-1596

Jean Bodin's academic abilities were so well thought of that he was considered to be the **Aristotle** of the sixteenth century. He was a leading Juri consulter, or rather a leading member of the Parliament of Paris. He was a highly respected intellectual of his day and time.

Mr. Bodin believed firmly in the ability of mankind to be *so strongly controlled by an evil spirit,* that they could actually turn themselves by **Satan's** help into a violent beast. He believed they could not only become *werebeasts* at will, but they could also summon **incubi and succubi** in order to fulfill *carnal desires.*

In addition, he refuted the arguments the famous *Johann Weyer (Weir)* who stated that the transformation of man to animal extended only in the minds of witches and shape-shifters, because their minds were mentally disturbed. *Mr. Bodin* believed firmly that the transformation occurred **not** only in the minds of these people but also in the spirit and bodies. It was much more than a mental alteration but a psychological and spiritual one.

Bogey

I believe there are very few adults who as children were not scared by the tales of the *bogeyman*. If the children were *naughty*, then the *bogeyman* was going to come and get them and take them away. *Bogeyman* was used to frighten them into good behavior.

What we did not know or understand is that the tales of the *bogeyman* were not grounded in fairy tales, but in true life stories of children who were stolen and eaten by people believed to be cannibalistic *werebeasts.*

Perrenette Gandillon

In 1598 a *werewolf* was seen attacking a small girl in a village in the **Jura Mountains of France.** When the girl's sixteen-year-old brother came to help, the beast turned on him and killed him.

Hearing the cries and sounds of the battle, the villagers came to the rescue. They surrounded the notorious *beast* and clubbed it to death. The villagers were struck with amazement as they watched the *beast* in its death throes transform from a wild animal into the nude body of a young woman whom they all knew as *Perrenette Gandillon.*

The eminent judge of **Sainte-Claude in the Jura Mountains**, *Henri Boguet,* testified that when the *Gandillon family* was arrested and jailed he observed they were more comfortable walking on all fours than on two legs. He reported that he saw the actual change from man to beast. The members of the family *howled like wolves* and their teeth became long and sharp while their *fingernails grew claw-like*. Finally, dark coarse hair sprouted all over their bodies.

Judge Boguet was also a witness to the case of eight-year-old *Louise Maillat*, who in the summer of 1598, was possessed by five demons: wolf, cat, dog, jolly and griffon. In addition, the little girl was also charged with shape-shifting into the form of a wolf.

Boxenwolf

In the **Schaumburg region of Germany**, *werewolves* are called *boxenwolves* because it is believed that they have made a pact with the devil, which allows them to actually transform into wolves. This transformation is accomplished by buckling a diabolical strap around their midsection. It is believed the *boxenwolves* take great pleasure in tormenting their victims.

Bruxsa

The **Bruxsa** is a **Portuguese** *shape-shifter* that combines elements of both the werewolf and the vampire. The **Bruxsa** is usually a woman who has invoked a very powerful demon. The **Bruxsa** leaves her home at night, turns into a hideous creature and fellowships with others of her kind. She usually *lives off the blood of her children*.

Giraldus Cambrensis

Until the end of the eighteenth century, **Ireland** was known in **England** as the "*Wolfland*," a country that abound with accounts of *werewolves*. As early as the *twelfth century, Giraldus Cambrensis* spoke of a priest who was met by a *wolf* in **Meath** who beseeched the cleric to go with him to minister to his dying wife.

The wolf explained that they had been resident of **Ossory**, whose people had been cursed for their wickedness by *St. Natalis* to change their shapes into *wolves* for a period of seven years. The priest was finally convinced to minister the last rites to the *she-wolf* when she finally revealed her human nature as an old woman.

The Chindi – Navajo Legend

According to **Navajo legend**, the **Chind**i is a *shape-shifter* who acts as an avenging angel to those who show disrespect to any of the Earth Mother's creatures and can take on any shape. Almost every true **Navajo** has a **Chindi** story to share. Many will tell of coming home at night and seeing *a coyote walking as a man*. This is considered a **Chindi**.

The Chronicon of Denys of Tell-Mahre

For centuries, scholars have struggled to understand the **Chronicon** of Denys of Tell-Mahre, a leader of **Syrian Jacobites**. From what can be understood, these ancient scribes were born in **Mesopotamia**, which is now **Iraq**. They recorded an awesome tale of the appearance of extremely frightening and terrifying creatures just before the reign of the Greek-Byzantine ruler *Leo IV* in the year 774.

They wrote that these *terrifying* creatures feared no man. No matter how well the men were armed, the beasts would turn on them and kill them. They were described as looking like wolves, but their faces were smaller and longer and their ears were large. The skin on their spines resembled that of pigs. These mysterious creatures performed terrible ravages on the people of the **Abdin Rock region near Hoh**. In some villages they *devoured more than a hundred people*, and in many other places anywhere from twenty to fifty.

If men would pursue them, the creatures never became fearful or tried to flee. Instead, they would turn on their pursuers. These creatures would enter houses and yards and climb upon terraces. They stole children from their beds, tore them to death and left without opposition. When they appeared, even the most vicious dog would be afraid to bark. These creatures eventually roamed into another area like **Arzanene, a village in southern Armenia along the Assyrian border.** These creatures also ravaged every village in the area of **Maipherk** and along **Mt. Cahai** causing great damage.

Coyote People - Navajo Indians

Just as many cultures believe in the *werewolf*. The **Navajo Indians** believe in the *werecoyote* and of other creatures that are part human and part animal.
The **Navajo** say you can tell if an animal is a true animal or a *werebeast* by looking into their eyes(gates). If it is a *werebeast*, the eyes will be dead; there will be no light in them.

Dientudo

El Dientudo (big teeth) is a commonly reported *Bigfoot-like* creature in the region around **Buenos Aires, Argentina**. Many people have reported seeing this half-man, half-bear creature in the wooded area near **El Gato Cre**ek and outside the **city of Toloso.**

William Ramsey – Werewolf Possession

William Ramsey was a very quiet hard-working man whose life was turned upside down when the *demonic spirit of the werewolf possessed him.* The book entitled, Werewolf, written by *Ed and Lorraine Warren* from the state of **Connecticut**, gives the account of his story.
Mr. and Mrs. Warren had been used to help people plagued by demonic spirits until the death of *Mr. Warren in 2006.* **The Warrens**, along with four police officers, assisted *Bishop Robert McKenna* in the *exorcism of Mr. Ramsey*, which was successful.

The Case of a French Boxer

Father Pellegrino Ernetti, a *Vatican exorcist*, tells of a *French boxer* whose career recorded more losses than wins. Then this boxer made a pact with **Satan** to obtain the strength and power of a werewolf.

When the boxer finally realized the harm he was causing to his opponents in the ring, he went to the priest who successfully performed an exorcism.

Historical True Cases

In 1975, psychiatrists *Frida Surawicz* and *Richard Banta* of **Lexington Kentucky** published their paper *"Lycanthropy Revisited"* in which they published and presented two case studies of contemporary werewolves.

These historical cases of people who were actually affected one way or another by *werewolf* systems were written by psychiatrists, lay people, clergy, historians and occult experts like the *Warrens*. These conditions actually existed whether they were emotional, physical or spiritual. They truly existed and many lives were ruined.

In all actuality, there is a very <u>real spiritual strongman</u> behind every one of these cases which have spanned the centuries destroying not only the victim of these creatures, but also the very beasts themselves.

Following are the names of actual strongmen who are responsible for the demonic possession of people who are affected with this curse:

- **Lahmu** is the *controlling* spirit behind the beast men.
- **Maahes** was an **Egyptian** *lion-headed spirit* of massacre.
- **Mont** is an **Egyptian** spirit which appears as a bull-headed strongman of war.
- **Bhutas** is a *shape-shifting cannibal vampire spirit.*
- **Canaima** is a **Waika and Makiritare Indian** who is a notorious *shape-shifting* spirit.
- **Curiysira** is an *Amazon vampire spirit* who is able to *shape-shift* into many different creatures.
- **Wendigo**, of a **Canadian** legend, is a *flesh-eating beast*.
- **Achelous** is the **Greek** version of the **Egyptian spirit Mont**. He is a *river spirit* with the head of a bull and body of a man.
- **Bogies** and **Boggarts** are English *shape-shifters* who <u>steal children.</u>
- **Caacrinolaas** is a strongman of *darkness* which appears as a large black dog, as in the case of David Berkowitz.
- **Chordeva** is an *East Indian shape shifting cat spirit* who <u>visits the sick and kills them</u>.
- **Jestan** is a Hindukusch *dog-appearing spirit of disease, famine and war*.

Though these are the names of the strongmen of the *shape-shifters* across the nations from Egypt to Canada, there is ONE name these brutal evil spirits of death must listen to and obey – the name JESUS.

The strongmen dealing with vampires, cannibals and werebeasts may seem to be creatures of myth and Hollywood fantasies.

Do <u>not forget</u>! Legends and myths have a way of blurring the truth. Therefore, <u>we are blind to the facts behind the lies.</u>

Prayer Against the Shape-Shifting Strongman

Lord, we know there are many strange things in the world we are not aware of. We thank You because You are aware of all things, and You are faithful to protect us from the seen and unseen things which would cause us great harm. **(Psalms 91)** *We thank You Lord, seeing that You go before us as a shield of faith* (**Ephesians 6:16**) *to stop all the attacks of the Adversary and protect us from the plans of the enemy of our soul.*

Lord, we thank You for Your Blood, **(Luke 22:19)** *which keeps our spirit, soul and bodies from the invasion of this spirit. We pray for those who are ensnared by these shape-shifting spirits. We know You will come to them and rescue them from this stronghold of the spirit of great darkness which has invaded them.*

Arise, *O Lord God Almighty and let Your enemies be scattered.* **(Psalm 68:1)** *Let the shackles of spiritual darkness be shattered once and for all. Let the wonderful light of Your Holy Spirit arise in our souls and spirits to bring light, truth and freedom forever and ever, Amen. Let the darkness and influence of the prince of darkness be demolished in the lives of Your servants once and for all for eternity. Amen and amen.*

PRAYER FOR DELIVERANCE FROM OCCULT INVOLVEMENT

I unreservedly forgive all my ancestors for all the things they have done that have affected me and my life. I specifically renounce the consequences of their sins in Jesus' name. As a child of God I now claim that the power of the blood of Jesus is setting me free from the consequences of generational sins. I claim my freedom from the consequences of all occult activity on either my father or my mother's family lines (name specifically), from curses and pronouncements that have had an effect on my life, from hereditary diseases and from the effects of any of their sins that have influenced me. I put any and all sins of an occult nature that I may have committed under the blood of Jesus and ask for Your forgiveness for each of them **(specifically name as many of them as you can)**. *I take back any access I have given to any of Satan's forces through these sins. I pray this in the name of Jesus, who became curse for me on Calvary and died that I might be set free. Amen*

Prayer of Protection and Proclamation

Psalms 91:
Whoever dwells in the shelter of the Most High
will rest in the shadow of the Almighty.
2 I will say of the LORD, "He is my refuge and my fortress,
my God, in whom I trust."
3 Surely he will save you
from the fowler's snare
and from the deadly pestilence.
4 He will cover you with his feathers,
and under his wings you will find refuge;
his faithfulness will be your shield and rampart.
5 You will not fear the terror of night,
nor the arrow that flies by day,
6 nor the pestilence that stalks in the darkness,
nor the plague that destroys at midday.
7 A thousand may fall at your side,
ten thousand at your right hand,
but it will not come near you.
8 You will only observe with your eyes
and see the punishment of the wicked.
9 If you say, "The LORD is my refuge,"
and you make the Most High your dwelling,
10 no harm will overtake you,
no disaster will come near your tent.
11 For he will command his angels concerning you
to guard you in all your ways;
12 they will lift you up in their hands,
you will not strike your foot against a stone.
13 You will tread on the lion and the cobra;
you will trample the great lion and the serpent.
14 "Because he[b] loves me," says the LORD, "I will rescue him;
I will protect him, for he acknowledges my name.
15 He will call on me, and I will answer him;
I will be with him in trouble,
I will deliver him and honor him.
16 With long life I will satisfy him
and show him my salvation."

Study Notes

Chart 9: Strongmen of Destruction

1. **Abatu** – spirit of destruction	7. **Dre** – spirit behind death and destruction
2. **Amducious** – the destroyer	8. **Joetun** – giant spirit behind chaos and destruction
3. **Ardat-Lile** – spirit behind destruction of families	9. **Loki** – Norse god of evil tricks and destruction
4. **Befana** – spirit out to destroy children	10. **Shiva** – Hindu god known as the destroyer
5. **Bergmoench** – spirit of harm and destruction	11. **Xolotl** – strongman of destruction
6. **Bohten Dayak** – spirit of evil tricks/ destruction	

Chapter 9
Strongmen of Destruction

Amducious is the Hebrew spirit of *destruction* who seeks to destroy all goodness from the life of people.
Abatu is a powerful spirit of *destruction*.
Ardat-lili is a powerful spirit of *destruction* who seeks to completely destroy families by any means it can, whether it is by *lies, by divorce, or by death*.
Befana, a well-known **Italian spirit**, is the strongman of the *destruction* of children. He will use any means necessary to *ruin the lives of children*. It can be through *divorce, physical and emotional abuse, alcohol, drugs, sexual sin, or witchcraft*.
Bergmoench is the **German** strongman who brings *harm and trouble*. He is identical to **Amducious (Hebrew)** and to **Befana (Italian)** spirits of destruction.
Bohten Dayak is a **Krishna** type **Hindu** spirit of *evil tricks and of terrible destruction*.
Dre is the **Tibetan** spirit of *violent death, utter destruction and chaos*.
Joetun is a giant **German** spirit of *chaos, death and destruction*.
Xolotl is the **Aztec** strongman of destruction.

**Each of these spirits is the powerful force behind
the destructive force that occurs throughout the world.
I have been asked if they are all the same spirit. The answer is no!**

They are individual spirits with *similar power*. Just as in the human world, we have many people who specialize in the same occupations like doctors, nurses, lawyers and police officers all over the world. They are identical in trade but not in name or person.

The Adversary has an **unlimited** *amount of spirits* to carry out his commands. They are alike in their powers, but they are assigned to different countries, cities, towns and families.

**Therefore, we must pray faithfully for our families, cities, churches,
and for those who have authority over us.**

There may be some who don't believe in these strongmen because they believe they are not superstitious or they don't believe in fairy tales. Just because a person doesn't believe in these strongmen, doesn't mean they do not exist. However, it does mean we are leaving our loved ones without protection.

**I have made this statement many times: The greatest trick
the devil ever did was in convincing the world he doesn't exist.**

Prayer Against the Strongmen of Destruction

Dear Lord, we are very thankful we are covered by Your precious Blood.
But now in Christ Jesus you who once were far off have been **made near by the blood of Christ**. **(Ephesians 2:13)**

You have filled us with Your Holy Spirit and have put a hedge of protection around us. **(Psalms 91**)

Lord, the storms of chaos and destruction may circle all around us, but Lord, You are still the Master of the storm, whether it is physical, spiritual or emotional. **(Luke 8:24)** *At the sound of Your voice, the destructive winds of chaos and confusion must come to an end.*

(Exodus 17:15) *Lord, we thank You because You are the Banner which covers us.*

You are the strong tower where we can run into and be saved from our enemies. **(Psalm 61:3)**

(Psalm 132:14) *You are our Sabbath and our resting place.*

Lord, since You are in us, we are more than conquerors because Your strength is in us.
(Romans 8:31-39)

May Your name be forever praised! Amen.

Study Notes

Chart 10: Strongmen of Slavery

1. **Abdiel** – spiritual strongman behind slavery	3. **Ammit** – spirit behind torment and mental slavery
2. **Abraxas** – taskmaster over slaves	

Chapter 10
Strongmen of Slavery

These strongmen of slavery have been around for centuries and in every country of the world. History books, including the Bible, have many stories of man's enslavement of man.

Even today, in this so-called enlightened world, *slavery exists*. There are slaves which are forced to work in the diamond fields of Africa. Then there are women who are kidnapped and are sold all over the world as *sex slaves*. Sadly, this even happens in America where innocent children are stolen from their homes, or runaways who are taken from the street and forced into child pornography.

America is not the only nation of the world with a shameful history of slavery.

Africa has its own history of slavery among their many tribes. Rome enslaved the entire world at once, just as Babylon, Medes and Persia, Greece, and Egypt did.

Spirits, such as **Abdiel**, *the strongman of slavery* and **Abraxas**, the taskmaster, were the *powers behind the Pharaohs* who *enslaved the nation of Israel* for over four hundred years.

We can see the effects of these powerful dark spirits who despise freedom and seek to enslave the whole human race under the deception of Satan.

The results of *slavery*, whether it was that of the **American Negro** who was forced to work the plantations, farms and factories of America, or the **Hebrews** who were forced into manual labor for over four hundred years, are terrible.

The horrors of young women and children forced into sexual slavery can only be birthed from a dark mind embedded with great perversion.

Man is capable of terrible deeds on his own. We don't need the influence of an outward dark force to commit unbelievable crimes of darkness. Just look at the lives of *Hitler, Jeffrey Dahmer, the Boston Strangler*, the night stalker, *Jack the Ripper* and so many others. As terrible as their crimes against humanity were, they get worse when these demented minds submit themselves to the diabolical minds of these strongmen. The gates of hell are thrown open wide and unspeakable horrors are then performed on mankind.

As terrible as the physical effects of *slavery* on mankind are. There is another form of slavery which brings complete and total destruction into the lives of many people and from all walks of life.

It does not matter if you are rich or poor; it can happen. It is the enslavement of the mind by *drug or alcoholic abuse*. It is also the enslavement of perverted thoughts through the influence of prejudiced views and hate.

When a person's mind is enslaved by these influences, there is no evil they will not do.

When you are under the spell of hate and prejudicial opinion, you will not feel wrong if you enslave another or take their life because, as far as you are concerned, they are beneath you.

Growing up in the ghetto, I have seen people who had great physical and mental abilities to accomplish great things in their lives. They either ended up in jail or enslaved to drug or alcohol addiction. Some are even in the grave because their minds had become enslaved to mental influences that consumed them.

The leading general of Satan's army for the tormenting of the mind is a strongman called <u>Ammit.</u>

It is his ambition to completely suppress the mind, the emotions, and the spirits of mankind. <u>His job is to turn people into mental slaves without a free will of their own.</u>

Sadly, as a young man I saw many of my friends become so emotionally and mentally bound to drugs that all these hopeful young lives ended up looking like the man with the legion of spirits as told in the Gospels of Christ. Just like this man with a legion of spirits needed Christ, so do my friends.

Jesus is more than able to set them free and return them to their rightful minds.
He who the Son sets free, is free indeed. **(John 8:36)**

Indeed, *slavery, whether spiritual, physical or mental*, is strong and the chains are hard to break; however, there is one far more powerful than these strongmen of slavery.

He has come to break every fetter and destroy the chains that bind. He has come to turn man from slavery to true freedom, from darkness to light, from the kingdom of Satan to the Kingdom of God. He is our liberator, and His name is Jesus.

Prayer Against the Strongman of Slavery

*Lord, we thank You because You heard the prayers of Your people Israel when they were enslaved in Egypt (a symbol of the world) under the power of Pharaoh (a type of **Satan**). You set them free through Moses, and You have done the same for us through Christ.*

Many are sitting in caves and in prison houses: **(Isaiah: 44)** *yet, God desires for them to be set free and restored. No one has brought the goodness of freedom to these who are enslaved. So many of our loved ones need to be set free, but there is no voice crying out to be free and fully restored.*

We thank You Lord because You never fail, and soon and very soon these captives shall hear Your voice proclaiming, "You are free! Your chains are broken, and your prison doors are wide open. Come forth in absolute power and joy and total liberation from the god of this world into the Kingdom of God and of His Christ forevermore." Amen.

(John 8:36) *So if the Son sets you free, you will be free indeed.*

Chart 11: Strongmen of the Occult

1. **Amducious** – Egyptian spirit of destruction	13. **Diana of the Ephesians** – spirit behind the worship of the moon. Queen goddess of all divisions of witchcraft
2. **Andrealphus** – spirit behind astrology	14. **Ezeqeel** – Hebrew spirit of cloud worship
3. **Araqiel** – Hebrew spirit of earth worship	15. **Hecate** – three-faced goddess of witchcraft
4. **Armaros** – Hebrew spirit of enchantment	16. **Kasbeel** – Hebrew spirit of secret knowledge, Kabala, occult séances
5. **Balan** – spirit behind fortune telling and witchcraft	17. **Nybbas** – spirit of fortune telling
6. **Bannik** – fortune telling spirit	18. **Raum** – Hebrew three-faced god of destruction with a face of man, viper, and a cat
7. **Baphomet** – spirit of the occult and of secret rites, Knights Templar, Masons, Mormons, all secret societies	19. **Stolas** – spirit of star gazing and herbology
8. **Baraqijal** – Hebrew spirit of astrology	20. **Uvall** – fortune telling spirit
9. **Barbados** – fortune telling spirit	21. **Vapula** – spirit behind philosophy
10. **Bifrous** – spirit of astrology	22. **Vassago** – fortune telling spirit
11. **Buer** – spirit of vain philosophy and logic	23. **Zagan** – spirit behind false miracles and wisdom
12. **Dantalion** – three-face spirit of sexual perversion, bisexualism, gender confusion, mind reading and the worship of the occult	

Chapter 11
Strongmen of the Occult

When we talk about the occult, we are not only talking about Wicca, witchcraft and Satanism, but we are also talking about cults like Christian Science founded by Mary Baker Eddy, spiritualism founded by the Fox sisters, the Jehovah Witness, the Mormons, New Age, Freemasons, and of course the two of the fastest growing cults in the world today – Islam and the Church of Scientology. All of these religions stand in opposition to God and His church. In addition to the cults already named, there is Buddhism, Hinduism, Confucianism, Transcendentalism, Silva mind control, Santeria and voodoo. The list can go on and on, but as you can see there is much opposition to the truth at work in the world.

> **There are many voices crying out, "This is the way; walk ye in it."**
> **The concept that all roads lead to heaven is not true.**
> **There is only one way, and that is through Jesus.**

The *great apostle Paul in the book of Acts* **faced the same problem as we do today.** A young slave girl who was possessed with the spirit of the python followed him around. This young lady brought in a great amount of money to her master by her fortune telling abilities. For many days she followed after Paul yelling, "These men are the servants of the most high God showing the way to salvation."

Many people have wondered why Paul became so upset with the young woman. After all, she was proclaiming what Paul was saying was true. The truth of the matter is that what she was really saying in the Greek was:

> **"These men are showing you a way to salvation, not the only way to salvation."**
> **Her voice was like the voices of the religions of the world today proclaiming there is more than one way to salvation.**
> **This was not true then, and neither is it true today.**
> **Jesus is still the one and only way to salvation.**

Spirit(s) of Fortune Telling

No man cometh to the Father except through the Son (**John 14:6**). In the Greek, it proclaims that the spirit of the *python possessed the slave girl*. Perhaps it was the strong man known as **Musmahhu**, *the exalted serpent*. However, if as the English states she was possessed by the *spirit of fortune telling*, it could have been **Balan**, *spirit of fortune telling and witchcraft*, or maybe **Bannik**, *spirit of fortune telling*, or **Barbados**, or **Nybbas**, the Greek *spirit of fortune telling*, or **Uvall**, a *fortune telling spirit*, or finally **Vassago**, also a *strongman of fortune telling*.

Diana of the Ephesians

We know for sure the followers of **Diana** of the Ephesians confronted Paul. **Diana** was the spirit behind the temple of paganism in Ephesus. She is the strongman behind the movement of Wicca and witchcraft. Thousands of her followers worldwide proclaim this **Diana** as the *Queen of* heaven – the *Queen of all witches*. This spirit called **Diana** by the **Greeks** was not only **Diana** *of the Ephesians*, but she was also the strongman behind Jezebel and **Semiramis**, the wife of Nimrod. **Semiramis** was also known as the queen of heaven and the goddess of force.

Spirit(s) of Astrology and Witchcraft

Along with the fortune telling spirits and **Diana**, known as the goddess of all witches and the queen of heaven, there is **Bifrons**, the spirit of astrology, **Buer**, spirit of vain philosophy, logic and false wisdom. Then there is **Hecate**, the three-faced goddess of witchcraft symbolizing the maiden, the mother and the crone, the three stages of witchcraft. There is also **Dantalion**, a three-faced mind reading spirit (Irish), **Andrealphus**, Hebrew spirit of astrology, **Raum**, a *three-headed god of destruction,* and **Stolas**, the strongman of stargazing and herbology.

Simon the Magician

Also in the book of Acts, there is the story of Simon the magician who tried to buy the power of the Holy Spirit from the Apostle Peter. All the people feared Simon and thought he was filled with the power of God, but in all reality the spirit behind Simon the sorcerer was probably a spirit known as **Zagan,** *the power behind false miracles and wisdom.*

False religions more than likely receive their powers of deception from Buer, Vapula and Zagan.

Religions like Mormonism, Jehovah Witness, Christian Science, Silva mind control, spiritualism, and the Church of Scientology more than likely receive their powers of deception from spirits like **Buer**, the spirit of vain philosophy and logic, or **Vapula**, the spirit behind philosophy, or **Zagan**, the spirit behind false miracles and wisdom.

It is the mission of all these spirits of the occult from Diana to Zagan to lead everyone they can away from truth into the lies and deception of the dark world of the occult.

They want to bind them forever in the Satanic web of falsehood where they, like Samson are blind by the darkness of deception so they are unable to see the light of truth of the Kingdom of God.

Prayer Against the Strongmen of the Occult

Father, we know there are many voices out there proclaiming, "This is the way; walk in it." These are voices which would deceive us and ensnare us with the lies and falsehood of witchcraft, vain philosophy and false religion.

They are trying to lift up their banners and their false Christ by saying they are sent to enlighten us to show us the path to Nirvana or oneness with the universe. They also claim to help us escape the wheel of karma so we do not have to come back over and over again to repeat life until we get it right.

Thank You Lord, because You have revealed the true meaning of life through Your beloved Son, our Lord and Savior Jesus Christ. He has opened the only true way to eternal life so that we can be restored back to fellowship with You and enjoy the privilege of eternal life in Your Kingdom forever and forever. Amen.

PRAYER FOR DELIVERANCE FROM OCCULT INVOLVEMENT

*I unreservedly forgive all my ancestors for all the things they have done that have affected me and my life. I specifically renounce the consequences of their sins in Jesus' name. As a child of God I now claim that the power of the blood of Jesus is setting me free from the consequences of generational sins. I claim my freedom from the consequences of all occult activity on either my father or my mother's family lines **(name specifically)**, from curses and pronouncements that have had an effect on my life, from hereditary diseases and from the effects of any of their sins that have influenced me. I put any and all sins of an occult nature that I may have committed under the blood of Jesus and ask for Your forgiveness for each of them (specifically name as many of them as you can). I take back any access I have given to any of Satan's forces through these sins. I pray this in the name of Jesus, who became curse for me on Calvary and died that I might be set free. Amen*

Chart 12: Worldwide Leaders of the Strongmen

1. **Abaddon** – Hebrew god of destruction	31. **Maahes** – lion-headed man, Egyptian strongman of war and massacre
2. **Adbiel** – strongman of slavery	32. **Malphas** – Hebrew spirit, leader of lies and deceptions
3. **Abraxas** – Egyptian taskmaster	33. **Mammon** – Hebrew spirit, leader of greed
4. **Agaliarept** – commander of war gods	34. **Mars** – Rome's strongman of war
5. **Akatash** – leader over all evil spirits	35. **Mehen** – Egyptian divine serpent
6. **Alastor** – leader over murderous spirits	36. **Mephistopheles** – German name for Satan, complete leader of all strongmen, spirits of darkness, fallen angels and demons
7. **Aldinach** – leader over the spirits of natural disasters	37. **Melkiresha** – chief of the strongmen directly under Satan, an angel of darkness, a watcher in reptilian form
8. **Amy** – prince of the kingdom of darkness, giver of occult knowledge	38. **Moloch** – Old Testament pagan god, the strongman behind child sacrifices and death
9. **Apollyon** – leader over the spirits of the pit, a destroying angel, Greek god of destruction	39. **Mont** – Egypt's strongman of war
10. **Apophis/Apep** – snake spirits	40. **Nehebkau** – Egyptian serpent god of the underworld
11. **Aries** – Greek god of war	41. **Osiris** – Egyptian strongman of sun worship
12. **Aspis** – Hebrew snake spirit of evil and stubbornness	42. **Rabisu – strongman who lies in wait, the doorkeeper (Genesis 4:6)**
13. **Atazoth** – former Watcher, leader of the spirits of darkness	43. **Rabisu Basmu** – the venomous snake
14. **Avnas** – a leader of the strongmen	44. **Rabisu Girtablulu** – scorpion man king of all poisonous creatures
15. **Azazel** – leader of the former watchers, leader of all spirits of war and workers of metal, and all the fallen angels	45. **Rabisu Harbati** – lord of the wastelands, dry places, deserts
16. **Baal** – one of the main chiefs of the leadrs of the fallen angels	46. **Rabisu Kulullu** – fishman, lord of the seas and the oceans
17. **Beelzebub** – Hebrew fallen angel, one of Satan's generals	47. **Rabisu Kusarikku** – half man and half bull, lord of half man and half animal mutations
18. **Behemoth** – Hebrew spirit strongman of waterways	48. **Rabisu Lahmu** – known as the hairy one, strongman of the wild beasts and men
19. **Belial** – Hebrew spirit leader of all the	49. **Rabisu Musati** – lord of the unclean areas

spirits of darkness	
20. **Belphegor** – Hebrew spirit, strongman of hidden knowledge	50. **Rabisu Mushussu** – known as the furious serpent
21. **Botis** – snake spirit	51. **Rabisu Musmahhu** – called the exalted serpent
22. **Buer** – reigning spirit of all vain philosophies and logic	52. **Rabisu Nari** – strongman of the inland waterways and rivers
23. **Byleth** – one of the leading strongmen	53. **Rabisu Ugallu** – big weather beast (storm spirit)
24. **Caacrinolas** – strongman of Satan's kingdom, appears as a large black dog	54. **Rabisu Umudabrutu** – spirit of extremely violent storms (hurricanes, tornadoes)
25. **Caym** – strongman, leader of over thirty legions of demons	55. **Rabisu Urhi** – destructive spirit over the roads, highways, and travel
26. **Gaap** – one of the Hebrew ruling strongmen	56. **Rabisu Uri** – strongman over the high places
27. **Iblis** – Arabic, Islamic leader of the djins (demons)	57. **Rahab** – strongman who keeps people blind to the truth, hinders our prayers from going up and the answers from coming down
28. **Isis** – Egyptian strongman of moon worship	58. **Raum** – Hebrew three-faced god of destruction with a face of man, viper, and a cat
29. **Kasdeja** – former Watcher, Hebrew fallen angel, spirit behind abortions and miscarriages	59. **Siva/Shiva** – Hindu god of destruction
30. **Leviathan** – great sea serpent	60. **Udug** – Hebrew former Watcher now strongman of deception

Chapter 12
Worldwide Leaders of the Strongmen

The following are the names of *spiritual strongmen* from all over the world. Many of these spirits have the same assignments but are not the same spirit. For example, there is **Mont,** the *bull-headed Egyptian god of war*, and **Mars** and **Aries** the Roman and Greek gods of war. Then there is **Agaliarept**, *commander of all war gods*.

We know the horrors of war, the bloodshed, the loss of lives, the infirmed, and the damaged minds are all the product of a devious mind. Who is the perverted mastermind behind all destruction and violence? The actual power behind these strongmen of war, destruction and chaos is **Satan**, and he is definitely out to kill, steal and destroy. He goes about as a roaring lion seeking out anyone he can destroy. Do not let your guard down. Be sure you are ready for the battle at all times.

I am writing these names so that you can come to recognize the strongman who is out to destroy you, your family and your church. *Watchmen*, wake up and be ready to sound the alarm to prepare the people of God for battle.

In the following list of names, you will probably recognize many from Greek, Roman, Norwegian and Egyptian mythology.

Because the names appear in myth, people tend to believe these spirits are not real. However, if you do a research of many of these names, you can trace them back to an actual being that lived. For instance, if you study Hercules' various names and nicknames, his appearance, what he wore, and how he died you will find that the mythical character has actual roots in the Biblical person of **Nimrod**, *the son of Cush – the mighty hunter before God.*

As you read these names, you may realize there is some evidence of their working in your life and your family's life. You may see the strongman, the familiar spirit who has been working in your family lineage from the very beginning of your family history. Lord willing, you can finally break their hold over the lives of you and your family.

Maahes is the **Egyptian** god of massacre. You can see the proof of his existence in the violent deaths of Christians in Egypt. You can see proof of the existence of **Mont**, the bull-headed Egyptian god of war in the civil wars of Egypt.

Osiris and **Isis** are the Egyptian's god of the sun and goddess of the moon. Many of **Isis'** attributes can be seen in **Diane, Aphrodite**, and **Venus**, the Greek and Roman goddess of love, the hunter and the moon. **Osiris** is one of the many deities of the Freemasons where his violent death is played out over and over again. The legend of **Osiris'** life and death can be traced back to the life and death of **Nimrod**.

The *snake spirit* has many names like **Nehebkau**, the **Egyptian** *serpent god of the underworld*; **Mehen**, the divine serpent; **Basmu**, the poisonous serpent; **Mushussu**, the furious serpent; **Musmahhu**, the exalted serpent; **Apophis** or **Apep**, the snake serpent; **Aspis**, the **Hebrew** snake spirit of *evil and stubbornness*; and **Batis**, the snake spirit.

Throughout the history of the world the serpent has been *worshipped as a divine creature*. This creature has been deceiving mankind ever since the Garden of Eden. **Satan** is still known as the old serpent. Just as the *serpent is quite cunning and deadly* and does **not** need a large entrance to come into places, so it is with **Satan**.

> **All he needs is a crack in your armor, and he can strike swiftly and deadly; so be sure your armor is secured and sealed against that great serpent called the devil.**

Abraxas is the Egyptian god of slavery. We can see her effect in the lives of the **Hebrew** people when they were enslaved in Egypt for over four hundred years.

Then there is the strongman over all the so-called gods of war. He is the five-star general *over all the other war spirits*. He takes his orders directly from **Satan** himself. It is his desire to bring about the final battle where he thinks God will be defeated and all of mankind enslaved. His name is **Agaliarept**.

Joined Forces of Mass Murder and Destruction

The **next spirit** is a master of causing great evil. He delights in destroying all that is good and replacing it with evil. His name is **Akatash**, and he works well with **Alastor**, who is one of the strongmen behind the *acts of murder*. When these *two join forces,* they produce mass murder and destruction. It is not just one person affected, but hundreds and thousands of people as in the concentration camps of World War II, the killing fields of Vietnam, the war in the Middle East, and the destruction of the Twin Towers in New York.

The massacre, which took place in **Waco, Texas**, was horrific. Young children were first rendered helpless by tear gas, which is illegal to use against our enemies in war. Then after becoming *paralyzed*, they were burnt to death by the fires of the compound being destroyed.

> **Lately the world has experienced many natural disasters like typhoons, hurricanes, tornados and earthquakes.**

All of these events are happening at a greater and faster rate than ever before in history. When we were living in Tennessee, my wife and I lived through a hundred and four tornados of all sizes in just about a month's time. I believe God will sometimes use nature to warn a nation of coming judgment. I also feel that many of these disasters are the works of a strongman called **Aldinach**. He may even have been the power behind the storm on the **Sea of Galilee** that Jesus took authority over.

There are *spirits which work in the lives of people to bring destruction, and they destroy* all good things. There is the Hindu god of destruction, **Shiva**; the Greek god, **Apollyon**; and the **Hebrew** spirit, **Abaddon**

Today we have an increase of the occult among the young people all over the world.

This is due largely to the influence of occult movies and books like Harry Potter, which ensnares the mind of the young, video games and even board games have opened the minds of our youth to be invaded by a demonic spirit. There are three very powerful strongmen working behind the scenes of these movies, books and games.

When you pray for your children, bind these three spirits.

The spirit of the world wants to inhabit the minds and gates of this generation so he or she is made unclean and defiled. (Please read Matthew 15:11 and Mark 7:15.)

The first is **Belphegor**, the Hebrew spirit of *hidden knowledge* who taught women to *practice witchcraft*. The second is **Atazoth**, a leading spirit of the spirits of spiritual darkness. The third is **Melkiresha**, *the leader of all spirits of spiritual darkness*. Moving forward, we have **Rabisu Uri**, the strongman of the *high places*, along with **Azael**, the *spiritual leader of the fallen angels*, and **Avnas**, another leader of the fallen angels.

I know I may come off as an alarmist, but from my own involvement with the occult, I know first hand that these spirits are very real, and they are out to ensnare your children and anyone else they can. Fathers, you are the patriarch of your family – the shepherd. Mom, you are the matriarch of the family.

Stand strong against the bear and the lion, which would attack the sheep of your flock, your children.

Along with **Baal**, whose *false prophets that Elijah*, the one true prophet of God, defeated, is **Beelzebub**, one of **Satan's** chief rulers. There is also **Belial**, the Hebrew spirit of darkness, foolishness and drunkenness. Isn't it ironic that we call alcohol drink "spirits"?

One of the *ruling principalities* is **Buer**, *the reigning ruler of vain philosophy and logic*. He tries to replace the wisdom of the Holy Spirit with the foolishness of man's wisdom. I believe along with **Buer**, you also have **Malphas**, the strongman of lies, falsehood and deception. They work with **Mammon**, the spirit of greed.

These strong spirits work in absolute unity to ensnare mankind in any way they can.

They work together to spread war, death, sickness, slavery and total destruction. If one is being beaten in battle, the others will come to its support.

> **The Christian churches must get over their division and strife over petty differences. We must put up a unified show of force if we ever wish to defeat them.**
> **Satan's plan is to Keep Us Divided.**

Many times we face a being called **Melkiresha**, a former watcher, now a chief angel of absolute darkness. He appears to his followers in the *form of a reptile* walking like a man. He is the cause of the legend of *the lizard people*, who are believed by **New Age** researchers and authors, to have started the human race.

In **Genesis 4:7**, God warned Cain that if he did wrong then sin waited to possess him.

> **There is a spirit called Rabisu, which simply means 'chief'.**
> **He lies patiently waiting for a crack to appear**
> **so he can enter into a person's life and take control.**

Rabisu Uri is the strongman of the *high places* where *altars to false gods*, like **Baal**, **Moloch** and **Dagon**, were established in order to offer up human sacrifices to them. **Rabisu Nari** is the strongman of the inland waterways and rivers, along with **Leviathan**, **Behemoth** and **Rahab**, the **Hebrew** spirits of the water.

Leviathan is called the *great serpent*, and if you ever battle it, you will never ever forget it. In the book of Job, **Behemoth** is described as *drinking up whole rivers in one gulp*. **Rahab** is the **spirit of Egypt**, which appears in the form of a *giant squid* who specializes in blocking prayers going up and answers coming down.

This year alone I have received five calls from pastors telling me they could see this giant squid-like creature in their churches and have asked what they could do to get rid of it. I know these creatures seem to be a thing of science fiction, but they are very real. For example, when the *New York police* arrested *David Berkowitz*, he told them he received his orders to kill from his neighbor's *black dog called Sam*. Because of this, *Berkowitz* became known as the *"Son of Sam"* killer. Could this have been the physical appearance of **Caacrinolas**, a prince of hell who appears as a large black dog?

Since **Rabisu** means 'chief' then **Rabisu Harbati** means that **Harbati** is the *chief spirit over the wastelands, the dry places and deserts*. **Rabisu Musati** is the chief spirit over the unclean areas like *bar rooms, strip joints, x-rated bookstores, x-rated movies and pornographic magazines*. This one is a very busy spirit – spreading his filth even into the lives of Christians. **Rabisu Urhi** is the *lord of the roads and highways of travel*.

My wife and I travel much across the country. However, even when we are just driving locally, I ask the Lord to bind this spirit so no mishap happens. We have many friends who are truck drivers, and since they have asked the Lord to protect them on the highways against this spirit, they have had far less troubles on the road.

> **There is actually a *spirit over wild men* called Lahmu.**
> **This spirit drives men to act like animals.**
> **They end up doing violent crimes, rapes, murder and gang wars.**

I sincerely believe this is the spirit behind biker gangs like the Hell's Angels, Gypsies, Jokers, and street gangs like the *Bloods, the Crypts, the Latin Kings, the Brown Knights,* and groups like the *Aryan Brotherhood* and the *KKK Clans*. **Lahmu** works along with another spirit called **Uridimmu**, known as the *mad lion*. He affects animals just as **Lahmu** affects men.

We also have seen the power of God bind the **two strongmen**: **Ugallu**, the *big weather beast* and **Umu Dabrutu**, the **violent storm.** Many times, when my wife and I would be traveling somewhere to minister, violent storms would come out of nowhere.

For a while we thought it was just a coincidence until the Lord told us to take authority over these spirits of the storm in His name. We did and the assault against us stopped where we were able to finish our trips safely. **(Ephesians 6:12)**

A Prayer for Protection Against These Violent Strongmen – These Leaders of the Army of Darkness

Dear Lord Jesus, we thank You because You have hidden us from the eyes of our adversary and his many allies, whether they are humans or spirits. You have kept us safe from those who would harm us mentally, emotionally, physically, spiritually or financially.

You have spoken and have caused the masters of the violent storms, earthquakes, hurricanes, tornados, rainstorms, hail and blizzards to stop their attacks against Your people.

You have protected us from violent men and animal attacks and have given us safe journey as we go our way to serve You. Thank You, Lord, for keeping a watchful eye on Your children. You are our wonderful Deliverer. Amen.

Ephesians 6:12

For we wrestle not against flesh and blood, but against principalities, against powers, against the rulers of the darkness of this world, against spiritual wickedness in high places.

Chart 13: Hebrew Strongmen

1. **Abaddon** – Hebrew name for the leader over the spirits of the pit, a destroying angel	7. **Beelzebub** – Hebrew fallen angel, one of Satan's generals
2. **Apollyon** – Greek name for the leader over the spirits of the pit, a destroying angel	8. **Behemoth** – Hebrew strongman of the waterways
3. **Azazel** – fallen prince of the fallen angels	9. **Belial** – Hebrew spirit leader of all the spirits of darkness
4. **Baal** – false god worshipped, used as a title meaning master or lord	10. **Leviathan** – great sea serpent
5. **Baal Shamin** – lord of the sky, a sun god	11. **Rahab** – strongman who keeps people blind to the truth, hinders our prayers from going up and the answers from coming down
6. **Bel** – a title meaning lord; a strongman of the Hebrew often associated with other strongmen from surrounding countries	

Chapter 13
Hebrew Strongmen

The Bible lists a number of false gods and other type of strongmen Israel faced over and over again. There are spirits like the Philistine's god, **Dagon**, whose statue was found lying face down on the threshold of his temple with his hands and head cut off.

In **Revelation**, John speaks about the angel from the bottomless pit, who is released in the latter days. He is called **Abaddon** in the **Hebrew** and **Apollyon** in the **Greek**, which means *'the destroyer'*. When he is released in the last days, he will be in charge of the locust-like creatures that will *torment mankind* for a *six-month period* of time.

There is **Azazel**, the *fallen prince of the fallen angels*. He is the one who has *taught* all *unrighteousness* on earth and *revealed the eternal secrets* which were preserved in heaven, which men were striving to learn. He taught men how to make swords, knives, shields and breastplates. He taught man about the metals of the earth, the use of antimony and the art of working them and bracelets and ornaments, and the beautifying of the eyelids, and all kinds of comely stones, and all coloring tinctures.

The *Phoenicians* worshipped a *false god*, which **Israel** began to build altars to and worship as well. The false god, **Baal**, most commonly spoken of in Scriptures means *'Lord of the sky'*. It is quite probable he was a sun god.

Another false god worshipped was the great **Bel**. He was the father of **Mot** and **Aleyin** and **Anat,** and killed by his rival, **El** (not the El of the Bible). There is another strongman worshipped by Israel, which was a Babylonian god called Bel; however, this was a version of **Enlil**. Here Bel is just a title meaning, 'lord'. The Apocrypha story shows us he was widely worshipped in Babylon.

His daily sacrificial offerings were forty sheep, twelve great measures of fine flour and six vessels of wine. **Bel** was often identified with **Enlil**, the Sumerian sky and mountain god. He was also identified with **Marduk**, the **Assyro-Babylonian god** of the *spring sun*. Originally he was vegetation god.

Beelzebub, another *strongman of the Hebrews*, is known as the *prince of the flies*. He is a spirit of *vast darkness and evil*, and many felt his name was another name for **Satan**. The spirit called **Belial** is the strongman over the *spirits of darkness, drunkenness, extreme foolishness and rebellion against righteousness*.

In the book of **Job**, the Lord speaks of *two terrible water monsters*. The first is **Leviathan**, the *great sea serpent* who is invincible to any weapon of man. This beast seems to be undefeatable by anything except the Lord Himself. We are warned that if we put our hands against him, we will never forget the battle.

Experience has taught me that this is absolutely true. When I have faced him, I stood firmly hidden in the Lord. Although I was victorious each time, I knew it was the Lord Jesus and definitely **not** me.

The battle belongs to the Lord, and so does all the praise.

The same can be said about the next *two water monster strongmen*, **Behemoth** and **Rahab**. Though we have mentioned these in several chapters before, it will be a great benefit to repeat their importance so that we are well informed.

Behemoth was so monstrous in size that the Bible said he could swallow up whole rives with one gulp. Many people try to compare him to the hippo and the crocodile; however, neither of these two creatures measures up to **Behemoth**.

Praise God! At the mention of the name of Jesus, this beast must bow and obey.

You must not confront this spirit without the power of the Holy Spirit, the shed Blood of Jesus and the Name of Jesus. If you do not have these, I would suggest you run as fast as you can, and don't stop for anything until you come to Jesus.

The **third spiritual beast** is a creature called **Rahab**, whose symbol is the giant *squid or octopus*. It has a many tentacles and works hard to keep people blind to the truth. In fact, it struggles to keep our prayers from going upward to the Lord and to hinder the answers from coming down.

Rahab is similar to the strongman in the **book of Daniel**. When Gabriel came to answer Daniel who had prayed and fasted for twenty-one days, he was hindered by the spiritual being called the **prince of Persia**. This spirit was so strong because it was able to stand against God's messenger until Michael the protector of Israel arrived and helped Gabriel to escape. After the angel finished speaking to the prophet Daniel, he warned him that a more powerful spirit than the prince of Persia was coming. He called him the prince of Greece (*Please see* **Daniel 10:12-13, 20-21**).

Daniel also spoke of other spirits which *would stand against God* and His people. They were the **spirit of Babylon** (*lion*), the **spirit of the Medes and Persians** (*bear*), the **spirit of Greece** (*the four-winged leopard*), **and the spirit of Rome** (*terrifying beast*).

Finally, there is the **kingdom of the antichrist** that is the end time dictator, and the little **horn of Daniel**. All these beings are real, and we need to know how to stand against them and how to set people free.

We must be willing to prepare for war

Prayer Against the Hebrew Strongmen

Lord, we thank You because You have revealed to us our secret enemies which fight against us and try to hinder our prayers from going up to You and to stop Your answers from coming down to us.

Father, we have complete and total confidence in You. Just as You sent Michael, the great warrior, to help Gabriel so he could bring to Daniel Your answer, so will You also do for us. We need to hear from the throne of heaven so we can expand Your kingdom here on earth and destroy the kingdom of the Adversary everywhere we go.

Yes, Father, we acknowledge that these strongmen are real. Without Your help, we can do nothing. However, with Your Son's Name to empower us, and His Blood to cover us, and His Spirit to fill us, we can do all things through God who strengthens us.

With God all things are possible. We are more than conquerors through Christ our Lord. Amen!

Romans 8:31-39

[31] What, then, shall we say in response to these things? If God is for us, who can be against us? [32] He who did not spare his own Son, but gave him up for us all—how will he not also, along with him, graciously give us all things? [33] Who will bring any charge against those whom God has chosen? It is God who justifies. [34] Who then is the one who condemns? No one. Christ Jesus who died—more than that, who was raised to life—is at the right hand of God and is also interceding for us. [35] Who shall separate us from the love of Christ? Shall trouble or hardship or persecution or famine or nakedness or danger or sword? [36] As it is written: "For your sake we face death all day long; we are considered as sheep to be slaughtered."

[37] No, in all these things we are more than conquerors through him who loved us. [38] For I am convinced that neither death nor life, neither angels nor demons, neither the present nor the future, nor any powers, [39] neither height nor depth, nor anything else in all creation, will be able to separate us from the love of God that is in Christ Jesus our Lord

Read: Romans 8:36 and Psalm 44: 22

Chart 14: The Watchers of Enoch

1. **Ananel (Hanane)** – one of the fallen watchers	14. **Kasbeel** – sinful angel whose name means sorcery
2. **Arakiba (Artaqifa)** – evil fallen angel, one of the chiefs of ten troops	15. **Kasdaye** – fallen angel who taught men abortion
3. **Araqiel** – one of the fallen watchers who taught men the signs of the earth	16. **Kokabel (Kokabiel)** – one of the fallen watchers whose name means star of God
4. **Arariel** – one of the seven angels with dominion over the earth	17. **Rameel** – one of the fallen watchers
5. **Armaros** – one of the fallen watcher who taught enchantments	18. **Ramiel (Rumja)** – one of the fallen watchers
6. **Asael** – one of the fallen watchers whose name means 'who God made'	19. **Samsapeel (Shamshiel)** – one of the fallen watchers
7. **Azazel** – considered to be responsible for teaching mankind about war and how to work with metals and make weapons.	20. **Sariel** – recorded as both a holy and a fallen angel
8. **Baraqijal (Baraqel)** – one of the watchers who taught astrology	21. **Satarel (Jetrel)** – one of the fallen watcher whose name means God's side
9. **Batarel (Batarjal)** – one of the fallen watchers	22. **Semiaza (Samjaza)** – supposed to be the actual leader of the fallen watchers
10. **Busasejal (Basasael)** – one of the fallen watchers	23. **Tamiel (Turael)** – one of the fallen watchers whose name means perfection of God
11. **Daniel (Danjel)** – one of the fallen watchers whose name means God is my judge	24. **Tumael** (unknown) – one of the fallen watchers
12. **Ezeqeel ((Neqael)** – one of the fallen watchers who taught men the knowledge of clouds	25. **Turel** – one of the fallen watchers whose name mean the rock of God
13. **Jomjael (Rumael)** – one of the fallen watchers whose name means *day of God*	26. **Zaqiel** – one of the fallen watchers

Chapter 14
The Watchers of Enoch

In the book of Enoch, which was at one time in history an accepted canonized book, we are given a list of names of beings. They were at one time angels of righteousness known as watchers. These were the sons of God mentioned in Genesis 6, which crossbred with the daughters of men.

The book of Enoch, along with the book of Jubilees, gives a list of the leaders of these rebellious sons of God. They are recorded as **Semjaza** the leader, **Arkiba, Rameel, Kokabiel, Tamiel, Ramiel, Danel, Ezeqeel, Baraqijal, Asael, Armaros, Batarel, Ananel, Zaqiel, Samsapeel, Satarel, Turel, Jomeael,** and **Sariel**.

Enoch mentions **Azaziel (Azazel)**, who taught men how to apply makeup for beautification. He was also the scapegoat in rabbinic literature and Targum. In The Zohar (Vayeze 153a), the rider on the serpent is symbolized as the evil **Azazel**. Here he is stated to be the chief of the order of *bene elim* (otherwise *ischim*, lower angels, "men-spirits").

> **Azazel – known as seducer of mankind,
> and refused to bow down before Adam.**

Irenaeus called **Azazel** *"that fallen yet mighty angel"*. In The Apocalypse of Abraham, he is referred to as the *"lord of hell, seducer of mankind"*, and here his appearance, when revealed in it is so called true form, shows him to be a *demon* with *seven serpent heads, fourteen faces* and *twelve wings*. Jewish legend proclaims **Azazel** as the angel *who refused to bow down before Adam* (In the Koran, the angel is **Eblis** or **Iblis**.) when the first human was presented to God to the assembled hierarchs of heaven. For refusing to do so, **Azazel** was then dubbed the ***great Satan*** (*Ref. Bamberger*, Fallen Angels). *Bamberger* also recorded that the *first star to fall from heaven* was **Azazel**. According to **Islamic legend**, when God commanded the angels to worship Adam, **Azazel** refused stating, *"Why should a son of fire bow down to a son of clay (mortal)?"*

For saying this, God cast **Azazel** out of heaven and changed his name to **Eblis**. *Milton* described **Azazel**, in his work Paradise Lost, as a cherum – tall, but also a fallen angel, and he was the standard bearer of **Satan**. It has also been written that **Azazel** was an ancient *Semitic god of the flocks* who was degraded to the level of a demon.

Samjaza, referred to as **Semyaza** (or **Semiaza, Shemhazai, Shamazya** or **Amezyarak**) is probably a combination of Shem that means *'name'* and Azza. He was the leader of the *fallen watchers,* the *bene of Elohim* (the sons of God). In legend, he is the *seraph* tempted by the maiden **Ishtahar** to reveal to her the explicit name of God. According to Graves in **Hebrew Myths**, it is said that **Semyaza** now hangs upside down between heaven and earth and is the *constellation Orion*. **Levi** in Transcendental Magic suggests that *Orion* would be *identical of Michael* doing battle *with the dragon*, and the appearance of this sign in the sky would be for the cabalist, a portent of victory and happiness.

According to The Zohar (**Genesis**), **Semyaza's** sons, **Hiwa** and **Hiya**, by one of *Eve's daughters*, were so large that they consumed 1000 camels, 1000 horses, and 1000 oxen daily. In *Byron's* version of the *legend* "*Heaven and Earth, a Mystery*", **Semyaza** is transformed into **Azaziel**, and the female **Ishtahar** is transformed into **Aholibamah**. A recently uncovered version of the **book of Enoch** (*Qumran collection*) contains a letter from Enoch addressed to **Semyaza (Shemazya)** and his companions.

Armaros (Armers, Pharmaros, Abaros, Arearos) is one of the leaders of the fallen angels recorded in **Enoch I**. He is responsible for teaching the resolving of enchantments. It is believed that **Armaros** may be a corruption of the name **Araros**.

Baraqijal, as noted in the **book of Jubilees**, is one of the *former watchers* (**Grigori**) who united with the daughters of men, which is touched on in **Genesis 6**. **Baraqijal** is now a demon who *inhabits* the nether realms and is a *teacher of astrology*. In **Enoch I**, he is recorded as a leader (*one of the chief of ten*) of a troop of fallen angels. It is believed that **Baraqijal** may be merely a variant of **Barakiel**.

Kokabiel is also known as **Kakabel (Kochbiel, Kokbaiel, Kochab** – star of God). He is a great angelic prince who exercises dominion over the stars and constellations. In *The Book of The Angel Raziel*, **Kakabel** is a *high holy angel*; however, in the *apocryphal lore*, as in **(Enoch 1)**, he is an evil fallen angel and a resident of the nether realms. According to legend, whether he is in heaven or hell, he still *commands 365,000 surrogate spirits* who do his bidding. Among his other duties, he is an instructor of astrology.

Ezeqeel in Hebrew means '*strength of God*'.

Ezeqeel in Hebrew means '*strength of God*'. In **Enoch I**, he is recorded as a leader of the fallen angels who taught mankind the art of augury from the clouds.

Arakiba (Arakab, Aristiqifa, Artaqifa) is an *evil fallen angel* who brought sin to the earth as cited in **Enoch I** (where **Arakiba** is designated as one of the chiefs of ten apostate troops).

Ramiel, (Remiel, Phanuel, Uriel, Yerahmeel, Jeremiel), in the Syriac Apocalypse of Baruch, is the angel who presides over the true visions *Baruch* saw and spoke of. In this vision, **Ramiel** appears as the angel who destroys the hosts of *Sennacherib*, a feat also credited to *Uriel, Michael, Gabriel*, and other redoubtable hierarchs. **Ramiel** *is chief of thunder* as is **Uriel** and he has charge over the souls, which come up for judgment on the last day.

In the book of **Enoch, Ramiel,** or **Remiel**, is both a *holy angel and a fallen angel* (**Enoch I, 6 and I, 20**). In **verse 20**, he is the leader of the apostates. In **verse 6,** he is one of the holy angels standing before the throne of God. In Paradise Lost VI, **Ramiel**, along with **Ariel** and **Arioch**, is overcome by **Abdiel** in the first day of fighting in Heaven. *To Milton*, **Ramiel**, being on the side of **Satan**, makes him evil.

In **Sibylline Oracle II 2, 5, Ramiel** is *one of five angels* who lead the souls of men to judgment. The five angels cited are **Arakiel, Ramiel, Uriel, Samiel** and **Aziel**. A number of Milton scholars (*Keightley and Baldwin*) have longed believed that Milton coined **Ramiel** as well as **Ithuriel** and

Zophiel. The names of these angels; however, have come to light in early *apocryphal., apocalyptic, Talmudic* sources. Therefore, *Milton*, who was familiar with such sources, had no need to invent these angels.

Danjal, or Daniel, means 'God is my judge'.

Danjal, or **Daniel**, means *'God is my judge'*. According to *A. E. Waite* in <u>The Lemegeton</u>, he is an *angel of the order of the principalities*. **Daniel**, as **Danjal**, is one of the fallen angels listed in Enoch 1. In the lower regions, he exercises authority over lawyers. His sigil is reproduced in R. Ambelain's, <u>La Kabbale Pratique</u>, pg 289, but in other accounts, he is still considered a holy angel – one of 72 who bears the name of God, Shemhamphorae.

Ezeqeel's name in Hebrew means 'strength of God'.

Ezeqeel's name in **Hebrew** means *'strength of God'*. He is also recorded in the book of **(Enoch 1)** as a *fallen angel* who defiles himself with the daughters of man, and taught augury from the clouds.

Asael's name in the Hebrew means 'who God made'.

Asael's name in the **Hebrew** means *'who God made'*. He is an angel under **Semjaza** who cohabited with the daughters of men, and as a result became a fallen angel.

Tamiel (Tamel, Temel, Tamuel) means 'perfection of God'.

Tamiel (Tamel, Temel, Tamuel) means *'perfection of God'*. He is known as the *angel of the deep*, which puts him in the sphere of **Leviathan, Behemoth** and **Rahab**. He is listed as one of the leaders of the fallen watchers in the book of **Enoch I**.

Arariel (Azareel, Uzziel) means 'curer of stupidity'.

Arariel (Azareel, Uzziel) means *'curer of stupidity'*. He is <u>one</u> of the *seven angels with dominion over the earth*. **Arariel** is specifically an angel who *presides over the waters of the earth, according to the Talmud.*

Araqiel (Araquiel, Arakiel, Araael, Arqael, Saraquael, Arkiel, Arkas) means *'one who exercises dominion over the earth'*.

Araqiel (Araquiel, Arakiel, Araael, Arqael, Saraquael, Arkiel, Arkas) means *'one who exercises dominion over the earth'*. He is one of the <u>two hundred fallen angels</u> recorded in **Enoch I**. **Araqiel** <u>taught</u> humans the *signs of the earth*. However, in the *Sibylline Oracles*, **Araqiel** does **not** seem to be a fallen angel. He is believed to be one of *the five angels who lead the souls of men to judgment* along with **Ramiel, Uriel, Samiel** and **Aziel**.

Batarel is one of the *fallen watchers*. He is invoked in *ceremonial magic rites*. The name **Batarel** appears in **Talisman 4** of the *Sage of the Pyramids* and also in the *Book of Black Magic*.

Samsapeel (**Samsaveel**, **Shamshiel**) is believed to be an *evil archangel* and is listed among the *apostates* in the book of **Enoch I**. He was one of the 200 who left their place in heaven to cohabit with the daughters of men.

Satarel, or Sartael, means *'God's side'*.

Satarel, or **Sartael**, means *'God's side'*. He is recorded as an evil archangel in control of the secret and hidden things. Along with being mentioned in the book of **Enoch I**, he is also in mentioned **(Talmud Berakoth 576).**

Sariel (**Suriel**, **Zerachiel**, **Sarakiel**, **Uriel**) is one of the *seven archangels* originally listed in the **book of Enoch** as **Saraqel** and differentiated from **Uriel**, although he is identified as **Uriel** in *T. Gaster's Dead Sea Scriptures*. **Sariel** is recorded as both a holy angel and a fallen one. In occultism he is one of the nine angels of the summer equinox and is effective as an amulet against the evil eye. He supposedly governs the zodiac sign of the Ram (Aries). In addition, he teaches the course of the moon, which was at one time considered forbidden knowledge.

In recently discovered knowledge found in the *Dead Sea scrolls*, one of the books, *The War of the Sons of Light Against The Sons of Darkness*, speaks of the angel, **Sariel**, as *a name which appears on the shields of the third tower*. The term *'tower'* here means a *fighting unit*. There were *four towers or four fighting units in all*.

Turel (Turiel, Turael) means *'the rock of God'*.

Turel (**Turiel**, **Turael**) means 'the rock of God'. He was one of the 200 angels listed in the **Book of Enoch**, who followed **Semyaza** in the descent from heaven to intermingle with the daughters of men as recorded in **Genesis 6**. The sigil of the fallen **Turiel** is pictured in *The Secret Grimoire of Turiel*, pg. 39. As **Turiel**, **Turel** is a *messenger of the spirits of the planet Jupiter* and also a *messenger of the angel* **Sachiel** or **Setchiel**.

Jomjael or Yomyael means *'day of God'*.

Jomjael or **Yomyael** means 'day of God'. All we know about him is that he is one of the sons of God who left his first estate and was cast out of heaven along with **Satan** and these others.

Zagiel was the *last* of the leaders of the watchers who lost their positions in heaven.

Zagiel was the *last* of the leaders of the watchers who lost their positions in heaven and were cast out for their sins of fornication with the daughters of men. His sorry testimony is simply stated: *He is an evil archangel*.

Kasbeel (Kazbiel, Kaspiel) means *sorcery*.

Kasbeel (**Kazbiel**, **Kaspiel**) means *sorcery*. He is a *sinful angel*, referred to as *chief of the oath*, whose original name was **Biqa**, meaning *good person*. (**cf Akae**) But **Karbeel** fell, and after he *lied* *to God*, his name was changed to **Kazbiel**, meaning '*he who lies to God*'. He supposedly asked Michael for the hidden name of the Lord, which of course Michael refused to give him. It is recorded in **Enoch I 69:13** and commented on in <u>Fallen Angels</u>, pg. 264, by *Bamberger*.

Kasdaye taught man how to terminate the life in the womb.

Kasdaye (**Kesdeya**, **Kasdeyae**, **Kasdeja**) is a *fallen angel* who teaches a variety of demonic practices <u>including abortion</u>. This is the spirit who taught man how to terminate the life in the womb. **Kasdaye** is one of the seven angels reputed to have led the apostate angels according to the book of Enoch.

In closing this chapter on the Hebrew strongmen, I would suggest buying a copy of the book of Enoch I and II and reading it.

Prayer Against the Strongmen of the Book of Enoch

Father, we thank You because You are our strong tower, our hiding place. **(Psalm 61:3)** *You are our protector and go before us as a shield of faith to quench the fiery darts of the adversary and his allies.* **(Ephesians 6:16)**

Lord, these strongmen are different from all the others. Everyone of these strongmen was bene Elohim, the sons of God. They abided at one time in Your kingdom and beheld Your glory. Yet, they chose to rebel against You and Your beloved Son, to turn their back on You and truth, to walk in darkness, and to deceive man to follow in their ways. **(Psalm 106:43)**

Oh Lord, keep us from deception, from following after them and being overcome by their lust and schemes, from their deception of <u>half-truths</u>.

Help us put on the full armor of God so we are not ignorant of the tactics of the enemy. **(Ephesians 6:10-18)**

For we do not wrestle against flesh and blood, but against principalities, against powers, against the rulers of the darkness of this age, against spiritual hosts of wickedness in the heavenly places. Therefore take up the whole armor of God, that you may be able to withstand in the evil day, and having done all, to stand. **(Ephesians 6:12-13)**

Father, please help us to see through the falsehood of the angel of light and his fallen angels. Thank You for keeping us out of the snare of these strongmen. Amen.

Psalm 61:3
…for you are my safe refuge, a fortress where my enemies cannot reach me.

Ephesians 6:16
In addition to all this, take up the shield of faith, with which you can extinguish all the flaming arrows of the evil one.

Psalm 106:43
Again and again he rescued them, but they chose to rebel against him, and they were finally destroyed by their sin

Ephesians 6:10-18

[10] Finally, be strong in the Lord and in his mighty power. [11] Put on the full armor of God, so that you can take your stand against the devil's schemes. [12] For our struggle is not against flesh and blood, but against the rulers, against the authorities, against the powers of this dark world and against the spiritual forces of evil in the heavenly realms. [13] Therefore put on the full armor of God, so that when the day of evil comes, you may be able to stand your ground, and after you have done everything, to stand. [14] Stand firm then, with the belt of truth buckled around your waist, with the breastplate of righteousness in place, [15] and with your feet fitted with the readiness that comes from the gospel of peace. [16] In addition to all this, take up the shield of faith, with which you can extinguish all the flaming arrows of the evil one. [17] Take the helmet of salvation and the sword of the Spirit, which is the word of God.

[18] And pray in the Spirit on all occasions with all kinds of prayers and requests. With this in mind, be alert and always keep on praying for all the Lord's people.

Chart 15: Strongmen of Emotions

1. **Aclahayr** – spirit behind mental anguish and disorders	30. **Chil Gazi** – seducer of women
2. **Aeshma** – controlling spirit behind violence, wrath, anger, rage and fury	31. **Daevas** – spirit behind drunkenness, envy, and impure sexuality
3. **Afrit** – relentless spirit of revenge	32. **Danglathas** – spirit behind violent crimes and murder
4. **Agares** – spirit behind false courage	33. **Dantalion** – three-face spirit of sexual perversion, bisexualism, gender confusion, mind reading and the worship of the occult
5. **Agathodemon** – driving force behind deception	34. **Druj** – spirit that works through perversion and corruption
6. **Agramon** – powerful spirit behind fears	35. **Erzulie** – spirit of fornication and adultery
7. **Aka Manah** – spirit behind the perverted mind and evil deeds	36. **Furfur** – spirit that works through perversion and corruption
8. **Akatash** – spirit behnd evil thoughts	37. **Gresil/Gressil** – spirit behind laziness
9. **Aku Aku** – spirit behind unstable, troubled, aggravated mind	38. **Incubus** – male demon of sexual lusting
10. **Alastor** – spirit behind murder	39. **Indra** – Iranian name for spirit of violence
11. **Alperer** – spirit that preys and troubles lonely women	40. **Inguma** – Biskian name for the spirit of fear
12. **Alu-Demon** – night spirit behind nightmares and bad dreams	41. **Jaldabaoth** – spirit of lust
13. **Ammit** – spirit behind spiritual torment	42. **Jezebeth** – spirit of falsehood and lies
14. **Andras** – spirit who works through quarrels and strife	43. **Joetun** – giant spirit of emotional chaos and destruction
15. **Angra Mainyu** – spirit behind pain, suffering, and torment	44. **Malphas** – spirit that works through deception and lies
16. **Ansitif** – spirit that possesses people	45. **Mammon** – New Testament spirit of greed
17. **Aosoth** – spirit that works through passion and death	46. **Mastema** – spirit behind hostility
18. **Apasmara** – spirit of mindlessness and glare (staring, daze) and belief in reincarnation	47. **Murmur** – spirit of lies, slander, accusations, falsehood, and deceit
19. **Ardat-Lile** – spirit behind destruction of families	48. **Ornias** – spirit of homosexuality
20. **Arioch** – spirit that works behind revenge	49. **Philatanus** – Jewish strongman of sodomy
21. **Ashtaroth** – spirit of lust and seduction	50. **Proserpine** – spirit who helps in establishing the act of sodomy

22. **Aspis** – Hebrew snake-like spirit of evil and stubbornness	51. **Pruflas/Busas** – spirits of war, discord, quarrels, and poverty
23. **Awar** – spirit behind laziness	52. **Pyro** – spirit that works behind falsehood
24. **Az** – spirit of extreme evil	53. **Rabisu – strongman who lies in wait, the doorkeeper (Genesis 4:6)**
25. **Azathoth** – powerful spirit of chaos	54. **Samael** – Hebrew spirit, which is a former Watcher who works through slander, accusation, and seduction
26. **Bael** – spirit of shrewdness and deception	55. **Sonneillon** – spirit of hate
27. **Belial** – Hebrew spirit of emotional darkness, uselessness, and desperation	56. **Succorbenoth** – Hebrew spirit behind jealousy
28. **Bilwis** – German name of the spirit of envy and absolute meanness	57. **Succubus** – female demon of sexual lusting
29. **Caym** – spirit of vain logic and puns	58. **Uphir** – spirit of pharmaceutical drug abuse and chemical and substance addictions

Chapter 15
Strongmen of Emotions

Emotions are quite natural and everybody has them. I am not saying that just because we are emotional we are under the control of spiritual strongmen. Neither am I saying that if someone suffers from an emotional or mental illness they are demon possessed. My own father was an epileptic for well over forty years of his life. I have had friends and associates in the ministry who were epileptics as well as patients I saw while working in the medical field. Evil spirits did not control them. However, I have seen many people who, when the unclean spirits were cast out of them, no longer suffered from seizures.

Everyone who suffers from emotional problems is **not** necessarily demon possessed. On the other hand, everyone who is demon possessed suffers from emotional problems. For example, we see this in the young boy who was brought by his father to Jesus because the disciples could not help the boy. Then there is the demoniac of the Gadarenes who lived among the graves.

Damaged emotions can bring on mental illness

It's obvious there are strongmen who work behind and through *damaged emotions*. There is **Aclahayr**, the spirit behind *mental illness*, who seeks to *enslave* the minds of men and bring them to ruin. The **Aeshma** spirit works through *wrath, anger, rages and fury*. He drives men to cause *great harm, destruction and even murder*.

Deception, Lies, Accusations, Broken Relationships, Marriages

Agathodemon is a very powerful spirit of *deception and lies*. He *perverts the truth and ruins lives through slander, false accusations and defamation of character.* He leaves behind him a vast tract of *broken relationships, marriages, friendships and partnerships* – forever destroyed because of his deception.

Afrit: Revenge, Threats – He stops man from hearing the Lord proclaim, "Stop the gates from hearing and obeying."

The powerful spirit of *revenge* is called **Afrit**. He causes people to seek not justice for an act done to them, but for revenge. He cries out "an eye for an eye", "a tooth for a tooth", and "a life for a life". He *deafens* you to the words of Jesus: "If your brother strikes you on one cheek, turn to him the other." He stops man from hearing the Lord proclaim: "*Revenge is Mine,*" says the Lord.

He keeps plaguing the mind of man until he cries out "blood for blood", and he is not satisfied until he extracts his pound of flesh for the acts done against him. **Afrit** works well with other strongmen known as **Alastor** and **Danglathas**, which are spirits of murder. **Afrit** has an evil twin, who is also a terrible spirit of *revenge*, called **Arioch**.

Agares is the spirit of fake courage who works extremely well with **Agramon**, the spirit of fear, and **Inguma**, a **Baskian** *spirit of fear*.

This spirit works to rob man of any peace, joy, or confidence he may have in God, his fellow man or himself.

Aka Manah: Perverted Minds – Lust and Seduction of All Facets Night Spirit

Aka Manah, spirit behind *perverted minds and deeds.*

There are spirits like: **Aka Manah**, a spirit behind *perverted minds and deeds*; **Ashtaroth**, spirit of *lust and seduction* and a leader of the <u>Incubus and Succubus</u>; **Alu-Demon**, a <u>night spirit</u> that works when men are asleep; **Jaldabaoth**, strongman of lust; **Ornias**, strongman of *homosexuality*; **Dantalion**, spirit of *bisexualism*; **Ezuli**, spirit of *fornication and adultery*; **Philatanus**, a very powerful strongman behind *sodomy and pedophile acts;* **Proserpine**, *a spirit of sodomy*; and **Druj**, a spirit of *perversion and corruption.*

The strongmen behind the acts of evil are **Akatash**, and the **Hebrew** *snake spirit* of *evil and stubbornness* is called **Aspis**, while **Az** is the strongman behind *evil desires.*

This tormenting spirit keeps a person from feeling forgiven and accepted by God.

Aku Aku is the spirit, which causes the mind to be *troubled and extremely aggravated*. He renders the mind unable to be at peace, to feel joy, happiness or love. **Ammit** is the spirit of spiritual torment. This *tormenting spirit* keeps a person from <u>feeling forgiven and accepted by God</u>. They feel constantly inadequate to be loved and redeemed from their past. They struggle with the concept that they have committed the unpardonable sin. **Ammit** works well with **Angra Mainyu**, the spirit of pain, torment and suffering.

...tormenting and troubling minds of lonely women.

Aka Manah and **Ammit** will often join forces together with **Alperer**, a strongman who specializes in *tormenting and troubling the minds of lonely women*. **Alperer** opens the doors for another **Hunza** spirit, which specializes in tormenting women, called **Chil Gazi**, an <u>incubus</u> who *seduces women sexually and eventually leads them to perform suicides.*

There are also spirits of destruction, and chaos like **Azathoth**, and **Joetun** is giant *spirit of destruction and chaos*. **Ardat-Lile** is a strongman specializing in family destruction and chaos.

Apasmara is the spirit behind *mindlessness and confusion*. **Bael** is the **Hebrew** strongman of *shrewdness and deception*. **Caym** is the spirit behind *vain logic and puns.*

Hate, Violence, Slander, Accusation, Discord, Strife, Poverty

Indra is the **Iranian** spirit of *hate and violence*. He **hates the truth** and works with **Jezebeth**, the spirit of *falsehood and lies,* and also with **Malphas**, the spirit of *deception and lies*. There are several other lying spirits like **Murmur**, the master spirit of lies, deceit, slander, falsehood and accusations. He works with **Pyro**, the *spirit of falsehood*, and **Samael**, the **Hebrew** *fallen watcher* who is the leader of the spirits of *slander and accusation* and is a major seducer.

Then there are the vastly powerful spirits of *hostility* like **Mastema**, and the equally powerful spirit *of war, discord, quarrels, strife and poverty* – the strongman **Pruflas**. **Busas**, the spirit of *poverty*, works not only on the materialist but also very much so in the area of the mind and the spirit of man.

Laziness, Drunkenness, Jealousy, Pharmaceutical Drug Abuse and Addiction

Another strongman who also assaults us is **Gresil**, or **Gressil**, the spirit of *procrastination and laziness*. Then there are the very powerful principalities of *drunkenness, jealously and envy* called **Daevas**, with its Hebrew counterpart, **Sonneillon**, the spirit of *hate,* and **Succorbenoth**, the spirit of *hate*, and **Uphir**, the spirit of *pharmaceutical drug abuse and addiction*.

Daevas, the spirit of *drunkenness*, and **Uphir**, the strongman of *drug addiction*, and the *spirits of sexual perversion* and *thievery*, along with **Alastor** and **Danglathas**, the principalities of *murder,* are going to be the **five major sins of the last days.**

The **last two strongmen of emotions** do not at first seem to be strongmen of emotions; however, taking a **closer look,** we can see how they work hand in hand with all of the other spirits.

Ansitif, the strongman of possession, and Rabisu, the spirit that lies in wait, are two *very patient spirits*.

They are more than willing to wait patiently for a crack to appear in your armor so they can slip in and set up camp in you and keep the door open wide for all the others to enter. These are what used to be called the doorkeepers. When a pastor would do deliverance they would seek out the spirits, which kept the doors open so the lead spirit could enter with others.

Once these spirits were revealed, they would be cast out and the door sealed so they could no longer enter in. In **Genesis:4,** the Lord warned Cain that sin waits at the door patiently for a chance to enter in.

We must always be on our guard. Remember, Satan goes about as a roaring lion seeking whosoever he can devour.

Prayer Against the Strongmen of Emotions

Dear Lord, we thank You for the precious Blood that covers us (**1 John 1:7**) *and closes all doors or entryways to the enemy and his allies. We thank You, Father, for Your love and mercy and for Your forgiveness and compassion. We thank You, Lord, because You are our Good Shepherd. You are the One who protects us from the roaring lion.*

We thank You, Father, that Jesus came to give us peace – that wonderful peace which passes all understanding. He was more than willing to heal our troubled minds as well as our bodies and spirits.

We no longer have to depend on our troubled minds, but by faith we can have the mind of Christ. **(1 Corinthians 2:16)** *It is having the mind of Christ that no strongman can prevail against and brings peace to everyone who believes, even in the midst of the most chaotic emotional storms we will ever go through, in Jesus Name, Amen.*

PRAYER FOR THOSE WITH SELF-DESTRUCTIVE OR SUICIDAL TENDENCIES

In Jesus' name I renounce all suicidal thoughts and any attempts I've made to take my own life or in any way injure myself. I confess **(name each sin of self-destruction that comes to mind)** *and put it under the blood of Jesus. I renounce the lie that life is hopeless and that I can find peace and freedom by taking my own life. Satan is a thief and comes to steal, kill and destroy. I put any access any demons claim to my life or to my family under the blood of Jesus. In Jesus' name I cover all that with the blood of Jesus. I choose life in Christ Who came to give me life and give it abundantly. Thank You for Your forgiveness that allows me to forgive myself. I choose to believe that there is always hope in Christ. In Jesus name I pray. Amen*

Chart 16: Strongman of False Religions
Part 1: Vodou (Voodoo)

1. **Allah** – false god of Islam (Moslems)	11. **Lwas** – immortal spirits with supernatural powers
2. **Balan** – spirit of witchcraft	12. **Oloddumare** – God Almighty of Santeria
3. **Baphomet** – spirit behind Satanic worship and secret societies	13. **Olorun** – in Santeria he is the owner of the heavens
4. **Bondye** – god of Vodou	14. **Orishas** – personal gods of Santeria
5. **Dantalion** – three-faced spirit behind the worship of the occult	15. **Petros** – violent, aggressive, dangerous lwas in Vodou
6. **Diana of the Ephesians** – spirit behind the worship of the moon. Queen goddess of all divisions of witchcraft	16. **Pyro** – spirit behind spreading falsehood, lies, myths, and legends
7. **Eledaa** – in Santeria, he is the creator being	17. **Rada** – gentle and benevolent lwas in Vodou
8. **Kalfou** – in Vodou, he controls the evil forces of the spirit world	18. **Sariel** – Hebrew former watcher who taught the worship of the moon
9. **Kokabel** – Hebrew former watcher taught the worship of the stars (angel worship)	19. **Shamreel** – Hebrew former watcher taught mankind to worship the sun
10. **Legba** – in Vodou he is the door opener to the spirit world	20. **Ummar** – demon power behind the Qur'an

Chapter 16
Strongmen of False Religions
Part 1: Vodou (Voodoo)

Voodoo, which means spirit or God, was originally started in **Africa** and was basically a religion founded on ancestral worship. The birthplace of voodoo (Vodou) was in the great empire ruled by the Fon called *Dahomey*. This **West African** Empire spread across the countries known as **Benin, Togo** and **Nigeria**. The majority of Haitian slaves were taken from *Dahomey*. At the time of the slave trade, *Dahomey* was the most powerful kingdom of **West Africa**, and one of its *major merchandise* of trades was *slavery.*

People who were conquered in battles, sorcerers, criminals and all other undesirables were sold as slaves. Many of these people, who were taken from **Dahomey**, inhabit an island in the **Caribbean** known today as *Haiti*. When these slaves came to **Haiti**, they brought with them their religion called **voodoo**. However, they changed its name to **Vodou** to separate it from its history of *black magic and witchcraft.*

One of *Dahomey's* strongest rivals was the ***Oyo Empire*** known as the **Yoruba.** These people were a large ethnic group, which lived mostly in modern day **Nigeria**. It was the custom of *Dahomey* to take the gods of the countries they conquered, or had to pay tribute to, and incorporate them into their belief system. The ability to incorporate the different religions helped the relocated **Dahomeans** in **Haiti** to establish the religion we know as **Vodou** (voodoo).

Lwas With the Names of Catholic Saints

The influence of the *Roman Catholic church* began to spread to the **African slaves**. In order to protect themselves from their cruel slave masters they would replace the names of their **lwas** with the names of *Catholic saints*. In their *secret rites* kept well *hidden* from their white *slave owners*, they would resort back to the original names of their lwas.

The followers of ***Vodou*** not only believe firmly in the **lwas,** which are their protectors, but also in many kinds of spirits and in good and evil angels. These **Vodou lwas** (spirits) were not remote beings that stood afar off, but they were very active in the daily life of their worshippers. **West Africans** had personal relationships with their personal **lwa**.

The **West Africans**, as well as the **Haitians**, would serve their personal **lwas** (spirits) by rituals and offerings, and in return the spirits helped them to make decisions and brought good fortune to them. They also brought retribution and revenge on behalf of the faithful.

The thousands of **lwas** formed a hierarchy with the *lesser-known spirits* on the bottom and the more powerful spirits on top. Anyone could know another person's **lwa** and make it his or her own.

They could even take the spirits of their enemies and turn them against their own followers.

A powerful private **lwa** could be exalted to become a powerful public **lwa,** as in the case of **Agassu** who founded the *royal line* of *Dahomey* and who is still honored in **Haitian Vodou** today.

In order to perform the rites and ritual of Vodou (voodoo), you needed:

1.) Dancing, drumming and chanting in order to communicate with the spirits
2.) Animal sacrifices made as offerings to the spirits
3.) A priest or a priestess who could interpret the messages from the spirits
4.) Possession of the bodies for individuals participating in the rituals

All these elements of the rituals were intended to foster the relationship each individual had with the ancestral and nature spirits.

The main purpose of rituals was to communicate with and to receive instruction. It was the duties of the priest or priestess to show each person who their **lwa** was and how to worship him/her. Also, it was the priestess or priest's responsibility to receive messages from the spirits and to interpret them to the followers and to call on the spirits to appear.

If the **lwa** did show when it possessed a person, he or she would begin to dance all over in a great frenzy. *The act was called 'riding the horse'.* It was called that because it is believed the spirit rode on the back of the possessed person like a rider on a horse.

The priest and priestess inherited their portion from their mother or father. Therefore, it was said of them that they were born into the priesthood. The priests or priestesses were not only the spiritual leaders of the communities but also the political leaders as well.

Many rebellious priests were sold into slavery because of the power they held in their community. No matter where they went, the priest or priestess would hold the absolute power of spiritual and political leadership.

The religious practices of the **Fon** and other tribal peoples of **West Africa** live on today, not only in offshoots like **Vodou** in **Haiti**, but also in **Africa** itself. In modern day **Benin**, the *official religion*, **Vodun,** is essentially the same as practiced in *ancient Dahomey* and for thousands of years before the empire was founded. Vodun, or Vodoun, is also the dominant religion in **Togo** and southwest **Ghana** and **Nigeria**.

The powerful public **lwas** (*spirits*) of the **Fon, Yoruba**, and other **West African tribes** are the most venerated spirits in **Haitian Vodou** because they provide a direct link to Haitian's African roots. Although the characteristics, functions, and personalities of these spirits changed when they were imported to Haiti, they are still the oldest and most important spirits honored in **Vodou**.

In **Vodou** the *oldest* **African** spirits are called **Rada,** and since they originated in the Haitians original homeland, they stand for stability and tradition. In **West Africa, Rada** acts as protectors and parental figures, helping to keep order and passing along ancient wisdom. They are supposedly *benevolent, gentle and kind.* They are called upon in the pursuit of goodness, such as the insurgence of good health and fortune. They are thought to help the communities against evil, to supposedly help make ethical decisions and of course to find love.

One thing to consider is the **African Vodun** with **Rada** as gods is not the right way with **Vodou** in **Haiti** as with **Christianity**, **Islam** or **Judaism**. There is only ONE true God and creator.

> **In Vodou, the lwas or spirits are the <u>immortal souls of the ancestors, the spirits of people who were all once alive.</u> That is why the spirits are honored or served and are never worshipped as gods.**

One important fact about the **lwas** is that they are truly spirits but **not spirits of humans** who once lived and died and are evolved into guardian spirits to benefit mankind. They are all demonic spirits sent forth to deceive man and to lead him into damnation.

I took the time to go over the history of **Vodou**, or **Voodoo**, written from the hands of **Vodou** participants, to show the deception these spirits have over their followers – even to the point where they invite these spirits to ride them as a horse. I have seen the faces of men and women who were being ridden by their personal **lwa**. There was nothing holy about them; instead, they wore expressions of absolute evil and torment. Many of these participants almost die from the experience of being controlled by these spirits. After observing them, you will understand these spirits do not serve them, but dominate them. There is no love for their devotees – only hate.

Rada is one of the most *important branches* of **Vodou**. Rituals, using special drums, chants and clothing, characterize it. Most rituals performed in **Vodou** are of the **Rada** type, which are the original ceremonies of the Fon. Through these rituals, practitioners of **Vodou** experience a direct link to their ancestors in **West Africa** – especially *Dahomey*. They keep themselves in bondage to their traditions and beliefs, which have enslaved their people for centuries.

Communication to the Departed Loved Ones

It is very interesting to see the familiarity of the practitioners of **Vodou** and the followers of the <u>Fox Sisters</u>, the <u>founders of spiritualism in America.</u> Both believe they are talking to the spirits of departed loved ones who have managed through spiritual evolution to evolve into higher beings and are now able to communicate with the living as wise guardians. *God, open the eyes of both groups to see the evil spirits pretending to be ancestral souls sent to help men to evolve into godhood.*

Vodou *embraces the saints of the Catholic church.*

It is not difficult to see why those who practice **Vodou** *embrace the saints of the Catholic church.* To them their **Vodou** spirits, which are former humans who have evolved into guardian spirits sent back to help them, is <u>no</u> difference than the *Catholic* saints who were once human. *Catholic* saints are humans who have died and are now resigned to sainthood – ready to hear the prayers of the *Catholic* and to intercede on their behalf to God.

> **I guess they never read that Jesus Christ is the only mediator between God and man, Who alone lives forever to make intercession for the true believers.**

Let us look now at some of the **lwas** and **Rada** of the **Vodou** believers. I believe these strongmen of *deceit* are not only involved in **Vodou**, but in *spiritualism* and even in the *sainthood of the Catholic church*. As I have said before, the *Dahomey Empire* did **not** have any problems with taking the spirits of their neighboring tribes – even those of their enemies. One of the spirits of *Dahomey* adopted from the **Yoruba** was a spirit called **Fa**.

Fa became one of the most important spirits in *Dahomey*. His domain was that of fate, and he held absolute control of divination – empowering his priest and priestess to be able to foretell the future. His job was to reveal the personal lwa of each person. These lwa would be the one that their follower would be responsible for honoring and to make clear the proper rites each person was supposed to do in order to get in the good graces of these lwa. Thus, **Fa** was responsible for helping the priests and priestesses to guide their followers in their spiritual lives.

The counterpart of **Fa** was incorporated from the **Ibbo** and **Yoruba tribes**. While **Fa** represented fate, his counterpart, **Legba**, represented change; through him, fate could be thwarted and the future altered. **Legba** was actually the same as **Rabisu**, the spirit who lies in wait, and **Uvall** and **Vassago**, the strongmen of fortune telling.

Legba was the *door opener of the spirit world*, and the priests and priestesses of the other spirits could communicate with them only through **Legba**. He was therefore always invoked or summoned first at every ritual. In **Vodou (Voodoo)**, **Fa** and **Legba** were blended into one personality who is now called **Papa Legba**. This made **Legba** become the head of the **Vodou's** *pantheon of spirits*, who is always invoked first and honored the most.

Next in the Vodou realms we have the **Serpent, Rainbow and Fire**. There are **two** other **Fon spirits**, which have key positions in the **Vodou** hierarchy. They are **Danbala** and **Ayida Wedo**. **Danbala** is related to the serpent god, **Da**, revered by the Fon. His *symbol* is the *snake*, while his supposed *wife,* **Ayida Wedo's** *symbol* is the *rainbow*. These two spirits, according to **Vodou** belief, are always together, and for the Fon, are important for gaining wealth and prestige.

Another strongman, whom the **Fon** appropriated from the **Nago tribe**, is a spirit called **Ogun** by the Nago and called **Gu** by the Fon. **Ogun** *rules* the realm of war, iron and fire. He is the **Vodou** counterpart to **Mars** and **Aries**, the *gods of war and iron*, **Vulcan**, the god of fire, and **Azazel**, the **Hebrew strongman** of war who taught man how to make weapons of iron. **Ogun** was always invoked when making weapons and metalwork. His qualities were blended together, and **Shango**, who was the **Yoruba spirit** of *thunder and warfare*, was the counterpart to **Thor**, the *god of thunder*, son of **Odin**. **Ogun** and **Shango** became known as one powerful spirit called **Ogu**.

The **Haitians** continue to honor the spirits of *Dahomey* and the other **West African tribes**. The **Haitian** slaves kept to their homeland and tribal traditions even knowing that their own people sold them into slavery. However, they felt their physical homeland of **West Africa** was lost to them forever, so they invented a spiritual homeland called **Ginen** after the **Gulf of Guinea** where *Dahomey* was located. Although the **Haitian's** ancestors and the land of their origins are separated from them by the horrible history of slavery, they can keep their memory alive in the perfect world of **Ginen**. There is an old Haitian proverb, which said: **Haiti** is the child of *Dahomey*, **Haiti** is the child of **Ginen**.

Ginen is not a physical kingdom. It is spiritual and can only be reached by communication with the spirits or by death. **Ginen** is the ancient birthplace of the ancient African spirits of **Vodun**, called the **Rada** spirits. It is also where these spirits live. During **Vodou** rituals, the spirits are called from **Ginen** to earth. The spirit, **Papa Legba**, is the gatekeeper to **Ginen**. Only he can open the way between the physical world and **Ginen** and allows communication with the spirits.

Ginen, according to **Vodou**, is the only place a soul goes to after it dies. In **Ginen** the soul gains immortality and sacred knowledge and is elevated to the role of an ancestral spirit. The spirit then can return to earth to benefit its descendant. This is what we would call in our belief as a familiar spirit. Finally, to the **Vodou** practitioner, **Ginen** represents the high moral traditions and spiritual wisdom of the African homeland. In **Vodou**, the goal is to always move toward the state - **Ginen**, a righteous state of being. Ginen supposedly is where you find the totality of yourself – where you can connect fully with the ancient traditions of **Africa**. Then after death, you can be reborn as one of the wise spirits of **Vodou**.

Haitian slaves adopted many of the Catholic rites and customs.

In order to protect themselves, the **Haitian** slaves adopted many of the Catholic rites and customs. Since the only days a slave got off from their labors were on the *Catholic* holidays, the slaves would use these days as their important religious ceremonies. Even the *act of baptism*, which many slaves chose to do four or more times, was integrated into their **Vodou**.

In the Catholic church when you are baptized,
you are being baptized in their church and not into the kingdom of God

They believed every time they were baptized, it brought them more magical powers. These baptisms eventually became what are known in **Vodou** as luck baths.

Taking *luck baths* is an old **Vodou** custom. Just as its name implies, their baths are performed to bring good luck, protection, and healing from the aquatic lwa, **Danbala** (snake god), **Ayrda-Wedo** (rainbow goddess), **Ezili** or **Erzulie** (*spirit of love and beauty*), **Agwe** (*god of fish and water activities*), and **Simbi** (**lwa** of magicians who live in fresh water). The luck baths are usually performed by an oungan or houngan (priest) who will become possessed during the ritual by the lwa being provoked.

The rites of baptism and Catholic holidays
were not the only *Catholic symbols* used in Vodou ceremonies.

The practitioners of **Vodou** also used the cross and the saints. *Saint Patrick* who chased the snakes out of **Ireland** became the symbol of **Danbala**. *Saint Peter* who was given the keys to the kingdom and is the supposed guard of the gate of heaven became **Papa Legba**, the guardian between the world of humans and spirits. *Saint Jacques* who is always depicted as an attacking soldier became the symbol of **Ogun**, the *god of war and iron and the sword*.

A Spanish Vodou priest named *Don Pedro*, who created the *Petro rituals*.

The **lwas** and **Rada** were considered to be good, loving protective spirits, but the revolution and rebellion of the slaves gave birth to another darker kind of spirits called **Petros**. A **Spanish Vodou** priest named *Don Pedro*, who created the *Petro rituals* and gave the group of spirits their names, brought these spirits into existence. Although fully **Haitian** or **African** in origin, these spirits shared many characteristics with the war-like spirits of the **Carib Indians**, once again showing the influence of their creator *Don Pedro*.

Vodou practitioners *believe in only one true God.*

With all of **Vodou**'s history of spirits (**lwa**) **Rada**, and **Petros** (*dark spirits*) it is quite surprising to find out that **Vodou practitioners** *believe in only one true God*. They believe God created all of the **lwas** (*spirits*) to serve him and to carry out his will as the people serve the spirit. The *monotheistic god of Vodou is a distant god*, difficult or impossible to develop a personal relationship with, which is why the spirits (**lwas**) play such a fundamental role in **Vodou**. While it is important to know who God is and to acknowledge his lordship over all of the elements of life, it is even more important to know the **lwas** (spirits) of **Vodou** because they are the ones who the practitioners of **Vodou** interact with daily.

In order for a person to understand whom the **lwas** are, they must understand God and his relation with the spirits. Also, you need to know where they come from, and how they express themselves in the world of man. Finally, you should understand that the spirits, with their individual personalities and temperaments, are closer to us than God and that is what enables humans to establish relationships with the spirits – to serve them so they can in turn serve us.

The god of Vodou may resemble the Christian's God; however, he is very different.

He is called **Bondye**, which is Creole for *Le Bon Dieu*, the 'good God' and also referred to as *Gran Met*, or the 'Grand Master'.

Although he shares some of the traits of the *Christian God*, **Bondye** is very much an **African god.** To them he is an eternal being who made the entire world and every thing in it. Since **Bondye** made the world, then parts of him is in all of creation, which means a part of **Bondye's** spirit animates us and gives us awareness.

Bondye does not have a personality or even human emotions.

Bondye is not personified in **Vodou**. Unlike the spirits, he does **not** have a personality or even human emotions. **Bondye** is an eternal force. To the followers of Vodou, **Bondye** represents the *inevitability of fate*, the *implacability of the forces of nature*, and finally the *constant movement of the universe*. **Bondye** is considered to be too great to become personally involved in the lives of men.

Unlike the **lwas** (*spirits*) who have personal relationship with mankind, **Bondye** is remote and unreachable. To the practitioner of **Vodou**, it is useless to plead with **Bondye** or to give him offerings because you cannot change his mind. Therefore practitioners of **Vodou** do not use much reason to serve or worship him directly. Neither are there any rituals held in his honor, nor are there any sacrifices made to him, and he, unlike the **lwas**, never possesses anyone.

Since **Bondye** is too busy to be involved in the lives of his creation, he has given this responsibility to **lwas** (*spirits*). The **lwas** are not gods; instead, they are immortal spirits with supernatural powers. They fall between God and mankind – symbolizing the saints, angels and devils of the *Catholic* religion. Each **lwa** represents a part of the natural world such as death, the ocean, the forest, animals and love.

In every **lwa**, a different attribute of **Bondye** divinity is manifested. The lwas oversee all human activities like marriage, work, health, money, childbirth, farming, war, art and music. There is no realm of human life which **lwas** do not preside over. Through the **lwa,** everything in life, every feeling of joy, anger, compassion, sorrow, work and rest finds meaning. We, according to **Vodou**, are always and completely surrounded by lwas. They live in dolls, crosses, jars, and other items consecrated to them. The word **"lwa"** means law, and the **lwas** represent cosmic laws.

Although the **lwas** are immortal supernatural beings, they were not always so. Lwa were at one time humans who died. Their souls were then transformed into eternal spirits. Through death they obtained supernatural powers and wisdom that extremely superseded those of the living. The **lwa** are divided into different groups called **nanchons**. The nations of **lwa** were originally established to give the intermixed slaves from different ethnic groups their own turn in honoring their own ancestral spirits during rituals.

Over time, the **nanchons** lost their original geographical and racial identity. They came to be associated more with the personalities of the **lwa**, which formed the nations. The more gentle, benevolent **lwa** belonged to the **Rada** nation, while the more violent aggressive dangerous **lwa** belonged to the **Petro nation**.

Here is a list of lwa's nations

Rada, lwa who originated in *Dahomey*; **Petro**, the **lwa** who came from **Haiti** and created by *Don Pedro*; **Kongo**, the **lwa** who originated in the **Congo**; **Ibo**, the **lwa** of the powerful **Yoruba** tribes; **Nago**, the lwa of another powerful **Yoruba tribe**; **Ginen**, the lwa who came from **Guinea**, **Bambara**, the **lwa** who originated in the **Sudan**; **Wangol**, the lwa who began in **Angola**; and **Siniga**, the **lwa** who originated in **Senegal**.

The **lwa** rule realms and have symbols that represent them and their **Petro** counterparts. For instance, **Danbala** rules the realm of wisdom and ancestral knowledge. His symbol is the snake and his *Catholic* counterpart is *Saint Patrick* and *Moses*. **Danbala** and his wife, **Ayida-Wedo** are the oldest and wisest of the **Rada lwa**. **Da Adyido Hwedo** is one of the *incarnations of the snake god*, **Da. Ayida-Wedo** has no **Petros** counterpart, but her Catholic counterpart is Our Lady of the Immaculate Conception. Her symbol is the rainbow, and she rules the realm of fertility.

Papa Legba is the most powerful **lwa** because he is the *gatekeeper*. His **Petros** counterpart is called **Kalfou**, and he is a dark spirit who is a trickster spirit like **Loki**. He delights in causing confusion, complicating simple situations, and inciting conflicts between people. Through him, *bad luck, destruction and injustice* can come into the world. Where **Papa Legba** brings order, **Kalfou** brings chaos. While **Papa Legba** represents fate, **Kalfou** provides the means to which fate can be thwarted. Where **Papa Legba** is associated with the positive *life-giving sun*, **Kalfou** is associated with the darkness of night and the pale light of the moon.

Kalfou is descended from the **Ibo god, Legba**, who symbolizes change and free will and stands as a counterpart to **Fa**. **Kalfou** controls the evil forces of the spirit world. He is honored at the crossroads by an evil sorceress and aids her in casting spells. **Kalfou's Rada** counterpart, **Papa Legba**, is represented by the cross which does **not** stand for the Christian cross, but for the crossroads where the worlds of the spirits and men cross each other and where **Papa Legba** stands. *Three Catholic saints* represent **Papa Legba**: *Saint Peter*, who holds the key to heaven and thus is also a gatekeeper; *Saint Lazarus*, who walks with a crutch and finally *Saint Anthony*, who helps find lost objects.

Ezili Freda is the **lwa** whose realm is love and beauty. She has a **Petros** counterpart called **Ezili Danto**. **Ezili Freda** is probably the most beloved of all lwa because she rules over the realm of love, and her symbol is the heart. But **Ezili Freda** has a very dark side, and it is **Ezili Danto**, a spirit that is very spiteful and *jealous and demanding*. She is prone to malicious fits of rage, and she feels she is not getting the attention she deserves.

Ezili can either fulfill all your great dreams or dish out severe punishment if she feels neglected. As the perfect woman, all aspects of **Ezili** are associated with the *Virgin Mary*. Therefore, **Ezili Freda's** *Catholic* counterpart is the *Mater Dolorosa de Monte Calvario,* a light-skinned Mary wearing a crown and surrounded by jewels and finery. As **Ezili Freda**, her symbol is the heart and is represented by a light-skinned Mary.

However, her **Petros** counterpart, **Ezili Danto** is a fiercely independent single mother who would fight to the death for her children. Her symbol is that of a heart pierced by a dagger and is represented by a large attractive dark-skinned woman. During the slave's rebellion, according to the legend, the male slaves couldn't trust her to keep a secret, so they cut her tongue out, so even when she possessed a person she could not talk. **Ezili Danto** can be very malicious toward women because of jealousy, but she has been known to marry women so she is considered the patron of *lesbians*.

A third part of **Ezili Freda** is **Grande Ezili** or **Grandmother Ezili**. As an old woman, she is nobody's lover, but is an old woman so crippled and arthritic that she cannot walk unless she drags herself using a stick. She is filled with grief with all the loss of love in the world.

Ogou, the *warrior* **lwa**, is a vast *family of spirits*, which embodies all the realms of the masculine, war, politics, machinery, metalworking, male fertility, and fire. He is the balance to the feminine ideal that **Ezili** represents, and the two are lovers. Descended from the powerful **Nigerian god** of lightning, **Ogun**, who has a fierce fiery temper, **Ogou** belongs to the **Nago nanchon**, but is honored alongside the other **Rada lwa**. Since **Ogou** rules over everything which has to do with fire, war, metal, and machinery, he is considered the patron of soldiers and is believed to be a great soldier himself. His *Catholic* counterpart is *Saint Jacques* who is always depicted on horseback in battle.

Ogou is the patron of anyone who works with metal tools or machinery, including blacksmiths, barbers, surgeons and truck drivers.

The family of **Ogou** spirits is larger than the family of any other **lwa**. Each aspect of **Ogou** takes on a slightly different, but related, role. For example, one **Ogou** rules over metal working, another is lord over fire, and another controls lightning, but in all of his aspects, the strength and power and masculinity of **Ogou** is evident. The list of the major aspects of **Ogou** is:

Ogou Baba – represents a military general
Ogou Badagris – lwa of the phallus
Ogou Batala – patrons of surgeons and doctors
Ogou Fer – lwa of fire and war
Ogou Feray – patrons of blacksmith and metal workers
Ogou La Flambeau – represents fiery rage of battle
Ogou Shango – lwa of lightning
Ogou Tonneree – lwa of thunder

The next **lwa** we will look at is **Agwe** who, with his wife **La Sirene**, are **lwa** of *the sea, the king and queen of the ocean*. Together they rule over the seas, but have no authority at all on land. **Agwe** is depicted as a mulatto with fair skin and sea-green eyes. He wears the uniform of a naval officer, and the sound of gunfire or any method of signaling always brings him great pleasure.

His symbols are small boats, oars painted blue and green, and small metal fish. His *Catholic* counterpart is the saint, Ulrich, who is often shown holding a fish. He's never pictured taking the form of a sailboat. In his **Petro** aspect, he is **Agwe la Flambeau** and represents the boiling of water and the heat of steam.

The power of the **Petros Agwe** is evident in volcanic eruptions under the sea, which boils seas and raises new islands. Most of the ceremonies for **Agwe** are held on the ocean. These services are very elaborate and very expensive, taking days to prepare for.

Agwe's supposed wife, **La Sirene**, has two aspects, resulting in one **Rada** and one **Petro.** In her **Rada** guise, she is a supposed wise mermaid. She is described as a beautiful white woman with long blonde hair and the tail of a fish. According to legends, she is so alluring, she can tempt men to jump into the sea where they end up drowning in the vain attempt to catch her. She is thought of as the aquatic version of the lwa, **Ezili**.

La Sirene makes eerie music on the bottom of the ocean.

Perhaps you can see the connection between **La Sirene** and the famous Sirens of Greek mythology. Because of her musical acts, she is the patron of musicians. She will also share her wisdom with **Vodou** priestesses, who dive to the floor of the oceans to receive instructions from her concerning sacred rituals and divine knowledge.

Her symbols are mirrors and seashells, and her Catholic counterpart is Saint Martha, the sister of Mary and Lazarus.

La Sirene's Petro side is **La Baleine**, the *whale*. Described as large, black, and extremely terrifying, the **Petro** side has a very fierce temper. If **La Baleine** is offended, she will lure the person who is responsible for the offence to a watery grave. **La Sirene** and **La Baleine** are so much connected that they are both worshipped together.

The **lwa** family of death is many and is called **Gede**. The leader of the Gede family is called the **Baron** and his wife is **Maman Brijit**. In **Vodou**, death plays a major role, so much so that an entire family of **lwa** is required to oversee the realm of death and watch over the spirits of those who have passed over before us. These lwa of death are neither **Rada** (*good*) nor **Petro** (*evil*). They are an entirely different kind of category unlike any of the other **lwa.** They produce great fear because of the mortality they are the representatives of. They balance the fear they cause by being great clowns. This aspect enlivens any ritual to get the **Vodou** practitioners to face death by making light of life.

The **Gede** family of **lwa** forms a hierarchy with the strongest and most honorable one at the top and the weakest and not well known at the bottom. **Gede** is an enormous group made up of the spirits of formerly living people who after death was elevated to the status of **lwa**. They do not belong to any of the **Vodou nanchons**, but they form a group separate from all other **lwa**. They have their own peculiar characteristic personality traits and ways of behavior. As a *group*, they form a family that generally appears together. Unlike the other **lwa** family, the **Gede** are completely Haitian in origin, and have no African tribal spirits.

The **Taino and Carib Indians** of **Hispanola** are the main influence of the personality traits of the Gede. **For example**, the **Gede** are very fond of tobacco (a native plant of **Hispanola**) and are given cigarettes or cigars as an offering to them. Since the **Gede** oversees death and everything connected to it, they are greatly feared and honored. They have enormous power because they have the ability to save a life by refusing it entrance to the realm of the dead. They also have the ability to translate the soul of a deceased person to that of an **lwa**. They are a sick person's last chance to be healed since they have the right to stop a person from dying. They have the special role as guardians of children.

The **Gede** supposedly want children to live a long life. So, according to myth, they are responsible to protect children from having their life cut short. **Gedes** are always portrayed as wearing the clothes of the death. They sometimes dress as undertakers in top hats and formal, but threadbare, coats. They also at times wear mourning dresses with black and mauve veils. Other times they may appear as corpses with their faces powdered white and strips of cloth tied around their chins and with cotton stuffed in their ears and noses. They, like *Jim Jones*, always wear dark sunglasses to protect their sensitive eyes, since they are accustomed to the dark realm of the dead, and not to sunlight. Their typical colors are black, purple and white – the colors of mourning and funerals.

Gede, the Blood from Animal Sacrifices

In the ritualistic ceremonies held for the **Gede**, the blood from animal sacrifices, which is usually a black rooster or a black goat, is collected in a bowl especially made from calabash gourd. The blood is then poured out on an altar or a black cross. The offerings to **Gedes** are placed in black boxes decorated with skulls and crossbones. The *Catholic* counterpart to the **Gede** is *Saint Gerard,* who is already shown wearing a black robe seated next to skulls and lilies which are both symbols of death.

The **lwa of death** live in *cemeteries and dark underground places,* and like all the other **lwa**, they are constantly around us. The **Gede** are greatly loved even though they are a steady reminder that we must all eventually die. The reason why they are so loved is because of their so-called fun loving nature and penchant for practical jokes. Because our death is so unavoidable, making fun of it helps us to get over it. In this aspect, the **Gedes** are the master of the human's libido, and everything they do makes fun of sex.

Their open celebration of human sexuality affirms the continuity of life, even in the face of death. **Gedes** are not shy of their rampart sexuality, but rather flaunt it out in the open. **Gedes** are greatly amused by their victims' contradictory attitude about sex – both being embarrassed by it and obsessed by it at the same time. As the masters of the realm of human sexuality, the **Gede** not only oversees death but also the source of life itself. Therefore, the **Gede** represents the balance between life and death. According to these **lwa**, sex is a natural part of life as inevitable as death itself.

The **Gedes** are subjected to no rules, but instead make their own, unlike the other **lwa**, which can possess a person only at certain times. **Gedes** can possess anyone they want at any time, and they often appear unexpectedly at ceremonies where they are not invited or invoked. This sounds like demon possession to me.

No matter how unexpected their appearance may be, they are for the most part welcome because their appearance supposedly enlightens even the most somber mood and turns a solemn ceremony into raucous party. They usually appear last after all of the other **lwa**. When they manifest through possession, they dress in ridiculous clothes, tell obscene jokes and stories, and since **Gede** are mostly male, they flirt outrageously with all the women present and dance the very suggestive dance called the **banda**.

> **These lwa are extremely notorious for using profanity and sexual language when they possess people (sounds like demon possession to me).**

They do not care about breaking the taboos or laws of society. They are supposedly dead, so what more can be done to them. Because of this, they constantly defy authority and social morals. They represent the rebellious nature of **Haitian** peasants who forever mistrusted authority.

These **lwa** seem to be on a perpetual mission to expose the ridiculous side of human nature.
When they possess a person, they delight in exposing the boldest lies and the greatest scandalous secrets of the people of the community. They love to expose illicit love affairs – telling all the dirty details. They also take great pleasure in possessing snobby prudish uptight people and making them look foolish in the eyes of everyone present.

In spite of all this, these **lwa** are considered to be very wise. They supposedly are the keepers of the entire body of anointed wisdom, and so they are knowledgeable about pretty much everything. They give their advice on all matters relating to fertility, from the planting of crops, to the breeding of animals, and to the best time to conceive children.

It is believed that when a **Gede** possesses a person, if you can pull that person aside and ask him a serious question, you will always get a reliable answer. There are more than **30 major Gede** who are recognized by everyone and hundreds, if not thousands, of lesser **Gede** whose names are not known until they suddenly choose to reveal themselves.

> **The Gede's symbols are:** the black cross, skulls and shovels.
> **Baron Samedi's** symbols are the cross, coffin, and the phallus.
> **Baron Cimetiere's** symbols are bones and the cemetery.
> **Baron La Croix's** symbol is the cross.
> **Maman Brijit** is the wife of the **Baron**, and her symbols are the cemetery, elm, and the weeping willow.

Since the **Gede** rule the realm of the dead, they are supposedly endorsed with great powers, especially in regards to magic, *which uses the bodies or the spirits of the dead (zombies)*. They can offer help to magicians – casting dark spells or protection from dark magic. They can also open tombs and command the dead to perform tasks for them, or for evil sorcerers.

These following **Gede** are also leaders. **Azaka** is the farmer's friend whose realm is agriculture and his symbol is the *djakout*. The *djakout* is a small sack made of woven straws that Haitian peasants wear over their shoulder and is used in the field to carry tools and harvest crops. It is firmly believed that **Azaka** will appear in physical form and limp from farm to farm begging for a glass of rum or a bit of cassava to eat. If you refuse him, disaster will come to your family. **Azaka's** *Catholic* counterpart is *Saint Isidore* who was also a farm laborer.

> **Gran Bwa is the patron of the forest and the protector of all wildlife, These lwa are extremely notorious for using profanity**

He personifies the strength of the tallest tree. He always has a joke or good advice to all who consult him. His symbol is **Mapou**, a silk cotton tree that is indigenous **Haiti**. Along with **Kalfou** and **Baron Cimetiere**, **Gran Bwa** forms a trinity of magicians which collectively oversee initiations and healings. Thus, he has a dual role. He knows the secrets of herbal medicine which the forest can offer, as well as the secrets of magic that the dark branches can camouflage. **Gran Bwa** is depicted as half-man and half-tree, with a body like a tree trunk, branches for fingers and roots for feet. His colors are brown and green. His *Catholic* counterpart is *Saint Sebastian* who died by arrows while tied to a tree.

Next are two **lwa**: **Loko** and **Ayizan**, who represent the **ancestral spirits** of the first priest and priestess, which are two of the oldest **lwa** in the **Vodou** pantheon. In rituals, they are honored right after **Papa Legba** and before all the other **lwa**. They preside over all the rituals. If they are offended, the ceremony cannot take place, and the other **lwa** cannot be invoked. Because of their officiating roles in **Vodou** rituals, they rarely manifest through possession. As patrons of the **Vodou** priesthood, **Loko** and **Ayizan** are also the **lwa** of medicine and herbal healing because one of the **Vodou** priest's primary roles in the community is as a folk doctor. They are consulted whenever a member of the community falls sick, and requires protection from black magic.

Loko acts as custodian and protector of the **Vodou** temple and guardian of all the **Vodou** ceremonies. He symbolizes the spiritual authority which the priest provides in the community. He gives the **Vodou** priest all his secrets and sacred knowledge and provides solutions to problems with the **lwa**. As a great *herb doctor*, **Loko** is associated with all plant life, and trees are sacred to him. He gives healing powers to the herbs and leaves of trees. He can diagnose healing and diseases for the **Vodou spirit**. His *Catholic* counterpart is *Saint Joseph*, and his colors are white and red with the red rooster as his symbol.

Ayizan, **Loko's** wife, is the protector of all priestesses and female initiates of Vodou. She shares her husband's guardianship of **Vodou's** religious traditions, healing powers, and the reverence due to ancestors. She also acts as guardian to the marketplaces – a common meeting place of **Haitian** women.

Ayizan is personalized as an elderly woman with a good and loving heart. However, she does punish those who abuse the weak, such as the very young, the very old, the poor and the sick. She is the protector of abusive wives and children. Her favorite colors are white and silver.

She chose women to be priestesses and is invoked at the initiation of priesthood. She bestows knowledge of healing through plants and herbs. Her symbol is a palm frond that is shredded during rituals and worn as a mask by her initiates.

The next strongman of the **lwa** is called **Simbi**. He is considered to be a master magician, and is the **lwa** of all fresh water from the still pools to the raging rivers – even to rainfall itself. His devotees say he supposedly is a shy, very bashful and somewhat withdrawn. He does not like to enter the temple. He only does so through permission. Instead, he prefers the solitude under the water. Therefore, he guards all the wells, ponds and streams, and he is responsible for bringing the rain.

In the cities, he oversees the flow of the electromagnetic energy through power lines and telephone wires. His symbol is the green snake which lives in fresh water. His *Catholic* counterpart is the **Magi** (the three wise men) and his colors are black and gray. **Simbi** was originally a **Kongo** spirit, and is the master of all magicians – whether black magic or white. He is not only the protector; he is also the *destroyer*.

He is known to kidnap fair-skinned children and bring them under the water where they are made to serve him for seven years. When they are released, he grants them the power of clairvoyance.

Even though **Simbi** is the master magician for both white and black magic, there is another powerful black magic sorceress whose name is **Marinette**. She is a very powerful and violent lwa and one of the most dreaded members of the Petro matron.

Marinette is a sworn servant of evil. She is invoked to help with all underhanded activities, especially those that invoke black magic. Werewolves particularly celebrate her and hold services for her whenever they need her help.
Marinette is also known as **Marinette Bwa Chech** which simply means *"Marinette of the dry arms"*. She is called this because she is believed to be a skeleton. Her symbol is the screech owl, and her domain is the dark wood, where, according to legend, she wanders at night.

> **Marinette's servants bury her offerings in secret places in the forest, where, under the cover of darkness, she retrieves them.**

She does this so that she doesn't have to share them with the other lwa. The ceremonies honoring her are held under a tent in the open country, in which gasoline and salt are thrown on a huge bonfire. **Marinette's** husband is the leader of the slave revolt and founder of the Petro nation of **lwa (dark lwa)**.

After *Don Pedro* died, he became a powerful **lwa** as in the cases of *Jean-Jacques* Dessalines, the first ruler of independent **Haiti**, Queen Marie Laveau, the Voodoo Queen of **New Orleans**, and the black magician, *Doctor John. Don Pedro's* **lwa** name is **Ti-Jean-Petro**. He is the spiritual leader of the **Petro** nation, and oversees resistance against oppression and violent revolutions. He often assists black magicians. He appears as a one-foot dwarf, and his passionate nature is seen when he violently manifests in possession.

The next **lwa** who can be either good or evil is the three-horned bull called **Bosou**. He is a mighty bull spirit with an unpredictable, fiery temper. In his *Dahomean* form, he was a sacred monster worshipped by kings, and at times he is honored in the **Petro** nation. He appears as a three-horned bull or as a hot-tempered man with three horns who likes to eat beef. The three horns stand for wilderness, strength and extreme violence. His colors are red, black and white. His *Catholic* counterpart is *Saint Vincent de Paul*. **Bosou** is associated with male virility; therefore, he is strongly identified with the soil and seeds for planting crops.

During times of war he is often summoned and works with the practitioners of the black arts. **Bosou** helps with the creation of small evil spirits which wreak havoc and cause trouble. He will also act as a spiritual bodyguard who protects his followers as they travel at night.

The **lwa of the storm**, who are not as widely served today as they once were in the past, are three inseparable spirits known as the lwa of storm, thunder and wind. As **Petro lwa** they are violent earthquakes, thunderstorms and hurricanes. When a person has this particular lwa the possessions are extremely violent and can even result in death.

Their **lwa** names are **Agau**, whose symbol is thunder, **Sogbo**, whose symbol is the thunderstorm, and **Bade**, whose symbol is the wind. There are slaves who have been struck by lightning and are believed to house spirits.

> **lwa temporarily displaces the soul of a person and takes complete control of that person's body.**
> **While the lwa possesses the person, its spirit literally lives in the person.**

In **Vodou**, the only way to truly commune with the **lwa** is to be possessed by them. This possession takes place when the **lwa** temporarily displaces the soul of a person and takes complete control of that person's body. While the **lwa** possesses the person, its spirit literally lives in the person. During this time, all of the body's actions are controlled completely by the **lwa,** and all the words spoken are the words of the **lwa**. Possession by the **lwa** is accepted as the norm to those who practice **Vodou**. In fact, if possession does not occur during a **Vodou** *ceremony*, it is considered to be a failure. When possession occurs, it is thought to be a sign that the lwa are pleased. If it does not, then it is believed that the **lwa** are not happy and perhaps even angry.

Those who practice **Vodou** consider possession by **lwa** a good thing and beneficial to the person possessed. However, this is not the case. The person possessed by the **lwa** has no control over his or her *physical actions* or the words coming out of their mouth. In fact, the possessed person cannot hear the voice of the **lwa**. He must be told the message after the **lwa** leaves him.

> **Many try to compare the baptism of the Holy Spirit to that of possession by the lwa.**

> **This is not true at all because the Holy Spirit is gentle and never takes complete control of a person's actions or speech, and the person being used by the Holy Spirit can always hear what is being said.**

The **lwa** is unlike the Holy Spirit because many times the **lwa** comes through quite violently. The possession by the **lwa** is nothing more than demon possession. They are not the spiritually evolved spirits of dead people who return to bring help. They are demonic spirits ruled by fallen angels to bring chaos, destruction and enslavement to the possessed person.

Let's look at what happens when people becomes possessed by an **lwa**. People who are about to be possessed by an **lwa** will all of a sudden look anguished and suddenly tense up. They may even start to tremble and pant. They could also feel a twinge of pins and needles in the neck or legs as the **lwa** tries to enter. Alternatively, possession may be preceded by extreme tiredness. They will have a hard time keeping their eyes open and will be filled with a strange heaviness throughout their bodies. However, possession may come abruptly without warning.

People being mounted by **lwa** will struggle against the spirits at first. They often stagger around in circles crying out, swaying and throwing their arms out to balance themselves. They tremble all over, their muscles tense up, and many times they convulse quite violently. Other people close to the ones being possessed take control of them by removing all jewelry, hairpins, shoes or any other item that may get lost or stolen. They make sure the people do not fall or hurt themselves, which can and does happen.

All of a sudden the ones being possessed stop all resistance. This is the sign that the people being ridden have had their souls removed from their bodies, and the **lwa** are now in complete control of those possessed. The intensity of the act of possession can actually be so violent the ones possessed can be seriously hurt or even die from the results. When the people are possessed they will take on the physical and personality characteristics of the **lwa.** They will walk, talk and act like the **lwa.** They will even take on the facial expression of the **lwa.**

> **Children who are possessed by older lwa
> will take on the character of an old person.**

Old people possessed by younger **lwa** will dance as if they had no infirmities. Men possessed by *female* **lwa** will act like women, and women possessed by *male* **lwa** will act like men.

> **Since lwa will enter either males or females,
> there is much cross-dressing involved.**

Those who are possessed by **Danlala** will *change into serpents* and will slide across the floor hissing like a snake and climb poles or trees, falling down head first like the **lwa.** Since **Danbala** cannot talk, but only make hissing sounds, another **lwa** must interpret **Danbala's** message to those assembled.

> **They try to compare this with the gift of tongues
> and interpretation of tongues in the New Testament.**

If **Papa Legba** is the possessing lwa, it is quite violent and brutal. The person is forcefully thrown down on the floor. He or she will limp around using a crutch and twist his or her limbs in a grotesque contortion. If **Ezili** is the *possessing spirit*, she will immediately be dressed in a pink and blue gown made from silk, stain and sheer lace. When she enters the temple, she will begin to sway her hips and flirt with all the men present. She gives and receives gifts from them. With the women present, she is more reserved with them, simply extending a hooked finger at them. **She always speaks in perfect French**, even if the only language the person being possessed speaks is **Creole**.

> **But toward the end, she always collapses in tears
> weeping for unrequited love and unfulfilled dreams.**

The next **lwa** who possesses people is a very violent and vulgar one. **Ogou** will appear as an energetic soldier who is quite rough. The musicians will play the **Haitian's** national anthem to herald his appearance, and gunpowder is thrown into the fire to cause small explosions. He always dresses in military clothing or wears a red scarf around his head or arms. He constantly waves a sword or machete and chews on a cigar. He struts around the temple demanding rum with an old phrase, *Gren mwe fret*, which means 'my testicles are cold'. Rum given to him is poured on the ground and set on fire rather then drunk. **Ogou's** strength and resistance to fire often manifests during possession. At times he will use flaming rum to wash his hands or hold a red-hot iron in his hand to prove the possession is authentic.

> **When a person is possessed by lwas like Agwe and La Sirene, <u>king and queen of the oceans</u>, or Simbi, <u>lord of the bodies of fresh water, the person can end up drowning</u>. When possessed by Agau, Sogbo and Bade, the lwa of thunderstorms, earthquakes, lightning and wind,
> the person becomes so violent that it can end with
> the death of a weak practitioner.**

When **Bosou** and other **bull-like lwa** called **lwa-taureaux possess someone**, the person is *seized with a great rage and the urge to destroy things*. When **Marinette** possesses someone, the person will *act like a screech owl*. The person will lower her head and let her arms hang like wings and turn hands and fingers into claws. Through the mouth of her horse, she will boast of the people she had eaten and confess her crimes. She will brag about the life energy of people she has drained, and finally, she will throw the possessed person into the bonfire and stamp around until the fire is put out.

The reports I have written here are not written from an opponent to **Vodou**, but are the actual events which happen when a practitioner becomes a horse and is ridden by the **lwa**.

This is the normal occurrence that takes place again and again at Vodou ceremonies.

No matter how severely a person is treated by their **lwa** they continue to return over and over again to be willing slaves of the **lwa**.

(Isaiah 5:20) In the latter days men will be lovers of self and will call good evil and evil good.

It is proof of what the great apostle Paul said, "In the latter days men will be lovers of self and will call good evil and evil good, they will go after false gods and have a form of godliness but deny the power thereof."

It is amazing what man is willing to tolerate in the service of these beings that claim to be god, but are not. It is slavery that they are more than willing to accept for the vain secret knowledge of the occult instead of coming to Jesus and receiving wisdom and true freedom from above.

Prayer for Protection Against the Strongman (Lwa) of Vodou

Dear Father, Thank You so much for Your love and protection. Lord, we thank You that we do not have to perform strange and dangerous ceremonies in order to receive Your blessing.

Father, we do not have to give sacrifices of materialistic possession. All we need to do is offer up the sacrifice of praise, and as we praise O Lord, You draw near to us your people. Lord, You desire to fellowship with us, to talk and walk with us.

Lord, all we need to do is ask You for wisdom, and You will freely give it to us. Father, how wonderful it is that You don't force us to make constant sacrifices to You to receive Your blessing. But instead Father, You, the God of creation, made the awesome sacrifice of Your beloved Son Jesus, so that we could have the wonderful opportunity to become Your children because of the shed blood of the Lamb of God.

Thank You, Lord, in Jesus name Amen.

Study Notes

Chart 16: Strongmen of False Religion
Part 2: Santeria

List of Orishas, Their Catholic Counterparts, and Their Feast Days

Orisha	Saint	Feast Day
Eleggua	St. Anthony	June 13
Orunmila	St. Francis of Assisi	October 14
Obatala	Our Lady of Mercy	September 24
Chango	St. Barbara	December 4
Oggun	St. Peter	June 29
Ochosi	St. Norbert	June 6
Aganyu	St. Christopher	November 16
Babalu-Aye	St. Lazarus	December 17
Yemaya	Our Lady of Regla	September 7
Oshun	Our Lady of Charity	September 8
Oya	Our Lady of La Candelaria	February 2

Chart of the Orisha in Yoruba (Nigeria), Santeria (Cuba), and Candomble (Brazil)

Yoruba (Nigeria)	Santeria (Cuba)	Candomble (Brazil)
Esu	Eshu, Eleggua	Exu
Orisa-nla	Obatala	Orixala, Oxala, Obatala
Orunmila	Orunmila, Orunla	Orunmila
Sango	Chango	Xango
Ogun	Oggun	Ogum
-	Ochosi	Oxossi
Sonponno	Babalu-Aye	Obaluae, Omolu, Xanpana
Yemoja	Yemaya	Iemanja
Osun	Oshun	Oxum
Oya	Oya, Yansa	Oia-Iansa

Chapter 16
Strongmen of False Religion
Part 2: Santeria

When the **Yoruba of West Africa** were brought to **Cuba** as slaves, they brought their own religious beliefs with them. They managed to preserve their faith the same ways that the slaves brought to **Haiti** did. They simply disguised their gods (**orishas**) behind the images of the *Catholic* saints to protect them from their cruel *Catholic* slave masters. As you read this chapter on **Santeria** you will notice many common traits between Vodou (**Haitian voodoo**) and **Santeria** (**Spanish voodoo**).

Both come from the same foundation. In both religions the priest and priestesses are the only ones who can reveal to you what **lwa** (spirit in **Vodou**) or **orishas** (gods of **Santeria**) you belong to and must serve. You do not have the right to choose which one you will serve. The choice is made for you.

To the **santeros**, as well as the **Yoruba**, *their god* is known as **Oloddumare**. The origin of the name is very hard to trace, but its connotation is that of one whose enemy transcends our ability to comprehend it. **Oloddumare** is immanent, omnipotent, and omniscient. He is the all and is greater than the all. **Oloddumare** is not an orisha because he was never created. He has always existed.

There are other names associated with **Oloddumare**. As **Olorun**, he is the owner of the heavens (orun), as well as the deity whose dwelling place is in heaven. According to Yoruba scholars, the Yoruba use **Olorun Oloddumare** as a composite name to describe the creator, but never Oloddumare Olorun. The use of this double name refers to the supreme being who lives in heaven and is almighty and dependable.

To the **santeros, Oloddumare** is god as the almighty, and **Olorun** is god as the creator of the physical world. **Orun**, in **Santeria**, is identified with both heaven and the sun. The **babalawos** never fail to greet the sun every morning. The ceremony is done quite early before sunrise and is called **nangale** (or **nangare**). The ritual is usually accompanied with a petition.

Yoruba also use the name **Eledaa**, which means creator and implies a being that is the source of all things. In **Santeria**, **Eledaa** is the spark of god that lives in everyone. It is referred to, or associated with, one's personal guardian angel. Many santeros associate it with one's ruling **orisha**. Although the Haitian's **Vodou** and **Santeria** have the same foundation, and **Vodou**'s belief in their god and **lwa** resemble that of **Santeria**'s belief in their god and orisha, I believe that the Santeria pantheon of orisha and the name for **Oloddumare** (god) is much more complicated.

Yoruba use the names **Oloddumare, Olorun** and **Eledaa** interchangeably. But please understand that each name shows a different aspect of god. Another name for god, which comes from **Oloddumare**, but is not identical to his, is **Ori**. **Yoruba** also use this name for the supreme deity, but it is far more complex. **Ori** is the physical head, as well as the driving force that guides it. **Ori** is not the soul, which is actually more easily equated with **Elidaa, Ori** is related as awareness, pure being, and consciousness.

In **Santeria**, there is another name that is applied to deity, which is never used by the Yoruba. The name is **Olofi** (or **Olofin**), and is the most common name used for their god. We do not really know where the name of **Olofi** – like that of **Oloddumare** – came from. The Santeria make a distinction between **Oloddumare** and **Olofi**. **Oloddumare** is a transcendent being who is the essence of everything and much more. **Olofi** is the creation itself, rather than the creator. He is **Oloddumare** manifested through **Olorun**, the true creator. **Olorun**, **Oloddumare**, and **Olofi** are three different aspects of the same supernatural being.

Oloddumare is divine essence, the creative will; **Olorun** is the creative act; and **Olofi** is the creation. **Eledaa** is the spirit of god manifested in man. **Ori** is the driving force – the awareness of the presence of that spirit. **Olofi** can be best described in **Santeria** as man's personal god, a manifested force that is in charge of creation – being creation itself.

The **santeros** refer to **Oloddumare** rather vaguely and obliquely. They do recognize him as the central ruling force of the universe, but do not deal with him directly. All of their work and petitions are made through **Olofi** through the powers of the orishas. **Olofi** is considered as Jesus Christ.

According to the legends **(patakis)** of **Santeria**, **Olofi** created the **orishas** by gathering together a number of flat stones (*otanes*) and putting some of his ashes into them. From these smooth flat stones filled with the divine power of **Olofi**, the **orishas** were born. Among the first of these **orishas** created from these smooth stones (*otanes*) were **Orunmila**, **Orisanla** (also know as **Obatala**), **Olokun** and **Eshu** (known as **Eleggua** in Santeria).

All of these **orishas**, except for **Olokun**, lived in heaven. **Olokun** lived on earth, which was, at this period of time, a marshy waste. When **Olofi** decided to create the solid ground, he gave the responsibility to **Obatala**, who is the symbol of pure intellect and purity. To assist **Obatala** in this assignment, **Olofi** gave him the orisha, **Orunmila**, the personification of wisdom who could divine the future by means of sixteen palm nuts (*ikin*). The new ground created by **Obatala**, with the help of **Orunmila**, became **Ile-Ife,** the holy city which today is considered sacred to **Obatala**. Some time after the creation of Ile-Ife, **Olofi** called **Obatala** to heaven to instruct him on how to make man. According to Santeria legend, **Obatala** was told by **Olofi** to form man and woman out of clay and lay them side-by-side to dry. Then **Olofi** would come and breathe his essence into them.

Obatala followed **Olofi's** instructions carefully, but according to the legend, **Obatala** became thirsty, so he decided to drink some palm wine to quench his thirst. Very soon his hands became clumsy from all of the wine he had drunk. So the new figures he now produced became twisted and deformed. He set these figures out to dry next to the well-formed ones. When he had finished, he called out to **Olofi** to come and breathe life into the figures he had made.

Trusting **Obatala** completely, **Olofi** came and breathed into them without checking them out first. That is why we have deformed people in the world. When **Obatala** sobered up, he saw what he had done and was very grieved over it. He swore never to drink wine again, and He became the **orisha** or patron of those who are deformed or abnormal in any way.

This legend **(pataki)** is also the basis of **Yoruba** belief that **Obatala** shapes the newborn in their mother's wombs. Among the orishas who first came down to earth were **Aganyu**, who was given the power to melt stone with his breath – creating the volcano. There was **Orisha-Oko**, who was given the secret of the harvest - therefore creating the four seasons and all growing things. To **Osain**, he gave the secrets of the herbs and plants, thereby resulting in the creation of the woods. To **Babalu-Aye** (**Sonponno**, **Shanpanna** to the Yoruba), he gave the power to cause and to cure sickness – especially smallpox.

The first **orisha** we will look at is the one called **Eleggua**. In **Nigeria**, this **orisha** is known as **Esu** (*pronounced Eshu*). He is one of the most powerful of **orishas**. This particular deity is worshipped in almost every household and village. It does not matter what other **orisha** they may worship, **Eleggua** must be propitiated first before any other divinity because it is believed he is the one who carries the offerings to the other orishas, and he will not do so if he is not honored first. According to **Awolalu**, without **Esu**, the dynamics of ritual would not exist. If he did not receive the necessary elements needed to fulfill his constructive function, he would retaliate by blocking the way of goodness and opening up the ways that are inimical and destructive to mankind. Hence, he is both feared and revered.

Because of this duo nature in some traditions as in the **Brazilian Candomble** where he is known as **Exu**, he is associated with the devil. But the **Yorubas** do not see **Esu** as an evil entity. The Yorubas also do not believe in the radically opposing forces of good and evil. **Esu** is one of functionaries of **Oloddumare**, and he is simply out to try to test the hearts of mankind. **Esu's** main purpose is to carry messages between mankind and the other orishas and to report the deeds of man to **Oloddumare**.

In **Santeria**, **Esu** is known as **Eleggua**, **Elegbara** and **Eshu**. As **Eleggua**, he is the essence of potentiality; as **Elegbara**, he is the wielder of power; and as **Eshu**, he is the eternal wanderer – moving with the speed of **Mercury**, the messenger of the Roman gods and goddesses. **Eshu** appears where he is least expected. He is considered to be beyond good and evil. He is justice personified and punishes or rewards with absolute equanimity. It is **Santeria** belief that **Eleggua** is a symbol of destiny and of perfect balance in nature. It is also believed that his vision surpasses that of all the other **orishas.**

Only he knows the past, present and future without recourse to divination systems. He knows the ills that affect mankind, and he knows the cures. Although his actions may be difficult to comprehend at times, supposedly he never acts irrationally. It is believed that he knows things no one else knows, and acts according to his own invariably perfect judgment.

In **Santeria**, **Eleggua** is a trickster who stands in corners and crossroads, guarding the home against danger. He is believed to keep evil at bay. **Eleggua's** punishments are usually mischievous – as in a child's prank. But when he is extremely displeased, the "pranks" can be quite heavy handed. They can result in theft, accident, or even in imprisonment.

The rewards of **Eleggua** are also quite distinctive – usually accompanied by a special sign of the orisha, such as his distinct colors (red and black) or by his number three or any multiple of three, with the number twenty-one as one of his favorites. **Eleggua** is said to have twenty-one paths (aspects known as avatars), and in each of them, he has a completely different set of characteristics. Each of these names is preceded by the name 'Eshu'. There is **Eshu Alabwanna**, an **Eshu Laroye**, an **Eshu Bi**, an **Eshu Aye**, an **Eshu Afra**, an **Eshu Barakeno**, and many more.

Eshu Alabwanna lives in the woods. **Eshu Barakeno**, the youngest of the Elegguas creates confusion wherever he goes. **Eshu Laroye** hides behind doors; **Esu Aye** works with **Olokun** – an aspect (name) of **Yemaya**. **Eshu Elufe** and **Eshu Anagui** appear as a very old man.

Eleggua is received as part of the initiation known as Los Guerreros, which means 'the warriors'. When the ritual is performed, **Eleggua** is formed with **Ochosi** and **Oggun**. Those practicing Santeria believe these three orishas work together in a powerful combination to protect the recipient from all harm and evil, and to assist him in all worldly matters. **Oggun's** symbols are a hoe, an awl, a spade and a hammer – representing **Oggun's** patronage of work. **Ochosi's** symbol – being the divine hunter – is the crossbow. **Eleggua's** symbol is usually a clay or cement head with cowrie shells to denote the eyes, the mouth, and sometimes the ears. When **Eleggua** is given in the form of a cement head, there is always a small blade protruding from its top, which symbolizes his power and his inexhaustible ashe.

> **Please understand that I am not giving any glory to the orishas and lwa of Santeria or Haitian Vodou. I am just sharing with you the background and history of these strongmen.**

If it seems that I am making these beings to have a positive side, that is **not** the case. I am giving an accurate account of their nature. I know some people do not find anything wrong with worshipping these beings if they bring blessing and healings to their followers. We must remember, however, that **Satan** is a master of deceit and can appear as benefactors for humanity, when in all reality he is using these positive actions to keep people in bondage. The difference between the miracles of **Satan** and the miracles of Jesus is that with **Satan**, you must pay his price in order to receive his blessing, and with Jesus, He paid the price so that, if we believe, we can freely receive without any strings attached.

Orunmila is the next **orisha**. According to Yoruba tradition, when **Oloddumare** commissioned **Obatala** to create the earth, he asked **Orunmila** to go with him to give him guidance. After the world came into existence, **Orunmila** divided his time between heaven and earth, so he was given the name **Gbaye-Gborun** which meant "one who lives both in heaven and earth". After the slave trade, the name became corrupt in **Iboru-Iboya** and a third name was also added: Ibochiche. This name came from an unknown source.

The combination **"Iboru-Iboya-Ibochiche"** became the common salutation that is given to the **babalawo** or *high priest* of **Santeria**, whose patron is **Orunmila**. Among the Yoruba, **Orunmila** is known as **Ibikeji-Edumare**, which simply means "next in rank to **Oloddumare**".

It is believed that **Orunmila** was present when man was created. He knows the ultimate destiny of every person, and because he does, he is able to give direction on how one can improve his fate. He also knows what is pleasing and what is offensive to the other orishas and can help mankind in their propitiation as well, as in communication with them.

In Santeria, **Orunmila** is most commonly known as **Orunla**. The Catholic saint that is **Orunla's** image is Saint Francis of Assisi. His colors are green and yellow. According to a legend, **Orunmila** tricked Death (known as **Iku**) into sparing the life of anyone who wears **Orunla's** ide, a bracelet made with green and yellow beads. According to Santeria tradition, only a man can become a babalawo, as **Orunla** refuses to share his secrets with any woman.

The **Yoruba** have a traditional <u>four-day week</u> in which each day is sacred to one of the major **orishas**. The first day, *Ojo Awo*, is dedicated to **Orunmila**; the second day, **Ojo Ogun**, is dedicated to **Oggun**; the third day, Ojo Jakuta, is sacred to **Chango**; and the fourth day, Ojo Obatala, is dedicated to **Obatala**.

Obatala is known as *"the king* of the *white cloth"*, as he is always dressed in impeccable white clothes. He is the symbol of peace and purity. He is also referred to as the father of mankind and the messenger of **Olofi**. In **Nigeria**, he is recognized as **Orishanla**. It is pronounced "**Orichanla**" or "**Ochanla**" in Santeria. In Santeria there are twenty-four paths (or avatares) for **Obatala**.

In some of **Obatala's** aspects, he is female. The most common example is **Ochanla**, who is believed to be the oldest of the twenty-four paths of **Obatalas**. In Yoruba tradition, **Obatala**, who is called **Orishanla** and **Oddudua** are androgynous deities, which simply means they are male and female – two in one.

Obatala is believed to control the mind and all thought. He is the owner of all heads and all bone structures and all white substances. Since all heads belong to **Obatala**, any person can receive him even if they have another ruling **orisha**. Often when it is difficult to determine whom a person's **orisha** is, they are initiated into the mysteries of **Obatala**.

Obatala's *Catholic* image is identified with our *Lady of Mercy,* although in his other aspects he is symbolized with other Catholic saints. For example, **Obbamoro**, one of the oldest, is identified with Jesus. **Obatala Ochacrinan**, who is said to be so old that he is constantly trembling, is identified with *Saint Joseph.*

Although **Obatala** has many aspects and is both male and female, he is considered one deity. He is called the owner of the world. **Obatala's** sacred numbers are eight, sixteen, and twenty-four. His feast is celebrated on September 24 – the same day as Our Lady of Mercy in the Catholic church is celebrated.

Oddudua is one of the most controversial of all the deities in the **Yoruba pantheon**. According to one legend, **Oddudua** is both a central divinity and a deified ancestor. The **Yoruba** of the **city of Ile-Ife** insist that it was **Oddudua**, and not **Obatala**, who created the earth, mankind, and the city of Ife. It is said that when **Obatala** became drunk on palm wine, **Oddudua** took over his creative work and completed what **Obatala** had barely started.

Another legend states that **Oddudua** came to the city **Ile-Ife** long after it was in existence, and conquered the original inhabitants. In this story, he is not an orisha, but a great warrior. To complicate things further, a third legend states that **Oddudua** is the wife of **Obatala** and is the chief female deity. **Oddudua's** necklace is made up of sixteen white beads and eight red ones. Some santeros identify **Oddudua** with Saint Anne and others with Saint Manuel.

The **Yoruba** have an **orisha** known as **Sango** (pronounced **Shango**), but is called **Chango** by the **Santeria**. According to legend, he is the fourth oba (king) of the city of Oyo in Nigeria. His reign as *king of Oyo* lasted seven violent years. A story claims **Chango** was absolutely impressed with magic and had great magical powers, so one day he inadvertently caused a thunderstorm, which destroyed his palace causing the death of many of his wives and children.

Full of sorrow and remorse, he abdicated his throne and hung himself. His enemies rejoiced at his disgrace and heaped scorn upon his name. Soon afterwards, a series of thunderstorms destroyed large parts of the *city of Oyo* and **Chango's** former followers proclaimed that **Chango** sent the storms because of his anger against his enemies. Many sacrifices were made in his name and in his honor. His followers proclaimed loudly, *"Oba ko so!"* which meant, *"The king did not hang,"* and from that moment of time, **Chango** was proclaimed an orisha, and his worship was established.

Chango represents power, whether it is procreative, authoritative, destructive, medicinal or moral. This power is visualized or centralized in **Chango's** staff called *oshe Chango*, which generally depicts a woman with a double-edged ax (*edun ara*) balanced upon her head. This ax is the symbol of **Chango's** thunderbolt which is also his power.

In **Santeria** the **oshe Chango** is a large double-edged ax made of wood and painted red and white. Sometimes the ax is adorned with cowrie shells. Among the **Yoruba**, women worship **Chango** by kneeling down and lifting up their breasts with their hands in supplication. Traditionally, it is the women who sing the praise songs (*oriki*) in honor of **Chango**. The deification of **Chango** can be traced to a **Yoruba** solar deity known as **Jakuta** (*the stone thrower*), who was a guardian of morality and goodness. Whenever people did evil in the eyes of **Oloddumare**, **Jakuta** would hurl down stones of fire.

Undoubtably, a syncretism took place between **Chango**, the deified king, and **Jakuta**, and now they are both worshipped as one. The Yoruba greeted thunder and lightning with shouts of *"Kabiesi!* This means, *"Hail, your Majesty!"* which is the same greeting given to all Yoruba's kings.

At the annual **Chango** festival in **Oyo**, the ritual *bataa* drums play in honor of the **orisha**, and those devoted to him dance to their rhythms until **Chango** possesses one or more of the dancers. The **elegun Chango** wears a red cotton coat, to which are fastened many cowerie shells and miniature symbols of **Chango**. Most of the elegun are males, but in some places such as in the **Egba** section of Nigeria. the elegun are females.

The **elegun** usually carry the *oshe Chango* and imitate, with extreme violent gestures, the devastating power of the deity of thunder and lightning. Sometimes they sit on the tip of an iron spear, and carry a pot of hot coals on their heads. They pierce their tongues and cheeks with knives or iron bars. They swallow fire, and some even catch bullets with their teeth. These extreme violent acts show the power of **Chango**, which can be released against the good as well as the evil. **Chango** is a dangerous **orisha,** and the **santeros** recognize his power and the dangers which could happen if he or one of his children is offended. **Chango** has killed and will kill again if he or his children are displeased.

According to **Santeria** traditions, **Chango's** colors are red and white, and his numbers are four and six. **Chango** is said to have twelve paths (or aspects). Some of the names of these paths are **Chango Ogodo, Alufina Crueco, Alafia, Larde, Yoda, Obakoso, Ochongo, and Ogomi Oni**. Although **Chango's** *Catholic* symbol is usually **Saint Barbara**, in some of his other paths he is symbolized with *Saint Patrick, Saint Expeditus, Saint Mark, Saint Daniel, and Saint George* the dragon slayer.

In **Yoruba tradition, Chango** has three wives. They are orisha **Oba, Oshun** and **Oya** – all of them river deities. His servant is the rainbow, **Ochumare**. In Santeria **Chango** is pictured as a notorious woman chaser and a lover of food and dance. His legal wife is **Oba**; however, his favorite concubine is the tempestuous **Oya** - the wind deity and keeper of the cemetery.

As we look at these **orishas** of **Santeria**, we see a double nature to everyone. What is strange is that even the good side can be extremely violent and destructive. We see this double nature in the life of the **orisha** called **Oggun**. He is the patron of all ironworkers and metal. He is also the protector of surgeons, police officers, and soldiers. He is one of three orishas received during the initiation of the warrior. The two others are **Eleggua** and **Ochosi**. These three **orisha** are inseparable.

Oggun provides employment and protection against criminals. On the other hand, **Oggun** is said to be the cause of all car and railroad accidents where there is much bloodshed. Oggun is also the force behind violent crimes where metal weapons are used. A very interesting story is told about one of **Eleggua's** aspects called **Eshu Ogguanilebbe** who is **Oggun's** faithful friend. It is said he causes car accidents and train derailments so that **Oggun** can feed on the blood of the victims.

As the symbol of war, **Oggun** is much feared and respected in **Santeria**. It is claimed by many **santeros** that **Oggun** is the father of tragedy, a symbol of all the pain and horror of war and violence. This **orisha** is worshipped and propitiated so that he will protect his followers from the very things he causes to happen. In Santeria, **Oggun** symbolizes the sacrificial knife and the act of slaying. Although **Eleggua** is said to be the first **orisha** to be honored in every ceremony of the religion, it is **Oggun** who eats first before any other **orisha**. This is because the blood of sacrifice touches the metal knife first, and **Oggun** is the **orisha** of weapons of metal and violent force used to slay the offering.

Oggun's violent nature has resulted in certain disrepute for the ironworkers, and many people live in constant fear of him. In spite of all the blood spilled and the violent force used by **Oggun**, the **santero** and **Oggun's** followers do not feel he is evil. Instead, they believe he is simply the archetype of the violent actions which results from man's weakness and lack of self-control. The **santeros** will tell you that, when a tragic event occurs, it is the result of the excess of evil in our society. Evil concentrates in the midst of society and then reveals itself through acts of extreme violence. **Oggun** is the **orisha** in charge of these violent deeds and actions in which man, by his lack of respect for divine and human laws, is the cause.

Oggun supposedly lives in the woods and is believed to represent the woods themselves. There is a legend which proclaims at one time he became so disgusted with mankind that he abandoned his forge and refused to come out of the woods. Without his metalwork, the advancement of civilization came to a standstill. **Olofi** was so concerned he sent in all of the **orishas** one at a time to convince **Oggun** to come out, but **Oggun** refused to do so. Then **Oshun**, the **orisha** of love, used her sensuality to trick him by dancing and applying honey to his lips. While dancing, she tied eight yellow handkerchiefs together to make a rope, and as **Oggun**, the ironworker, became captivated by her physical beauty, she tied the rope around his waist to lead him out of the woods. From that day forth, **Oggun** has pined for **Oshun**, who only has eyes for **Chango**, who symbolizes passion and desire.

Oggun has seven known paths in Santeria according to some **santeros**. Among them are **Oggun Sarabanda and Baumba**. His colors are black and green, although it was originally red – the color of blood. According to legend, **Oggun** lost the color red to **Chango**. **Oggun** wears a skirt made of *mariwo* (palm fronds) and a large straw hat; a machete hangs from his side. Dogs are sacred to him, among both the Yoruba and the **santeros**. **Oggun's** *Catholic* image is *Saint Peter*, and the two numbers most closely associated with him are seven and three.

Among the **Yoruba**, **Oggun** is worshipped as one of the first **orishas** and sometimes as a deified ancestor. To the **Yoruba**, **Oggun** is the patron of iron and of war, and is believed to protect hunters, blacksmiths, barbers, butchers, and all those who work with iron and steel. He is also believed to be the absolute symbol of justice and is called on to witness a pact between people. In Nigeria, this belief in **Oggun's** symbology as justice is so strong that, whenever a follower of **Oggun** appears in a court of law, he is made to swear on the name of **Oggun** instead of the Bible or the Koran.

The follower of **Oggun** will swear on the name of **m,** by kissing a piece of iron representing **Oggun**, and swear to tell the truth. No one would dare to break this solemn oath, for **Oggun** is known to inflict the most extreme violent punishment on anyone who swears falsely by his name.

Ochosi is the **third orisha** received during the initiation known as the warriors, Los Guerreros. **Ochosi's** name comes form the Yoruba title, **Osowusi**, meaning, "The night watchmen is blessed." He is the *divine hunter*, and his **Santeria** alter is *Saint Norberto*. In **Brazil**, it is *Saint Sebastian and Saint George*. His colors are blue and yellow, and his numbers are three and seven. His symbol is the crossbow made of iron.

Ochosi owes his importance to four things. First, he is the parton of all hunters whom he protects and helps to locate their prey. Second, he is said to have medical and healing powers since he is always in the woods with **Osain**, the **orisha** of plants and herbs, from whom he learned their magical and healing powers. Third, **Ochosi** is said to have power over new houses and cities, so if someone wants to move or buy a house they invoke him. Finally, **Ochosi** has judicial and administrative power; therefore, if someone finds himself in trouble with the police and the court, he will call on **Ochosi** for help.

Though this next **orisha** is one of the most powerful one, he is not well known. His name is **Aganyu**, and the volcano, which makes his power that of fire, symbolizes him. He is believed to be the father of **Chango**, the thunder god, and like his *Catholic* saint counterpart, *Saint Christopher*, he is a fiery man and the patron of travelers. His colors are red and green, and like **Chango**, his numbers are six and four.

> **The orisha made famous and immortalized by <u>Desi Arnaz</u> with drums and songs on the *I Love Lucy* show is Babalu-Aye.**

He is also known as **Obaluaye** which means the 'king who owns the earth'. He is also known as **Omolu**, meaning *'Son of the Lord'* and as **Sonponno**, the god of smallpox and contagious diseases. He is represented as a sick and frail old man leaning on a large staff. His *Catholic* counterpart is *St. Lazarus*. He is said to dress in sackcloth like a beggar, with a shoulder bag crisscrossed on his chest, carrying his favorite food – toasted corn.

Babalu-Aye is one of the most *respected and well loved* of all the **Santeria's orishas**. His powers are so significant that he is never initiated on the head of an individual. During the tambors or drum parties, **Babalu-Aye** and **Obatala** are the only **orishas** who can come down and take possession of any santero, even if that person belongs to another **orisha**. **Babalu-Aye** can either heal or bring about the most terrible diseases – from cancer and paralysis to syphilis, leprosy and epidemics of all kinds. He is also believed to bring great financial blessing and to be partial to lovers because of his great sexual drive and power. His colors are white and blue, and his number is seventeen.

According to legend, the magic of **Santeria** is natural magic. Its power is the power of herbs, plants and trees found in the woods or tropical forests of the **Antilles**. In the dark and mystical atmosphere of the deep woods live the spiritual entities of the Yoruba. The **santeros** claim that everything comes from the woods, from the fertile womb of the earth. After all, magic cannot be practiced without the help of the forest. Even the most basic spell requires a plant, an herb, a stone, a flower, a fruit, a seed or even an animal. With these items, the **santeros** is said to be able to cure a disease, a headache and even cancer. He supposedly can undo an evil curse, drive away bad luck, and bring to naught the evil intents of an enemy.

The woods can provide everything a **santero** will need to work his magic. However, he must never take a single leaf or stone without asking permission from the woods. Not only must he ask permission, but he must always pay the forest for everything he takes. The method of payment is items like rum, tobacco or a few copper coins. There are special times when a young chicken must be sacrificed. Normally, it is done at the roots of a large tree in the woods.

Osain is the **orisha** of the woods, and he is also known as the owner of the woods. According to legend, **Osain** was never born; he just sprang forth from the bowels of the earth – like Athena from Zeus's forehead. He is a one-eyed, one armed, one-legged deity, and his symbol is a twisted tree. **Osain** also has one huge ear, which he can hear nothing with and one very small ear, which he can hear the rustling of the grass two miles away. The entire ewe is the possession of **Osain**. Without asking for his help beforehand, no work can be done in Santeria.

One of the many stories, which explain how **Osain** lost parts of his body, is the time **Chango** and **Osain** fought a battle over **Oya**, a female orisha. **Chango** became so enraged when **Osain** flirted with **Oya** that he struck **Osain** with a lightning bolt – leaving him lame and half-blind for all eternity. Other santeros say this is not a true story. They say **Osain** is a pure deity with no sexual interest at all. and **Osain** and **Chango** are the best of friends.

Yemaya is an **orisha** of the seawaters and a symbol of maternity. Her name is derived from the Yoruba title, *Yeyeomo eja*, which means 'the mother whose children are the fish'. Her cult comes from the city of Abeokuta. She is represented as a beautiful maiden with prominent breasts. Her colors are blue and white, and her number is seven. In Santeria, her *Catholic* counterpart is *Our Lady of Regla*. (**Regla is a region of Cuba.**) In **Nigeria**, she is associated with the Ogun River.

According to legend, **Yemaya** has been married to several different **orishas,** including **Oggun** and **Orunla**, and she has had love affairs with many others. There are seven paths to her among which are **Okutti,** her most violent aspect; **Awoyo**, the oldest; **Malewo**, who *lives in lakes*; and **Asesu,** who lives in murky water and is *slow to answer prayers*. The most powerful aspect of **Yemaya** is **Olokun** who is believed to symbolize the depth of the oceans and is thought to either be a hermaphrodite or a siren. As Olokun, Yemaya is never initiated on the head of a person because the vastness of the sea cannot fit inside the head of a human being.

Yemaya is one of the most revered and popular of the **orishas**. There is a strong link between **Yemaya** and her sister **Oshun**, the orisha of the rivers. **Oshun** will always come to her sister as the rivers always come to the sea. When **Yemaya** possesses one of her followers, they imitate the movement of a wave and circle around very fast, swaying like seawater. **Yemaya** is a symbol of womanhood and is very often associated with the moon – just like **Diana** of the Ephesians. Her necklace is made up of seven white or crystal beads alternating with seven blue beads. The color scheme may vary according to the path the necklace represents.

Yemaya's *sister orisha* is called **Oshun**. According to legend, she is the divinity of river that crosses the region of **Oshogbo** in Nigeria. The title given to **Oshun** is *Yalodde* (iyalode), which is the highest honor given to a woman in that land. It means 'mother of nations'. **Oshun** is the symbol of river waters, without which life on earth would not be possible. Therefore, according to legend, she controls everything that makes life worth living, such as children, money, pleasure, love and marriage. In **Santeria**, her *Catholic* counterpart is *Our Lady of La Caridad del Cobre*, the patron of Cuba. **Oshun's** number is five, and her color is yellow.

The *stomach area* is very *sacred* to **Oshun,** and for this reason women who want to have children will propitiate her so she will help them conceive. Childbearing is not the only area she controls. She is also responsible for all stomach problems and operations. She is the counterpart to the **Greek** goddess of love, **Venus**. **Oshun** has five paths known as *Yeye Cari, Yeye Moru, and Yeye Miwa.*

Oya is an **orisha** who is also called **Yansa**. She is the orisha of the winds, the tempests and the **Niger River**, which is known as **Odo-Oya in Nigeria**. In **Santeria**, she is known as the owner of the cemetery. **Oya's** colors are wine or dark red, and her number is nine. Her initiates are the only ones whose hair is not cut off during the asiento. **Oya**, like her husband **Chango**, has power over fire. Her *Catholic* counterpart is *Our Lady of La Candelaria*. She also has another well-known *Catholic* counterpart, *Saint Teresa.*

She is a *warrior* **orisha** and is very aggressive in her behavior. She has constant battles with **Chango**, and because they are equal in power, they often end in a draw. However, **Oya** knows how to frighten **Chango**. All she has to do is show him a human skull, for that is the one thing the **orishas** fear. To get back at **Oya**, **Chango** will show to her the one thing she fears the most, which is a ram's skull. When shown this, she is completely under **Chango's** control. **Oya's** necklace is brown with white and red stripes, and her favorite animals are hens and goats.

The **orishas** we have looked at so far are the most popular in **Santeria**, and they are the ones initiated during the asiento, except for **Osain** and **Babalu-Aye**. They are **Eleggua**, **Obatala**, **Orunla**, **Oggun**, **Ochosi**, **Chango**, **Aganyu**, **Yemaya**, **Oshun**, and **Oya**.

This author has personally been in spiritual warfare against two of these spiritual strongmen referred to as **orishas** in **Santeria**. They are **Chango**, the **orisha** of thunder and storms, and **Oya**, the **orisha** of the wind and tempests. Before my conversion to Christianity, these were two of my spiritual guides. After my conversion, they tried many times to stop my ministry and take my life. Yes, they are real, and they are powerful, but compared to my Lord and Savior, Jesus Christ, they are powerless. I know what these two can do, but I also know what I can do because of the glorious Name of Jesus.

The next **orishas** we will look at are powerful but are never used in the asiento – the part of the major initiation. **Orisha-Oko** is the symbol of the earth and his *Catholic* counterpart is *Saint Isidro Labrador*. After **Oggun**, he is the next **orisha** to eat and take part of the sacrificial animal. He does this because he is the lord over the earth, and since the blood of the sacrifice falls to the earth, he has the right to partake and eat of the sacrifice.

Orisha-Oko's necklace is pink and blue. He has no special numbers. Among the Yoruba, both men and women can be priests of **Orisha-Oko**. As a symbol of their priesthood, they wear a red and white vertical line upon their foreheads. Only the priestesses become possessed by the **orisha** and are known as **Agegun Orisa-Oko**. An iron staff ornamented with cowrie shells represents this particular deity. The honeybees are said to be his servants, and the farmers bring their products to him before they go to the market.

Yewa (Yegua) is an **orisha** of many mysteries. She is said to symbolize **Iku** (death) or the transition of death, and because of this, she is very much feared and respected in **Santeria**. The **santeros** say that **Yewa** feeds on the dead, and **Oya**, who only comes into the cemetery to partake of the dead, consumes what is left after this dark feast. Most of the time, **Oya** lingers outside the cemetery gates; after all, she is known as the owner of the cemetery. However, the **santeros** say her real home is in the marketplace.

Yewa, according to **Santeria** tradition, is a virgin **orisha** who is very modest and severe. Those chosen to be her priestesses are women who are often past their prime and are celibate. This is because **Yewa** will not tolerate any sexual dalliances among her daughters. In **Cuba** she is initiated during the *asiento,* but in the U.S. her initiation is quite rare. **Yewa's** color is pink, and when she dances her ritual dance during the santero's funeral ceremony called *itutu*, she covers her face with two scepters (called *irukes*) made from the tails of horses. Her *Catholic* counterpart is *Saint Claire*.

The orisha, **Dada**, is said to be **Chango**, the orisha of the storm's half-brother. When their father, the *king of Oyo*, died, **Dada** (also known as **Ajaba** or **Bayanmi**) became king in his place. He was said to be a peaceful ruler who loved the arts. His half brother, **Chango**, was jealous of him and started a revolt, which ended with **Dada** being dethroned and **Chango** becoming king. When **Chango** died, **Dada** was once again crowned king of Oyo.

In **Santeria**, **Dada** is the *symbol of wealth and prosperity*. He is not normally crowned during the asiento, but those who are in need of help in their business endeavors receive his initiation. His *Catholic* counterpart is *Our Lady of the Rosary*.

The **Ibeyi** are known as the divine twins and also as the **Jimaguas**. They are the beloved of the **santeros** and are considered to be the messengers and children of **Chango**. The twins are propitiated with twin dishes of candy and fruit. They are said to be very helpful in obtaining material prosperity. Their *Catholic* counterparts are *Saint Cosme and Damian*. They are never crowned on the head.

Oba is the symbol of the family and the virtuous wife. She is the forsaken wife of none other than **Chango**, the *orisha of storms*. In Nigeria, there is a river named after **Oba**, which meets at one point with the river water of **Oshun**. Where these two rivers meet, the waters become so violent many believe the two orishas are still battling over their relationship with **Chango**. **Oba** has no assigned numbers, and her color is pink. In order for initiates to receive **Oba**, they have to first undergo **Oshun** initiation. **Oba** is said to partake in the bones of the dead and to have complete control of the bone structure of the body.

Inle is the symbol of doctors. **Inle's** *Catholic* counterpart is *Saint Raphael*. In the *apocryphal book of Tobit*, **Raphael** is the *angel* sent to help Tobias. He is also believed to be the angel who troubles the waters of the *pool of Bethesda*. The Catholics say he is the *patron of druggists, happy meetings, health inspectors, lovers and travelers*. Young people leaving home invoke his help against blindness. He is not crowned on an initiate's head directly, but through the initiation of **Yemaya**.

His necklace has white beads with green streaks. **Inle** carries a staff with two snakes intertwined just like **Mercury** or **Hermes** the messenger of the **Roman and Greek** gods and goddesses. This staff is the symbol of **Inle's** female companion, **Abbata** and is reminiscent of the *caduceus* which represents the healing arts.

Osun is received in **Santeria** at the same time as the Warriors. All of his secrets are contained in a small silvery metal cup topped by a tiny rooster and surrounded by small bells. **Osun** must be placed in a closet or anywhere that he will not be in danger of falling off or turning over. If **Osun** falls off or turns over, there is imminent danger surrounding the owner. He must contact the person who gave him the Warriors to discover what is wrong and take proper measures to avoid trouble. **Osun** represents one's personal guardian angel

Although the **orishas** are essentially considered by the practitioner of **Santeria** to be a comfort and help in times of need, they are also known to be severe punishers and firm upholders of moral behavior. Any straying from the path of the **orishas** will result in swift and terrible punishment by the saints (**orishas**). In order to have the blessings and protection of the **orishas**, the **santeros** must be highly respectable people. They who would dare to break any of the strict rules set by the **orishas** pay dearly for their misdeeds.

The **orishas** have been known to *extremely punish and even to kill* by the powers they are said to obtain. Any sudden or inexplicable death is believed to be the actions of an enraged **orisha**. **Chango**, who controls fire and lightning, has been known to punish his followers because of disobedience by burning their most precious possession. The practitioner may even be burned if the act of disobedience is too grave.

Chango will also take revenge on ones who will offend or come against his followers by destroying their property with a raging fire. **Oshun** and **Yemaya** will very often afflict the stomach and the reproduction area. **Babalu-Aye** brings on plagues, infectious diseases, and leg injuries. **Obatala**, who is often displayed as an infirmed old man with shaking limbs, will bring blindness, head injuries, brain tumors and palsy.

The **orishas** will not tolerate any anti-social behavior or disobedience from their initiates or followers. They are supposedly very generous with their blessing, but totally severe with their punishments. The **santero** is, after all, a priest who represents the **orisha** and his attributes. Therefore, he or she is expected to be a role model for the community and a servant of the **orishas** and mankind. When they fail in this, they become the recipient of the most terrifying wrath of the **orisha.**

Although there are slight changes in the **orisha** names in these countries, they are the same strongman. It is quite amazing to see that the attributes of the Catholic saints, who represent the **orisha**, are the same as these demonic strongmen.

I have shared the names and attributes of the lwa of the Haitian Vodou and the orishas of Yoruba, Santeria, and Candomble (better known as Macumba) and their *Catholic* counterparts.

This alone should be enough to show their diabolical natures. If I had space enough to show the worship ceremonies, which are performed to honor them, you would be appalled. The blood shed from innocent animals to appease them would probably make you wonder how people can be so blinded as to follow these beings of destruction.

It just goes to prove if people will not serve the one and only true God of the Bible, then they will worship anything just to get their own way. God, please open the blind eyes of these slaves to the false gods who are out to destroy mankind.

Prayer Against the Strongmen (Orisha) of Yoruba, Santeria and Candomble

Lord, we ask You to cover us from the ensnarement of these deceiving spirits of darkness. Help us all, Lord, to avoid the snares and lies of these false spirits which lie in wait to enslave mankind.

They want to deceive us with promises of false blessings and miracles, from fortune telling to the communication with the spirits of the dead through séances. They promise us supernatural power which is not theirs to give. They lure us towards secret wisdom obtained through occult means. They want to open our eyes to the deception that our ancestors who have died come back as guardian angels to protect and guide us in everyday living and make prayers on our part to You.

Father, we know there is only one high priest who lives forever and intercedes on our behalf to You, Father, and that is our Lord and Savior Jesus Christ. Amen.

Summary on the Strongmen

We have looked at the history of many spirits proclaiming to be gods like **Ra, Aamon, Horus**, and **Tammuz** from Egypt, Greece and Rome. They are proclaimed to be sun gods. Each demands to be worshipped as the one and only true sun god. Even the Pharaohs of Egypt claimed to be the sun god.

Then there is **Allah, Men, Khons, Abduxuel, Adriel, Anamelech**, and **Amaimon** – all claiming to be the one true god of the moon. It is amazing as in the case of **Allah**, the god of the Moslems and the Koran that he actually began as a female demon of the moon called **Alli**. Then Mohammed changed **Alli's** sex and name from a female moon demon, which his clan worshipped, to a male god.

These beings all claim to be a god of some force of nature, whether it is the sun, the moon, rain, waters, wind, fire, death, infirmity or sex. They all represent a symbol of nature, but the God we serve is not a sun god or a moon god, or a thunder god, or god of death or a god of the sea. He is the God of all creation.

These **so-called strongmen or lwa or orisha** claim to have power over one physical area of life, but the God we serve, the God of the Bible and creator of heaven and earth, has control and power over all aspects of creation, even death, hell and the grave.

Coming out of a background of the occult, which covered seven generations of my family, I refuse to submit myself to a created being, *lwa, orisha, thunder god, moon or sun god, fallen angel, ancestral spirit or any other strongman of the occult*. They only seek to enslave my family and me so they can gratify their desire to be equal to the one and only true God of the Bible.

We have looked at so many different kinds of strongmen demanding complete and total loyalty to them, with terrible punishment to those who disobey them. Even the most loyal of their followers receive terrible punishment. I have known people who faithfully served these vile creatures – refusing them nothing and submitting completely to them in everything; yet they end up dead or institutionalized for the remaining days of their life.

We have looked at some strange spirits; it seems difficult to believe they are real. Like I said earlier, the greatest trick the devil ever played on the world was to convince them he does not exist. As you read about the vampire spirits, the cannibal spirits, or the shape-shifting spiris, it's hard to fathom the reality that man can become any of these things. It is not so much that men become physically what these creatures represent, but they become emotionally and spiritually these things and eventually act out the characteristic attributes of these strongmen physically. This is true with cases like *Jeffrey Dahmer*, a real life cannibal, and *David Berkowitz*, the *son of Sam killer*, who took his orders from his neighbor's large black dog named Sam.

Then there is the leader of the *five families of vampires* who is called *Star* and lives in Anderson, S.C. He has many many young people across the nation who idolize him and have come to believe they are actually vampires. In my ministry, I have been used to set young people free from these spirits, which control them.

There is also the case of the gentleman in **England** who was set free from the spirit of the *werewolf* in the presence of doctors, nurses and police officers. *Mr. Ramsey* allowed his testimony to be put in book form, entitled <u>Werewolf,</u> *by Ed and Lorraine Warren*. There are many true stories of actual cases of murder performed by people over the centuries controlled by the spirit of the wolf.

I wrote this book to reveal the names of the strongmen, **not** to bring glory and recognition to them. We have to know who our enemies are. By knowing their names, it takes away their ability to stay hidden and to continue to work under the cover of darkness. I have spent countless hours in research on these beings and how they work in the lives of people to enslave them. I have also met many of these beings in the years I spent in bondage to the false gods and goddesses of my occult background. I have faced them again in the ministry of deliverance, which I have had the privilege to be used in the last thirty-eight years of ministry.

It is amazing that no matter what false religion these strongmen are a part of, you can begin to see the familiar spirits, which hold entire families in bondage for generations. I have seen entire families set free from drug and alcohol addictions and from physical and mental, as well as spiritual, abuse. I have seen the influence of the spirit of suicide broken off of people when the strongmen have been called by name and rebuked in the name of Jesus.

I know many people will say, "**I don't need to know the name of the spirit to have authority over it in Jesus name**." This is true; however, God honors the name of Jesus and whatsoever we ask according to His word; He will do it in the name of Jesus. What I have discovered as I've traveled to many nations is that when the name of the spirit was known, the power over it seemed greater and the deliverance was easier with no attention given whatsoever to the spirit possessing the person.

I know many people argue that, when Jesus spoke to the demon possessed and asked his name, the sprit answered, **"My name is Legion for we are many**." People say Jesus was asking the man what his name was, and the demons spoke up and gave their name as legion. I believe the devils knew Jesus was speaking to them and they immediately revealed who they were and their number. Every time Jesus performed deliverance, the spirit was revealed for what it was. Jesus always pointed out clearly whom the spirit was that was manifesting in the person. It was always known if it was a spirit of infirmity, a blind spirit, a deaf and dumb spirit or even Satan himself.

My sincere wishes is: I hope this book will help you to see clearly whom your enemy is and who has been working for generations to keep your family lines in bondages. May God bless you and your loved ones and bring freedom, joy, health, prosperity and salvation to those you love and care for.

A Final Prayer

Dear Lord, thank You for Your everlasting love, kindness and mercy. Thank You, Father, for being our strong tower and hiding place. You are the place of our rest and Sabbath and the banner which covers us.

You are the shield of faith which goes before us to quench the fiery darts of our adversary: the devil and his fallen angels, and the strongman who seeks to destroy us.

Thank You, Lord, that if any of us lacks wisdom and understanding, all we need to do is ask of You, and You will give it to us.

May everything we do and say bring glory to You, Lord, in Jesus Name, Amen

PRAYERS FOR DELIVERANCE AND HEALING

pgs 172-178

PRAYER FOR DELIVERANCE FROM GENERATIONAL BONDAGE

PRAYER TO BREAK UNGODLY SOUL TIES

PRAYER FOR FORGIVENESS FROM IDOLATRY-BASED SINS

PRAYERS AGAINST ORISIS AND ISIS: GOD AND GODDESS OF THE FREEMASON

PRAYER FOR FORGIVENESS FOR SIN AND DELIVERANCE

PRAYER FOR FORGIVENESS OF ANGER AND UNFORGIVENESS

PRAYER TO FORGIVE OTHERS

PRAYER FOR DELIVERANCE OF A SON OR DAUGHTER OR FAMILY MEMBER

PRAYER OF SUBMISSION TO THE HOLY SPIRIT

PRAYER OF THE ARMOR OF GOD

PRAYER FOR SPIRITUAL WARFARE IN GENERAL

PRAYER FOR A MARRIAGE

PRAYER FOR DELIVERANCE FROM GENERATIONAL BONDAGE

Gracious Father over all, I acknowledge before you the sins of my parents and ancestors. I know that they have sinned because all men and women are sinners. And so, I openly confess the sins of my parents and ancestors. I know I cannot do what only they could have done in attaining forgiveness of their sins, but I am sorry for their sins against you and I ask that you cover their sins with the blood of Jesus and not hold their consequences against me or my descendants. I claim the finished work of Jesus Christ, Who bore all my sin upon Himself. In faith I accept that work on the basis of your holy Word. I reclaim any consent given to Satan's forces by my parents' sin. Dear Jesus, please set me free from all evil influences coming from my parents and ancestors in the name of Jesus. I know I am a new creation in Christ. Old things have gone and all things have become new. I here and now reject and disown all the sins of my ancestors. As one who has been delivered from the power of darkness and translated into the kingdom of God's dear Son, I cancel out all demonic working that has been passed on to me from my ancestors. As one who has been crucified and raised with Christ and who sits with him in heavenly places, I reject any and every way in which Satan may claim ownership of me. I declare myself and my descendants to be eternally and completely signed over and committed to the Lord Jesus Christ. I now command every evil spirit and every enemy of the Lord Jesus Christ that is in or around me to flee my presence and never to return. I now ask You, heavenly Father, to fill me with Your Holy Spirit. I submit my body as an instrument of righteousness, a living sacrifice, that I may glorify You in my body. All this I do in the name & authority of the Lord Jesus Christ. Amen

PRAYER TO BREAK UNGODLY SOUL TIES

In the name of the Father, the Son and the Holy Spirit, I ask God to break all ungodly spirit, soul and body ties that have been established between me and (name person). I sever that linking supernaturally and ask God to remove from you all influence of the other person **(name them)** *and drawback to myself every part that has been wrongfully tied in bondage to another person. I now speak directly to every evil spirit that has taken advantage of this ungodly soul tie. You no longer have any rights here and I order you to leave now without hurting or harming me or any other person and without going into any other member of the family. In Jesus' name. Amen.*

PRAYER FOR FORGIVENESS FROM IDOLATRY-BASED SINS

Dear heavenly Father, You have said the pride goes before destruction and an arrogant spirit before stumbling **(Proverbs 16:18)**. *I confess that I have not denied myself, picked up my cross daily, and followed You* **(Matthew 16:24)**. *In so doing I have given ground to the enemy in my life. I have believed that I could be successful and live victoriously by my own strength and resources. I now confess that I have sinned against You by placing my will before Yours and by centering my life around self instead of You. I now renounce the self life and by so doing cancel all the ground that has been gained in my members by the enemies of the Lord Jesus Christ. I pray that You will guide me so that I will do nothing from selfishness or empty conceit, but that with humility of mind I will regard others as more important than myself* **(Philippians 2:3)**. *Enable me through love to serve others and in honor prefer others* **(Romans 12:10)**. *I ask this in the name of Christ Jesus my Lord. Amen.*

PRAYERS AGAINST ORISIS AND ISIS: GOD AND GODDESS OF THE FREEMASON

Father God, creator of heaven and earth, I come to you in the name of Jesus Christ your Son. I come as a sinner seeking forgiveness and cleansing from all sins committed against you, and others made in your image. I honor my earthly father and mother and all of my ancestors of flesh and blood, and of the spirit by adoption and godparents, but I utterly turn away from and renounce all their sins. I forgive all my ancestors for the effects of their sins on me and my children. I confess and renounce all of my own sins, known and unknown. I renounce and rebuke Satan and every spiritual power of his affecting me and my family, in the name of Jesus Christ. I renounce and annul every covenant made with Death by my ancestors or myself, including every agreement made with Sheol, and I renounce the refuge of lies and falsehoods which they have been hidden behind.

In the name of the Lord Jesus Christ, I renounce and forsake all involvement in Freemasonry or any other lodge, craft or occultism by my ancestors and myself. I also renounce and break the code of silence enforced by Freemasonry and the Occult on my family and myself. I renounce and repent of all pride and arrogance which opened the door for the slavery and bondage of Freemasonry to afflict my family and me. I now shut every door of witchcraft and deception operating in my life and seal it closed with the blood of the Lord Jesus Christ. I renounce every covenant, every blood covenant and every alliance with Freemasonry or the spiritual powers behind it made by my family or me.

I renounce every position held in the lodge by any of my ancestors or myself, including "Master," "Worshipful Master," or any other occult title. I renounce the calling of any man "Master," for Jesus Christ is my only master and Lord, and He forbids anyone else having that title. I renounce the entrapping of others into Masonry, and observing the helplessness of others during the rituals. I renounce the effects of Masonry passed on to me through any female ancestor who felt distrusted and rejected by her husband as he entered and attended any lodge and refused to tell her of his secret activities. I also renounce all obligations, oaths and curses enacted by every female member of my family through any direct membership of all Women's Orders of Freemasonry, the Order of the Eastern Star, or any other Masonic or occult organization. In the name of Jesus Christ I renounce the oaths taken and the curses and iniquities involved in any aspect of Freemasonry, by myself or my ancestors.

Holy Spirit, I ask that you show me anything else which I need to do or to pray so that I and my family may be totally free from the consequences of the sins of Masonry, Witchcraft, Mormonism and all related Paganism and Occultism.

Dear Father God, I ask humbly for the blood of Jesus Christ, your Son and my Savior, to cleanse me from all these sins I have confessed and renounced, to cleanse my spirit, my soul, my mind, my emotions and every part of my body which has been affected by these sins, in the name of Jesus Christ. I also command every cell in my body to come into divine order now, and to be healed and made whole as they were designed to by my loving Creator.

I ask you, Lord, to fill me with your Holy Spirit now according to the promises in your Word. I take to myself the whole armor of God in accordance with (**Ephesians, Chapter Six**), *and rejoice in its* *protection as Jesus surrounds me and fills me with His Holy Spirit. I enthrone you, Lord Jesus, in my heart, for you are my Lord and my Savior, the source of eternal life. Thank you, Father God, for your mercy, your forgiveness and your love, in the name of Jesus Christ. Amen.*

PRAYER FOR FORGIVENESS FOR SIN AND DELIVERANCE

Dear heavenly Father, You have told us to put on the Lord Jesus Christ and make no provision for the flesh in regard to its lusts **(Romans 13:14)**. *I acknowledge that I have given in to fleshly lusts which wage war against my soul* **(I Peter 2:11)**. *I thank You that in Christ my sins are forgiven, but I have transgressed Your holy law and given the enemy an opportunity to wage war in my members* **(Ephesians 4:27; James 4:1, I Peter 5:8)**. *I come before Your presence to acknowledge these sins and to seek Your cleansing* **(I John 1:9)** *that I may be freed from the bondage of sin* **(Galatians 5:1)**. *I now ask You to reveal to my mind the ways that I have transgressed Your moral law and grieved the Holy Spirit.* **(Then confess each sin that comes to mind one by one.)** *I now confess these sins to You and claim through the blood of the Lord Jesus Christ my forgiveness and cleansing. I cancel all ground that evil spirits have gained through my willful involvement in sin. I ask this in the wonderful name of my Lord and Savior Jesus Christ. Amen.*

PRAYER FOR FORGIVENESS OF ANGER AND UNFORGIVENESS

Dear heavenly Father, I thank You for the riches of Your kindness, forbearance, and patience, knowing that Your kindness has led me to repentance **(Romans 2:4)**. *I confess that I have not extended that same patience and kindness toward others who have offended me, but instead I have harbored bitterness and resentment. I pray that during this time of self-examination You would bring to mind only those people that I have not forgiven in order that I may do so* **(Matthew 18:35)**. *I also pray that if I have offended others you would bring to mind only those people from whom I need to seek forgiveness and the extent to which I need to seek it* **(Matthew 5:23-24)**. *I ask this in the precious name of Jesus. Amen.*

PRAYER TO FORGIVE OTHERS

Thank You, Jesus, for dying that I might be forgiven. By an act of my will I now choose to express the desire of my heart and forgive those who have hurt me. **(name the people)** *I release each and every one of these people into the freedom of my forgiveness. In Jesus' name. Amen.*

Father, I confess that, as a result of being hurt, I have allowed myself to hold anger, resentment and bitterness in my heart against **(name)**. *I acknowledge this as sin, and I now repent and turn from this behavior. I ask that You will forgive me and cleanse me. I take back any access this sin has given to any of Satan's demons. In Jesus' name. Amen.*

PRAYER FOR DELIVERANCE OF A SON OR DAUGHTER OR FAMILY MEMBER

*I humbly bow before you, heavenly Father, to intercede for my child. I bring him/her before You in the name of the Lord Jesus Christ. I thank You that You have loved with the love of Calvary. I thank You that You gave him/her to us to love and nurture in Christ. I ask You to forgive us that for all of our failures to guide him/her in the way he/she ought to go. Accepting my position of being "mighty through God to the pulling down of strongholds," I bring all of the work of the Lord Jesus Christ to focus directly against all of Satan's power in **(name)**'s life. I bind up all the powers of darkness set to destroying, and I loose him/her from their power in the name of the Lord Jesus Christ. I invite the blessed Holy Spirit to move upon **(name)**'s heart and to bring him/her to you. In my position as mother/father I put all their sin under the blood of the Lord Jesus Christ. I take back any access any of Satan's forces claim through any ancestral openings, and I put that under the blood of the Lord Jesus Christ. I plead the blood of the Lord Jesus Christ over **(name)**'s life. I ask that Your Holy Spirit would fill **(name)** and ever use him/her for your honor and glory, so that he/she would grow up to serve You. In Jesus' name I pray. Amen.*

PRAYER OF SUBMISSION TO THE HOLY SPIRIT

Dear heavenly Father, You have said that rebellion is as the sin of witchcraft and insubordination is as iniquity and idolatry **(I Samuel 15:23),** *I know that in action and attitude I have sinned against You with a rebellious heart. I ask Your forgiveness for my rebellion and pray that by the shed blood of the Lord Jesus Christ all ground gained by evil spirits because of my rebelliousness would be canceled. I pray that You will shed light on all my ways that I may know the full extent of my rebelliousness and choose to adopt a submissive spirit and a servant's heart. In the name of Christ Jesus my Lord. Amen*

PRAYER OF THE ARMOR OF GOD

Heavenly Father, I desire to be obedient by being strong in the Lord and the power of Your might. I see that this is Your will and purpose for me. I recognize that it is essential to put on the armor that You have provided, and I do so now with gratitude and praise that You have provided all I need to stand in victory against Satan and his kingdom. Grant me wisdom to discern the tactics and sneakiness of Satan's strategy against me. I delight to take the armor You have provided and by faith to put it on as effective spiritual protection against the spiritual forces of darkness present in the world today.

I confidently take the belt of truth that You offer me. I take Him who is the truth as my strength and protection. I reject Satan's lies and deceiving ways to gain advantage against me. Grant me discernment and wisdom to recognize the subtle and sneaky ways in which Satan seeks to cause me to accept his lies as truth. I desire to believe only the truth, to live the truth, to speak the truth, and to know the truth. I worship and praise You that You lead me only in the ways of truth. Thank You that Satan cannot stand against the truth.

Thank You for the breastplate of righteousness which you offer me. I eagerly accept it and put it on as my protection. Thank you for reminding me again that all of my righteousness comes from You. I embrace that righteousness which is mine by faith in the Lord Jesus Christ. It is His righteousness that is mine through justification. I reject and repudiate all trust in my own righteousness which is as filthy rags. I ask You to cleanse me of all the times I have counted my own goodness as being acceptable before You. I bring the righteousness of my Lord directly against all of Satan's workings against me. I express my desire to walk in righteousness before God today. By faith I appropriate the righteousness of Christ and invite Him to walk in His holiness in my life today that I might experience His righteousness in total context of ordinary living. I count upon the righteousness of my Lord to be my protection. I know that Satan must retreat from before God's righteousness.

Thank You, Lord, for the sandals of peace You have provided. I desire that my feet should stand on the solid rock of the peace that You have provided. I claim the peace with God which is mine through justification. I desire the peace of God which touches my emotions and feelings through prayer and sanctification **(Philippians 4:6).** *Thank You that as I walk in obedience to You the God of peace promises to walk with me* **(Philippians 4:9).** *I thank you that as the God of peace You are putting Satan under my feet* **(Romans 16:20).** *I will share this good news of peace with all others that Your Spirit will bring into my life today. Thank you that You have not given me a spirit of fear but of love and power and a sound mind* **(II Timothy 1:7).** *Thank you that Satan cannot stand against Your peace.*

Eagerly, Lord, I lift up the shield of faith against all the blazing darts that Satan and his hosts fire at me. I recognize that You are my shield and that in Your incarnation and crucifixion You took the arrows of Satan which I deserved. By faith I count upon You to shield me from above and beneath; on my right and my left; in front of me and behind me, that I might be protected, walled in, and encapsulated by You that Satan may gain no way to hurt me or keep me from fulfilling Your will today.

I am willing that any fiery darts of Satan You wish to touch me should do so, but I shall look upon them as refining fires permitted in Your providence and by Your love for my refining and Your glory. Thank You, Lord, that You are a complete and perfect shield and that Satan cannot touch me apart from Your sovereign purpose.

I recognize that my mind is a particular target of Satan's deceiving ways. I take from You the helmet of salvation. I cover my mind and my thoughts with Your salvation. I recognize that the Lord Jesus Christ is my salvation. I fill my head with Him. I invite His mind to be in me. Let me think His thoughts, feel His love and compassion, and discern His will and leading in all things. Let my mind be occupied with the continuing, daily, saving work of my Lord in and through my life. May You meet and defeat all Satanic thoughts in my mind.

With joy I take hold upon the sword of the Spirit, which is the Word of God. I affirm that Your Word is the trustworthy, infallible Word of God. I choose to believe it and to live in its truth and power. Grant me the love for Your Word which comes from the Holy Spirit. Forgive and cleanse me from the sin of neglecting Your Word. Create in me a hunger and thirst to study and know Your Word. Enable me to memorize it and to meditate upon its truth. Grant me proficient recall and skill in using Your Word against all of Satan's subtle attacks against me, even as my Lord Jesus Christ used the Word against Satan. Enable me to use Your Word not only to defend me from Satan, but also to claim its promises and to wield the sword strong against Satan to defeat him, to push him back, to take away from him ground he claims, and to win great victories God through Your Word. Thank You that Satan must retreat from Your Word applied against him.

Thank You, dear Lord, for prayer. Help me to keep this armor well oiled with prayer. I desire to pray at all times with depth and intensity as the Holy Spirit leads me. I trust the Holy Spirit to enable me and to intercede for me and through me. Grant me great supplication and burden for others in God's family of blood-washed saints. Enable me to see their needs and to assist them through prayer as the enemy attacks them. All of these petitions, intercessions, and words of praise I offer up before the true and living God in the name and worthy merit of my Lord Jesus Christ. Amen

PRAYER FOR SPIRITUAL WARFARE IN GENERAL

Gracious God, I acknowledge that You are worthy of all honor, glory and praise. I am thankful for the victorious work of Your Son, Jesus Christ at Calvary for me. I apply His victory to my life now as I willingly surrender every area of my life to Your will.

Thank you for the forgiveness and righteousness that has been given to me as Your adopted child. I trust in Your protection and provision daily. I know that your love for me never ceases. I rejoice in Your victory, my Lord, over all the principalities and powers in the heavenlies. In faith I stand in Your victory and commit myself to live obediently for You my King.

I desire that my fellowship with You become greater. Reveal to me those things that grieve You and enables the enemy to secure an advantage in my life. I need the Holy Spirit's powerful ministry in my life; bringing conviction of sin, repentance of heart, strengthening my faith and increasing perseverance in resisting temptation.

Help me to die to self and walk in the victory of the new creation You have provided for me. Let the fruits of the Spirit flow out of my life so that You will be glorified through my life. Fill me with your love, joy, peace, patience, kindness, goodness, gentleness, faithfulness and self-control.

Please place your hedge of protection around me, my possession, my family and all my descendants. Protect us from anything the enemy would try to do against us.

I know that it is Your will that I should stand firm and resist all of the enemy's work against me. Help me to discern the attacks upon my thoughts and emotions. Enable me to stand upon Your Word and resist all the accusations, distortions and condemnations that are hurled against me.

It is my desire to be transformed through the renewing of my mind, so that I will not compromise with the ways of the world, or yield to the enemy's attacks, but be obedient to Your will. So give me the mind of Christ in order that I may have His perspective, wisdom, compassion, holiness and truth.

I draw upon those spiritual resources that You have provided me and I attack the strongholds and plans of the enemy that have been put in place against me. I command in the name of Jesus Christ that the enemy must release my mind, will, emotions and body completely. They have been yielded to the Lord and I belong to Him.

Lord, enable me to become the person You created me to be. Help me as I pray to be strong in faith. Show me how to apply Your Word in my life each day. I know that I wear the full armor of God when I am committed to and stand firmly upon Your Word. I want You to have the supreme place in my life. Give me a hunger and thirst to know You better, to read Your Word more deeply, to pray more readily and to keep you first in all my thoughts all day long.

I surrender myself completely to You, Lord. You are always faithful and You extend Your grace to me constantly, even when I do not realize it. I claim Your promise of forgiveness and cleansing in its fullness. In faith, I receive the victory today that you have already put in place for me. I do this in the name of Jesus Christ, my Savior with a grateful heart. AMEN

PRAYER FOR A MARRIAGE

Loving Heavenly Father, I thank You for Your perfect plan for our marriage. I know that You planned marriage to be beautiful and satisfying, a picture of our relationship with you. I ask that You would do what is needed in and through me to make our marriage all it should be.

Please forgive me for my sins of failure in my marriage. I confess my sins: **(confess individually all the sins and shortcomings you are aware of.)** *I ask You to forgive me. I put them under the blood of Jesus and take back any access I have given to any demons through them. Open my eyes to see all areas where I am deceived and help me to apply Your truth to those areas.*

I pray for my mate as well and put his/her sins under the blood of Jesus as well. I intercede for them and ask for your mercy to cover their sins and shortcomings and to take back any access any of Satan's forces claim through him/her.

Father, I ask that You would fill each of us with Your Holy Spirit. Fill us with the fruit of Your Spirit: love, joy, peace, patience, goodness, kindness, gentleness, meekness, faithfulness and self-control. Heal us from the hurts we have caused ourselves and each other. Give us a spirit of forgiveness for each other. Put Your supernatural love in our hearts and help us to love each other as You love us.

Show me what I need to do to change to correct my hurts and errors from the past. Help me to apologize where necessary and to know what to do to restore our relationship. I submit myself to You to be used and changed as You see fit. I submit my marriage to You for You to do what is necessary to heal it and use it for Your honor and glory

Index

Chapter 1: Strongmen of War
Different Countries and Different names for their gods
Pages 12-21

Abigor – warrior demon
Agaliarept – Hebrew commander of armies
Aries – Greek god of war
Azazel – Hebrew god of war
Busas – another name of Pruflas
Jestan – Hindukusch demon of disease, famine, and war
Mars – Rome's strongman of war
Mont – Egypt's strongman of war
Pruflas – facilitates quarrels, wars, discord, and poverty
Rama – Hindu god of war
Siva (Shiva) – the destroyer
Thamuz – god of war, said to have started the inquisition and to have invented artillery
Udl – Austrian god of war.
Zaebos – god of war that appears as a soldier
Zepar – god of war that appears in the form of a soldier

Chapter 2: Strongmen of Sex
Different spirits of perversion
Pages 22-29

Agrat-bat-mahlaht – spirit of prostitution and sex slavery
Ashtaroth – Phoenician goddess of lust and seduction
Ardhanarisvara - bisexual personality of Siva
Chil Gazi – seducer
of women
Daevas – demon of addiction, drunkenness, sexuality, death by starvation and contagious diseases
Dantalion – three- face spirit of sexual perversion, bisexualism, gender confusion, mind reading and the worship of the occult
Druj – Iranian demon of lies and uncleanness, rape, and incest
Erzulie – spirit of fornication and adultery
Hermaphroditos or **Hermaphroditus** – spirit that is both male and female
Incubus – male demon of sexual lusting
Jaldabaoth – spirit that rapes women and starvation and contagious diseases
Lilith – spirit of sexual seduction
Ornias – spirit of homosexuality
Philatanus – Jewish strongman of sodomy
Proserpine – spirit who helps in establishing the act of sodomy
Succubus – female demon of sexual lusting

Chapter 3 Strongmen of Idolatry
Pages 30-35

Aamon – Egyptian sun god
Abduxuel – moon god
Adriel – moon god
Allah – moon god in Arabic mythology
Amaimon – Egyptian sun god
Ammon – another name for **Amon**, the Egyptian king of the gods
Amon – Egyptian king of the gods
Anamelech – moon goddess
Apollo – son of Zeus, god of the sun
Diana of the Ephesians – spirit behind the worship of the moon. Queen goddess of all divisions of witchcraft
Horus – Egyptian god of the sky and sun
Isis – Egyptian strongman of moon worship
Khons – Egyptian moon god
Men – Anatolian moon god
Osiris – Egyptian strongman of sun worship
Ra – Egyptian god of the sun and creator god
Tammuz – Egyptian vegetation god

Chapter 4: Strongmen of the Storm
Thor, the meaning of the lightning bolt, devil and fallen angels
Pages 36-41

Adad – Babylonian storm and thunder god
Addu – another name for Adad, Babylonian storm and thunder god
Agau – in Vodou, he is the violent god of storms
Babuala – strongman of the storm
Bade – in Vodou, he is the god of wind
Chango – in Santeria, he is the god of thunder and lightning
Focalor – spirit that has power over the winds and the sea and is the cause of death by drowning
Jeretik – in Russian mythology demon that spreads bad weather, storms, and sickness
Nicor – water demon that causes hurricanes and tempests, causes death by drowning
Shango – another name for **Chango**
Thor – Norse god of thunder
Ugallu – big weather beast
Umudabrutu – strongman of the violent storm
Vaya – Iranian demon of wind and causes death by numbing the body

Chapter 5: Strongmen of Infirmity and Disease
Pages 42-47

Aclahayr – spirit of mental illness
Ahazu – spirit of night seizures
Asakku – spirit of disease and death; plagues
Daevas – demon of addiction, drunkenness, sexuality, death by starvation and contagious diseases
Impundulu – vampire spirit of disease and death
Iya – cannibal spirit of sickness and death
Jeretik – spirit of storms and sickness
Jestan – spirit of disease, war, and famine
Shabriri – spirit of blindness
Xtabal – spirit of infirmity
Zarich – spirit of weakness and illness

Chapter 6: Strongmen of Death
The spirit of abortion, child sacrifics, death to children and animals
Pages 48-55

Abaddon or Apollyon – angel of bottomless pit and death
Amducious – in Hebrew, the destroyer
Ankou – death spirit of the elderly and the sick
Aosoth – spirit that specializes in passion and death
Astovidatu – spirit of death
Bajang – death spirit of newborns
Banshee – Irish death spirit
Baron Samedi – Vodou spirit of the dead
Basilisk – spirit of violent death
Befana – Italian spirit which destroys children
Buda – spirit of the death of children
Daevas – demon of addiction, drunkenness, sexuality, death by starvation and contagious diseases
Dengelmaennie – Alpine spirit of death
Dimme – Sumerian spirit of sickness and death
Dre – spirit of death and destruction
Drude – spirit of nightmares and death by strangulation
Duppy – spirit of terrible death
Focalor – spirit that has power over the winds and the sea and is the cause of death by drowning
Flauros/Haures – spirit of death by fire
Hemah – Hebrew spirit of death over domestic animals
Imdugud – Sumerian spirit of death of domestic animals
Impundulu – vampire spirit of disease and death
Iya – cannibal spirit of disease and death
Jahi – death by poison
Jigarkhvar – cannibal spirit of death; witch-like vampire

Kabala – Hebrew spirit of crib death called **Lilith** (supposed first wife of Adam and mother of all demons)
Kasdeja – spirit of death by abortion and by miscarriage, a former Watcher
Maahes – Egyptian spirit of massacre
Meshabber – spirit of death over wild and free animals
Milcom/Moloch – Ammorite demon who causes the death of children
Nicor – water demon that causes hurricanes and tempests, causes death by drowning
Siva or Shiva – in Hindu, the destroyer
Vanth – Etruscan spirit of death
Vaya – Iranian demon of wind and causes death by numbing the body
Vepar – fallen angel who brings storms and causes death by gangrene
Virikas – West Indian spirit of death
Wasco – demon who brings death to children by eating them
Wraith – death spirit
Yama – West Indian god of death
Yukki-Onna – Oriental spirit of death by freezing

Chapter 7: Strongmen in Serpent Form
Pages 56-61

Anantaboga – Hindu giant dragon-like creature
Apep – Egyptian snake spirit
Apophis – Greek snake spirit
Aspis – Hebrew snake spirit of evil and stubbornness
Banda – serpent that binds or ties men up
Basmu – a poisonous serpent
Basuki – Hindu giant dragon-like creature
Botis – snake spirit
Kundalini – spirit that is a coiled serpent at the base of the spine and is invoked during yoga
Mehen – Egyptian divine serpent
Musilinda – the great cobra
Mushussu – furious serpent
Musmahhu – exalted serpent
Nagas – Hindu serpent deities
Nehebkau – serpent god of the underworld
Ra Uraeus – divine cobra
Satan – that old serpent, the devil
Usumgallu – great dragon

Chapter 8: Strongmen of Mystical Legends
Part 1: Vampires
Pages 62-73

Adze – ghost-like vampire from Ghana
Alu – vampire spirit of the night
Asanbosam – in African folklore, vampire-like creatures
Aswang – Philippine vampire spirit
Aulak – temple vampire
Baital/Baitala – race of vampires
Baobhan – vampire spirit
Bhutas – vampire shape-shifter
Charmo Vetr – Hindukusch vampire spirit
Chordewa – vampire witch
Churel – vampire spirit in India
Civatateo – Aztec vampire
Danag – Oriental spirit
Dearg-Due – Irish vampire
Eretica – Russian vampire
Estrie – Jewish vampire
Gayal – vampire ghost from India
Gierach – Prussian vampire
Hanh Saburo – vampire from India
Hannya – Japanese vampire
Hant-pare – Indian vampire which clings to the wounds of a person
Hantu- Dor Dong – Indian vampire
Hiadam/Haidam – Hungarian vampire
Impundulu – vampire spirit of disease and death
Jaracaca – Brazilian snake vampire
Jigarkhvar – cannibal spirit of death; witch-like vampire
Kali – wife of Sita/Shiva, fierce vampire
Kuang-Shi/Chiang-Shi – Chinese vampire
Mah'anah – vampire spirit
Mmbyu – mischief-making vampire from India
Nachzeher – vampire spirit
Neuntoter – German vampire that is a carrier of plagues and pestilence
Pacu-Pati – vampire race from India
Penanggalan – Malaysian vampire
Pisacha – Indian vampire
Rakshasa – unrighteous Hindu vampire
Swawmx – vampire creature from Burma
Talamar – vampire creature of the Banks Islands
Vetala/Vetal – similar to Baital/Baitala, race of vampires
Vrykolakas – vampire on the island of Chios/Khios
Wichan Alwe – Araukanian vampire

Chapter 8: Strongmen of Mystical Legends
Part 2: Cannibals
Pages 71-79

Bachbakuala-Nuksiwae – man-eating creature among the Kwakiutl Indians
Baka – Haitian cannibal spirit
Belu – man-eating spirit in Burma
Blutschink – man-eating cannibal
Bolla – a cannibal spirit in Albania
Cherufe – giant cannibal spirit, which eats young girls
Curiysira – shape-shifting cannibal from the Amazon
Iya – cannibal spirit of disease and death
Jigarkhvar – cannibal spirit of death; witch-like vampire
Wasco – demon who brings death to children by eating them
Wendigo – shape-shifter, flesh-eating beast in the outback and woods of Canada
Wolba – flesh-eating spirit
Wutr – female cannibal
Xastur – kills people in their sleep and devours them
Yachemi – female cannibal
Yama-Onna – cannibal spirit of greed
Yamale – giant cannibal
Yara-Ma-Yha-Who – Australian cannibal
Yush – red giant cannibal spirit

Chapter 8: Strongmen of Mystical Legends
Part 3: Shape-Shifters
Pages 80-93

Achelous – river spirit with head of bull and head of man
Adlet – dog people
Almasti – Russian creature that was part man and part beast
Anubis – Egyptian jackal-headed god of the underworld
Bhutas – shape-shifting vampire spirit
Bisclaveret – French werewolf
Bogies & Boggarts – English shape-shifters
Boxenwolf – German werewolf
Bruxsa – Portuguese shape-shifter
Caacrinolaas – strongman of darkness, appears as a black dog
Canaima – notorious shape-shifting spirit
Chindi – Navajo shape-shifter
Chordeva – East Indian shape-shifting cat spirit

Curiysira – shape-shifting vampire spirit
Jestan – Hindukusch dog spirit
Kusarikku – bull man strongman of the half man and half animal mutations
Lahmu – spirit of the beast man
Maahes – lion-headed man, Egyptian strongman of war and massacre
Wendigo – shape-shifter, flesh-eating beast in the outback and woods of Canada
Were-being (can take the shape of any animal – record of cases in every nation)

Chapter 9: Strongmen of Destruction
Pages 94-97

Abatu – spirit of destruction
Amducious – the destroyer
Ardat-Lile – spirit behind destruction of families
Befana – spirit out to destroy children
Bergmoench – spirit of harm and destruction
Bohten Dayak – spirit of evil tricks/ destruction
Dre – spirit behind death and destruction
Joetun – giant spirit behind chaos and destruction
Loki – Norse god of evil tricks and destruction
Shiva – Hindu god known as the destroyer
Xolotl – strongman of destruction

Chapter 10: Strongmen of Slavery, Physically & Mentally
Pages 98-101

Abdiel – spiritual strongman behind slavery
Abraxas – taskmaster over slaves
Ammit – spirit behind torment and mental slavery

Chapter 11: Strongmen of the Occult
Pages 102-106

Amducious – Egyptian spirit of destruction
Andrealphus – spirit behind astrology
Araqiel – Hebrew spirit of earth worship
Armaros – Hebrew spirit of enchantment
Balan – spirit behind fortune telling and witchcraft
Bannik – fortune telling spirit
Baphomet – spirit of the occult and of secret rites, Knights Templar, Masons, Mormons, all secret societies
Baraqijal – Hebrew spirit of astrology
Barbados – fortune telling spirit

Bifrous – spirit of astrology
Buer – spirit of vain philosophy and logic
Dantalion – three-face spirit of sexual perversion, bisexualism
Diana of the Ephesians – spirit behind the worship of the moon. Queen goddess of all divisions of witchcraft
Ezeqeel – Hebrew spirit of cloud worship
Hecate – three-faced goddess of witchcraft
Kasbeel – Hebrew spirit of secret knowledge, Kabala, occult séances
Nybbas – spirit of fortune telling
Raum – Hebrew three-faced god of destruction with a face of man, viper, and a cat
Stolas – spirit of star gazing and herbology
Uvall – fortune telling spirit
Vapula – spirit behind philosophy
Vassago – fortune telling spirit
Zagan – spirit behind false miracles and wisdom

Chapter 12: Worldwide Leaders of the Strongmen
waterways, oceans spirit behind abortions, violent storms, hindered prayers, strongman over legions of demons
Pages 106 - 113

Abaddon – Hebrew god of destruction
Adbiel – strongman of slavery
Abraxas – Egyptian taskmaster
Agaliarept – commander of war gods
Akatash – leader over all evil spirits
Alastor – leader over murderous spirits
Aldinach – leader over the spirits of natural disasters
Amy – prince of the kingdom of darkness, giver of occult knowledge
Apollyon – leader over the spirits of the pit, a destroying angel, Greek god of destruction
Apophis/Apep – snake spirits
Aries – Greek god of war
Aspis – Hebrew snake spirit of evil and stubbornness
Atazoth – former Watcher, leader of the spirits of darkness
Avnas – a leader of the strongmen
Azazel – leader of the former watchers, leader of all spirits of war and workers of metal, and all the fallen angels
Baal – one of the main chiefs of the leadrs of the fallen angels
Beelzebub – Hebrew fallen angel, one of Satan's generals
Behemoth – Hebrew spirit strongman of waterways
Belial – Hebrew spirit leader of all the spirits of darkness
Belphegor – Hebrew spirit, strongman of hidden knowledge
Botis – snake spirit
Buer – reigning spirit of all vain philosophies and logic
Byleth – one of the leading strongmen
Caacrinolas – strongman of Satan's kingdom, appears as a large black dog

Caym – strongman, leader of over thirty legions of demons
Gaap – one of the Hebrew ruling strongmen
Iblis – Arabic, Islamic leader of the djins (demons)
Isis – Egyptian strongman of moon worship
Kasdeja – former Watcher, Hebrew fallen angel, spirit behind abortions and miscarriages
Leviathan – great sea serpent
Maahes – lion-headed man, Egyptian strongman of war and massacre
Malphas – Hebrew spirit, leader of lies and deceptions
Mammon – Hebrew spirit, leader of greed
Mars – Rome's strongman of war
Mehen – Egyptian divine serpent
Mephistopheles – German name for Satan, complete leader of all strongmen, spirits of darkness, fallen angels and demons
Melkiresha – chief of the strongmen directly under Satan, an angel of darkness, a watcher in reptilian form
Moloch – Old Testament pagan god, the strongman behind child sacrifices and death
Mont – Egypt's strongman of war
Nehebkau – Egyptian serpent god of the underworld
Osiris – Egyptian strongman of sun worship
Rabisu – strongman who lies in wait, the doorkeeper **(Genesis 4:6)**
Rabisu Basmu – the venomous snake
Rabisu Girtablulu – scorpion man king of all poisonous creatures
Rabisu Harbati – lord of the wastelands, dry places, deserts
Rabisu Kulullu – fishman, lord of the seas and the oceans
Rabisu Kusarikku – half man and half bull, lord of half man and half animal mutations
Rabisu Lahmu – known as the hairy one, strongman of the wild beasts and men
Rabisu Musati – lord of the unclean areas
Rabisu Mushussu – known as the furious serpent
Rabisu Musmahhu – called the exalted serpent
Rabisu Nari – strongman of the inland waterways and rivers
Rabisu Ugallu – big weather beast (storm spirit)
Rabisu Umudabrutu – spirit of extremely violent storms (hurricanes, tornadoes)
Rabisu Urhi – destructive spirit over the roads, highways, and travel
Rahab – strongman who keeps people blind to the truth, hinders our prayers from going up and the answers from coming down
Raum – Hebrew three-faced god of destruction with a face of man, viper, and a cat
Siva/Shiva – Hindu god of destruction
Udug – Hebrew former Watcher now strongman of deception

Chapter 13: Hebrew Strongmen
Pages 114-117

Abaddon – Hebrew name for the leader over the spirits of the pit, a destroying angel
Apollyon – Greek name for the leader over the spirits of the pit, a destroying angel
Azazel – fallen prince of the fallen angels
Baal – false god worshipped, used as a title meaning master or lord
Baal Shamin – lord of the sky, a sun god
Bel – a title meaning lord; a strongman of the Hebrew often associated with other strongmen from surrounding countries
Beelzebub – Hebrew fallen angel, one of Satan's generals
Behemoth – Hebrew strongman of the waterways
Belial – Hebrew spirit leader of all the spirits of darkness
Leviathan – great sea serpent
Rahab – strongman who keeps people blind to the truth, hinders our prayers from going up and the answers from coming down

Chapter 14: The Watchers of Enoch
Pages 118-125

Ananel (Hanane) – one of the fallen watchers
Arakiba (Artaqifa) – evil fallen angel, one of the chiefs of ten troops
Araqiel – one of the fallen watchers who taught men the signs of the earth
Arariel – one of the seven angels with dominion over the earth
Armaros – one of the fallen watcher who taught enchantments
Asael – one of the fallen watchers whose name means 'who God made'
Azazel – considered to be responsible for teaching mankind about war and how to work with metals and make weapons
Baraqijal (Baraqel) – one of the watchers who taught astrology
Batarel (Batarjal) – one of the fallen watchers
Busasejal (Basasael) – one of the fallen watchers
Daniel (Danjel) – one of the fallen watchers whose name means God is my judge
Ezeqeel ((Neqael) – one of the fallen watchers who taught men the knowledge of clouds
Jomjael (Rumael) – one of the fallen watchers whose name means *day of God*
Kasbeel – sinful angel whose name means sorcery
Kasdaye – fallen angel who taught men abortion
Kokabel (Kokabiel) – one of the fallen watchers whose name means star of God
Rameel – one of the fallen watchers
Ramiel (Rumja) – one of the fallen watchers
Samsapeel (Shamshiel) – one of the fallen watchers
Sariel – recorded as both a holy and a fallen angel
Satarel (Jetrel) – one of the fallen watcher whose name means God's side
Semiaza (Samjaza) – supposed to be the actual leader of the fallen watchers
Tamiel (Turael) – one of the fallen watchers whose name means perfection of God
Tumael (unknown) – one of the fallen watchers
Turel – one of the fallen watchers whose name mean the rock of God
Zaqiel – one of the fallen watchers

Chapter 15: Strongmen of Emotions

spirit behind pain, suffering, and torment, powerful spirit behind fears, controlling spirit behind violence, wrath, anger, rage and fury, spirit that preys and troubles lonely women, spirit behnd evil thoughts, addictions

Pages 126 - 131

Aclahayr – spirit behind mental anguish and disorders
Aeshma – controlling spirit behind violence, wrath, anger, rage and fury
Afrit – relentless spirit of revenge
Agares – spirit
Agathodemon – driving force behind deception
Agramon – powerful spirit behind fears
Aka Manah – spirit behind the perverted mind and evil deeds
Akatash – spirit behnd evil thoughts
Aku Aku – spirit behind unstable, troubled, aggravated mind
Alastor – spirit behind murder
Alperer – spirit that preys and troubles lonely women
Alu-Demon – night spirit behind nightmares and bad dreams
Ammit – spirit behind spiritual torment
Andras – spirit who works through quarrels and strife
Angra Mainyu – spirit behind pain, suffering, and torment
Ansitif – spirit that possesses people
Aosoth – spirit that works through passion and death
Apasmara – spirit of mindlessness and glare (staring, daze) and belief in reincarnation
Ardat-Lile – spirit behind destruction of families
Arioch – spirit that works behind revenge
Ashtaroth – spirit of lust and seduction
Aspis – Hebrew snake-like spirit of evil and stubbornness
Awar – spirit behind laziness
Az – spirit of extreme evil
Azathoth – powerful spirit of chaos
Bael – spirit of shrewdness and deception
Belial – Hebrew spirit of emotional darkness, uselessness, and desperation
Bilwis – German name of the spirit of envy and absolute meanness
Caym – spirit of vain logic and puns
Chil Gazi – seducer of women
Daevas – spirit behind drunkenness, envy, and impure sexuality

Chapter 15: Strongmen of Emotions
continued

Danglathas – spirit behind violent crimes and murder
Dantalion – three-face spirit of sexual perversion, bisexualism, gender confusion, mind reading and the worship of the occult
Druj – spirit that works through perversion and corruption
Erzulie – spirit of fornication and adultery
Furfur – spirit that works through perversion and corruption
Gresil/Gressil – spirit behind laziness
Incubus – male demon of sexual lusting
Indra – Iranian name for spirit of violence
Inguma – Biskian name for the spirit of fear
Jaldabaoth – spirit of lust
Jezebeth – spirit of falsehood and lies
Joetun – giant spirit of emotional chaos and destruction
Malphas – spirit that works through deception and lies
Mammon – New Testament spirit of greed
Mastema – spirit behind hostility
Murmur – spirit of lies, slander, accusations, falsehood, and deceit
Ornias – spirit of homosexuality
Philatanus – Jewish strongman of sodomy
Proserpine – spirit who helps in establishing the act of sodomy
Pruflas/Busas – spirits of war, discord, quarrels, and poverty
Pyro – spirit that works behind falsehood
Rabisu - strongman who lies in wait, the doorkeeper **(Genesis 4:6)**
Samael – Hebrew spirit, which is a former Watcher who works through slander, accusation, and seduction
Sonneillon – spirit of hate
Succorbenoth – Hebrew spirit behind jealousy
Succubus – female demon of sexual lusting
Uphir – spirit of pharmaceutical drug abuse and chemical and substance addictions

Chapter 16: Strongman of False Religions
Part 1: Vodou (Voodoo)
Pages 132- 151

Allah – false god of Islam (Moslems)
Balan – spirit of witchcraft
Baphomet – spirit behind Satanic worship and secret societies
Bondye – god of Vodou
Dantalion – three-faced spirit behind the worship of the occult
Diana of the Ephesians – spirit behind the worship of the moon. Queen goddess of all divisions of witchcraft
Eledaa – in Santeria, he is the creator being
Kalfou – in Vodou, he controls the evil forces of the spirit world
Kokabel – Hebrew former watcher taught the worship of the stars (angel worship)
Legba – in Vodou he is the door opener to the spirit world
Lwas – immortal spirits with supernatural powers
Oloddumare – God Almighty of Santeria
Olorun – in Santeria he is the owner of the heavens
Orishas – personal gods of Santeria
Petros – violent, aggressive, dangerous lwas in Vodou
Pyro – spirit behind spreading falsehood, lies, myths, and legends
Rada – gentle and benevolent lwas in Vodou
Sariel – Hebrew former watcher who taught the worship of the moon
Shamreel – Hebrew former watcher taught mankind to worship the sun
Ummar – demon power behind the Qur'an

Chapter 16: Strongmen of False Religion
Part 2: Santeria
List of Orishas, Their Catholic Counterparts, and their Feast Days
Pages 152-167

Orisha	Saint	Feast Day
Eleggua	St. Anthony	June 13
Orunmila	St. Francis of Assisi	October 14
Obatala	Our Lady of Mercy	September 24
Chango	St. Barbara	December 4
Oggun	St. Peter	June 29
Ochosi	St. Norbert	June 6
Aganyu	St. Christopher	November 16
Babalu-Aye	St. Lazarus	December 17
Yemaya	Our Lady of Regla	September 7
Oshun	Our Lady of Charity	September 8
Oya	Our Lady of La Candelaria	February 2

Chart of the Orisha in Yoruba (Nigeria), Santeria (Cuba), and Candomble (Brazil)

Yoruba (Nigeria)	Santeria (Cuba)	Candomble (Brazil)
Esu	Eshu, Eleggua	Exu
Orisa-nla	Obatala	Orixala, Oxala, Obatala
Orunmila	Orunmila, Orunla	Orunmila
Sango	Chango	Xango
Ogun	Oggun	Ogum
-	Ochosi	Oxossi
Sonponno	Babalu-Aye	Obaluae, Omolu, Xanpana
Yemoja	Yemaya	Iemanja
Osun	Oshun	Oxum
Oya	Oya, Yansa	Oia-Iansa

About the Author

Dr. Henry Lewis is the President of an Apostolic International ministry called Joshua International. Joshua International offers Biblical Leadership Training and Spiritual Over comers material. Henry Lewis is a Sicilian Jew and a descendent of Andrew Murray.

He is married to his wife, Patricia, for over 42 years. They have been in ministry since 1980 and have two children.

Dr. Lewis has authored 10 books. The first book called A Quest for Spiritual Power is now translated in Arabic and in French.
The Arabic book was printed in Egypt and the French book was assembled and translated in Switzerland and printed in France.

Dr. Lewis is a sought-after speaker and author, teaching at churches and conferences along with numerous TV guest media outlets teaching on subjects such as: spiritual warfare, revival, transformation, revelation, transformational prayer. Henry evangelizes and teaches with international prophetic leaders in 10 countries.

His testimony of his former occult leadership experiences of seven generations has enabled him to share the love of God and his delivering power.

Charisma magazine shared is testimony in 2000. 750,000 Hindus translated the article in their language and accepted Christ.

Dr. Lewis attended several colleges which led to obtain three Doctorates in Counseling, Theology and Christian Education.

Henry and his wife have established churches in the US. Their first church was by the assistance of Aimee Semple McPherson's son, Rolf McPherson, who believed in their calling. Later, Dr. Roy Hicks, Sr. (friend who worked at Angelius Temple with Rolf McPhearson) supported them as well.

Henry and Patricia's spiritual foundation was formed from: Dr. Leonard Heroo (Apostle and President of Zion Bible Institute), McPherson), Evangelist Robert Schambach, Prophet David Wilkerson and Derek Prince, Lester Sumrall etc.

Henry's passionate thirst for the knowledge and truth of God's word led him to obtain a deep relational experience with his Lord and Savior, Jesus Christ – and not a religion – so he could hear and know the voice of God.

His vision is to teach and train a courageous generation the incorruptible Word of God and introduce the power of the Holy Spirit. Henry and Patricia's goal is to bring restoration to all nations including the Native Americans. His wife, Patricia is of the Iroquois nation.

Henry & Patricia coordinated large transformation events in New England under the 'Vision for New England" network which began in Salem, Ma with the help of Rev Ken Steigler & local pastors. Daystar programming promoted the events for 2 years. A transformation video was edited that shares the signs and wonders and miracles that occurred.

Dr. Henry Lewis is ordained with the Assemblies of God.
Henry is also ordained Rabbi through Asher Intrater from the Revive Israel Ministries

He is available for speaking.

Books

A Quest for Spiritual Power - Redeemed from the Curse - testimonial
Choisi Par Le Maitre: En quête de puissance spirituelle - French translation
A Quest for Spiritual Power - Arabic translation
Nimrod - How religions began and how it applies today
Spiritual Opposition to the Five Fold Ministry
The Secret Names of the Strongmen - study material & prayer manual
Jezebel - human or the spirit of baal?
The Dispensation of the Lion and the lamb
The Return of the Days of Noah

Available on Amazon

For More Information

In the US write:

H.A. Lewis
Joshua International
P.O. Box 1799
Maricopa, AZ 85139

Email: Info@halewis.org
Email: Info@ joshua-edu.org

To order or inquire of additional products, visit us online

Website: www.halewis.org

Book Cover Artist: Debbie Wheat
Contact: izayu54@yahoo.com

Book Co-coordinators:
Grace Miller
Patricia Lewis

To order additional copies of this book or any other product, visit us online

Website: www.halewis.org

Visit us on Facebook
https://www.facebook.com/drhenrylewis

Book Cover Artist: Debbie Wheat
Contact: izayu54@yahoo.com